LITERARY AND
SOCIOPOLITICAL WRITINGS
OF THE BLACK DIASPORA
IN THE NINETEENTH AND
TWENTIETH CENTURIES

LITERARY AND SOCIOPOLITICAL WRITINGS OF THE BLACK DIASPORA IN THE NINETEENTH AND TWENTIETH CENTURIES

Kersuze Simeon-Jones

LEXINGTON BOOKS

Lanham • Boulder • New York • Toronto • Plymouth, UK

Published by Lexington Books
A wholly owned subsidary of The Rowman & Littlefield Publishing Group, Inc.
4501 Forbes Boulevard, Suite 200, Lanham, Maryland 20706
www.rowman.com

10 Thornbury Road, Plymouth PL6 7PP, United Kingdom

Copyright © 2010 by Lexington Books
First paperback edition 2013

British Library Cataloguing in Publication Information Available

Library of Congress Cataloging-in-Publication Data

The hardback edition of this book was previously cataloged by the Library of Congress as follows:

Simeon-Jones, Kersuze, 1974-
  Literary and sociopolitical writings of the Black diaspora in the nineteenth and twentieth centuries / Kersuze Simeon-Jones.
      p. cm.
  Includes bibliographical references and index.
  1. Black nationalism—Philosophy. 2. Pan-Africanism—Philosophy. 3. Black nationalism—History. 4. Pan-Africanism—History. 5. African diaspora in literature. I. Title.
  DT16.5.S56 2010
  320.54'6—dc22

                                                                    2010014360

ISBN: 978-0-7391-2253-2 (cloth : alk. paper)
ISBN: 978-0-7391-8036-5 (pbk. : alk. paper)
ISBN: 978-0-7391-4764-1 (electronic)

♾™ The paper used in this publication meets the minimum requirements of American National Standard for Information Sciences—Permanence of Paper for Printed Library Materials, ANSI/NISO Z39.48-1992.

Printed in the United States of America

For My Daughter, With Eternal Love

Contents

Acknowledgments

I THANK THE SUPREME BEING, the Universe, along with the spirits of the Ancestors for infallible guidance through my life journey and intellectual work. I thank the people, past and present (too numerous to name), who have contributed to my continuous personal and professional development. I thank my daughter for helping me better comprehend and appreciate life on earth.

Introduction

Il est des noms qui sonnent comme un manifeste. Tel me fut révélé le nom du Dr. Price-Mars. . . . Je lus *Ainsi parla l'oncle* d'un trait, comme l'eau de la citerne, au soir, après une longue étape dans le désert . . . Me montrant les trésors de la négritude qu'il avait découverts sur et dans la terre haïtienne, il m'apprenait à découvrir les mêmes valeurs, mais vierges et plus fortes sur et dans la terre d'Afrique. . . . Par quoi le 15 octobre 1956 sera le quatre-vingtième anniversaire de la négritude.

There are names that ring like a revelation. As such I was revealed the name of Dr. Price-Mars. . . . I read *Ainsi parla l'oncle* uninterruptedly, like water from the fountain, at night, after a long journey in the desert . . . unveiling to me the treasures of négritude he had discovered on and within Haitian soil, he was teaching me to discover the same values, but purer and stronger, on and within the soil of Africa. . . . This is the reason October 15, 1956 will be the eightieth anniversary of négritude.

—Léopold Sédar Senghor[1]

I read Hegel, Karl Marx, Lenin and Mazzini. The writings of these men did much to influence me in my revolutionary ideas and activities, and Karl Marx and Lenin particularly impressed me as I felt sure that their philosophy was capable of solving these problems. But I think that of all the literature that I studied, the book that did more than any to fire my enthusiasm was *Philosophy and Opinions of Marcus Garvey* published in 1923. Garvey with his philosophy of "Africa for Africans" and his "Back

to Africa" movement did much to inspire the Negroes of America in
the 1920s.

—Osagyefo Kwame Nkrumah[2]

A S WE CONTINUE INTO THE TWENTY-FIRST century, studies on, and the
teaching of, the history of the African Diaspora are increasingly gaining momentum and receiving the necessary consideration they have been
lacking. Intellectuals and activists hope that through thorough research of
a history long-neglected, as well as through the teaching of their findings,
they will help ameliorate the state of people of African ancestry throughout
the world—psychologically, educationally, economically, politically, and
socially. The purpose of this work is to contribute to the historiography of
Afro-Diasporic studies, by tracing and examining the historical development
of literary and sociopolitical movements of the Diaspora in the writings of
key political figures. Through the scrutiny of the various philosophies that
were fundamentally and largely anchored on education—formal, informal,
religious, secular, private, and public—this study analyzes the political,
economic and social past of the black Diaspora in relation to the future. In
extension, the goal is to encourage interdisciplinary, cross-geographic and
cross-lingual pedagogical approaches to black history, literature, and culture.
With the comparative and connective analyses of political leaders as well as
the movements they adhered to, I argue that throughout the nineteenth and
twentieth centuries the principles of Black Nationalism—in all its forms, i.e.,
both *avant la lettre* and nominal—fostered the emergence of the literary and
sociopolitical movements of the era. In turn, these movements contributed
to the conceptual evolution and functions of Black Nationalism. One of the
key elements of Black Nationalism was the advocacy for education; for, as the
leaders and scholars viewed it then—as it is still viewed today—education
was the locus of psychological strength and material advancement. From that
framework, the chapters examine the critical role education played in each
movement and the importance each leader accorded this fundamental element of nation-building, race-building, self-reclamation, and valorization.

The specific movements examined in the following chapters include Pan-
Africanism, Garveyism, Indigénisme, New Negro Renaissance, Négritude and
Afrocriollo. The political leaders and scholars associated with these move-
ments include Edward W. Blyden, Martin R. Delany, Ida B. Wells-Barnett,
W. E. B. Du Bois, Anna Julia Cooper, Zora Neale Hurston, Marcus Aurelius
Garvey, Amy Jacques-Garvey, Jean Price-Mars, Aimé Césaire, Paulette Nar-
dal, Jane Nardal, Nicolás Guillén, Langston Hughes, Jacques Roumain, Osa-
gyefo Kwame Nkrumah, George Padmore, Patrice Lumumba, and Malcolm
X. These figures were among a myriad of activists and scholars who investi-

gated, analyzed, wrote about, spoke of, and taught the history of their ancestors in order to motivate their contemporaries toward self-awareness, social
consciousness, conscientious leadership, as well as economic and political development. To this end, this study seeks to demonstrate the cross-ideological
effects among the figures listed, and dialogically examine their philosophies,
struggles, and achievements. Parenthetically, the figures and movements I
have elected to examine in this study neither suggest a hierarchy within the
various national liberation movements of the Diaspora, nor does it negate the
important sacrifices of countless activists—not mentioned here—who had
been imprisoned and/or died in the name of freedom and black advancement
across Africa, the Americas, and Europe. Instead, I view this work as part of
the historiography of people of African descent. This text adds to the body of
work that has already been published and those that will be published in the
future.

Within the context of Afro-diasporic studies, it is reasonable to say that
while the leaders and the movements examined in this work have been the
subject of much scholarly writing, less attention has been accorded to the
correlation between the educational philosophies embedded in the socioli-
erary movements and the various political dialogues across geographic and
generational boundaries.[3] Up to the early 1990s, scholars have tended to focus
on literary movements while glossing over the social and political circumstances surrounding these movements or vice versa, or they have limited their
analyses of both literary and sociopolitical movements as a result of linguistic
barriers and/or geopolitical divisions.[4] Though a number of writers have analyzed the political and literary trajectory of the black Diaspora, less emphasis
has been placed on the sociocultural links between literary and sociopolitical movements, and the influential dialogues held between movements and
leaders.[5] Building on the existing scholarship this study demonstrates, from
a transnational scope, the ideological and activist connections that existed
between leaders and various movements—synchronously, diachronically,
and cross-geographically. To accomplish this goal, two objectives have been
established. The first objective is to examine key ideologies that have served
as common threads and connective elements throughout the Diaspora. Particular focus is given to the philosophies of Black Nationalism, Black Internationalism, and Universal Humanism. The goal is to assess the degree to which
these philosophies have drawn upon common values such as self-reclamation,
self-respect, self-reliance, self-preservation, as well as liberation, and advancement. Further, it is to establish that the principles of Black Nationalism, Black
Internationalism, and Universal Humanism were essential to the conceptu-
alization of each literary and sociopolitical movement of the nineteenth and
twentieth centuries. The second objective is to examine the temporal and
spatial evolution of each social and literary movement. To the extent that each

leader and writer helped establish new dimensions to ongoing movements, it is important to examine the conceptual nuances that intellectuals and activists contributed to the sociopolitical struggle, both nationally and diasporically.

If the concept of Black Nationalism led Marcus Garvey to specific assertions and deeds, it certainly brought Jean Price-Mars and Aimé Césaire to different approaches. Also, if the precepts of the New Negro were molded into distinct ideological forms in Booker T. Washington's sociopolitical actions, men such as Alain Locke and W. E. B. Du Bois manifested their notion of New Negro and, by extension, the principles of Black Nationalism differently. Indeed, it is through the contemporaneous relational and dialectical analyses of each writer/leader and concept/movement that we are able to probe the dialogues that took place among black leaders, from the nineteenth to the twentieth century. In other words, one cannot thoroughly speak of Négritude with regard to the pioneer role of Aimé Césaire without examining the foundational intellectual and political contributions of the Nardal sisters. One cannot analyze the ideologies of Delany and Du Bois without examining Alexander Crummell's philosophies on the black struggle, including the importance of education and religion in the black community. Similarly, a study of Nkrumah's political life must take into account George Padmore's political engagement, as well as Patrice Lumumba's sociopolitical endeavors for freedom and African unity. Hence, it is crucial to follow the personal and political involvement of black leaders not solely in their respective countries, but also within the ecumenical context of the black Diaspora.

To probe the collective ideologies articulated throughout the black world while concurrently examining the geopolitical particularities of each nation, it is essential to look at leaders who psychologically, culturally, and/or physically traveled through Africa, the Americas, and Europe, and whose ideas reached a number of contemporaries and successors. While leaders such as Delany and Malcolm X sojourned in Africa, others such as Césaire and Price-Mars traveled to Haiti and the United States respectively, but often spoke of a psychological and spiritual return to Africa, the ancestral land. The comparative approach is thus inescapable if one is to investigate the extent to which leaders influenced one another. Furthermore, to understand the various dimensions of each ideology and movement it is necessary to dismantle geographic, language, time, and generation barriers. It was through the works that were passed from one generation to the next, that leaders learned the lessons of history, particularly the lessons of organizational strategies, which are requisite for leading and sustaining successful liberation movements. It is weightily meaningful that Nkrumah stated his greatest influence was Marcus Garvey, along with the reading of the activist's philosophical text, *Philosophy and Opinions of Marcus Garvey*. It is equally significant that Nkrumah warned the people of the Gold Coast (later renamed Ghana) of the responsibilities of independence to counter the staunch presence and continuous devastation of colonialism and neocolonialism, making Haiti a case in point. Martin Delany's novel *Blake; or the Huts of America* and his manifesto *The Condition, Elevation, Emigration, and Destiny of the Colored People of the United States* shed light on the psychological damage of politicized and ideologized Christianity, as early as 1852. Moreover, his texts ponder the absence of education for blacks, to outline the level of economic insufficiency, and mental bankruptcy educational deprivation perpetuates. Similarly, Aimé Césaire's triumvirate plays, *La Tragédie du Roi Christophe, Une Tempête*, and *Une Saison au Congo*, present the challenges of independence, governance, and autonomy. In his plays Césaire depicts Patrice Lumumba and King Henry Christophe as simultaneously tragic and heroic *symbols* from whom black leaders can learn about the effects of colonialism and neocolonialism, and from whose political circumstances successive leaders can study the impact of indirect ruling. These brief literary examples preamble the argument that nineteenth- and twentieth-century black Diaspora leaders maintained consistent dialogues with and consequential influences on one another, through their seminal works and activism. Moreover, such mode of examination reveals the ways in which they adopted and adapted each other's ideologies.

The relational approach based on social specificity is significant. As Nkrumah states in *Consciencism* (published in 1964), "philosophy always arose from a social milieu, and that a social contention is always present in it either explicitly or implicitly. Social milieu affects the content of philosophy, and the content of philosophy affects the content of social milieu either by confirming or by opposing it."[6] Hence, when a philosophy confirms the social milieu, it becomes the ideology of that society; when it opposes its environment, then it becomes an ideology of revolution. With the objective of social reformation, proponents of Afro-diasporic movements opposed and challenged repressive ideologies. As a response to the stifling status quo, they formulated ideas and undertook actions that modified existing social conditions. Nkrumah further affirms that every social revolution must have an intellectual revolution standing firmly behind it. The revolution he envisioned for Africans and, by extension, African descendants is "a revolution in which [their] thinking and philosophy are directed towards the redemption of [their] society. . . . The philosophy that must stand behind this social revolution is that which [he has] once referred to as philosophical consciencism."[7] With similar logic each leader postulated a three-dimension black advancement movement: intellectual-philosophical, social-cultural, and political-economic. To respond to attacks of "propagandism" concerning the philosophies of black advancement, Garvey interchanged the words "propaganda" and "dissemination." Garveyites did not recoil from accusations of propagandism, for them the term did not hold a pejorative connotation; instead, it was analogous to the idea of disseminating one's philosophy of pride and liberation. For centuries nations have propagated their history and culture through education, various texts—both religious and secular—and the media; thus, the *Negro World*, which was simultaneously a political and literary paper, assumed the responsibility of spreading the Garveyite seed of mental and social revolution. "We are not afraid of the word *propaganda*," he maintained, "for we use the term in the sense of disseminating our ideas among Negroes all the world over. We have nothing stealthy in this meaning."[8]

Chapters 1 and 2 offer a historical background to the social and political movements of the nineteenth and twentieth centuries. Chapter 1 probes the trajectory of the formation and interpretation of the concepts that became the ideological foundations of the literary and sociopolitical movements. The definition of each term, examined within specific eras, with concrete historical examples, permits a better understanding of subsequent chapters. Following the argument that the thirteen-year revolution in Saint-Domingue (1791–1804)—which led to the liberation of enslaved Africans and the proclamation of a new Black Republic—is the manifestation of the Black Nationalist concept, chapter 2 analyzes the Black Nationalist ideology in the leadership of Toussaint Louverture, with a particular focus on his vision on the indispensable relationship between education and nation-building. The historical background of Black Nationalism and struggles for independence elucidate the influence Louverture maintained on successive leaders of the Diaspora, starting with Frederick Douglass and Denmark Vesey. Chapter 3 explores the paradoxes of simultaneous progress and regression in the articulation of various religious precepts and educational curricula. The chapter examines the principles of race progress and nation-building through appropriate education, in the works and philosophies of Edward Blyden and Martin Delany. For a comprehensive examination of the role of education and religion, the perspectives of Blyden and Delany's predecessors, contemporaries, and successors are also studied dialogically. Chapter 4 investigates the pivotal role of black women within the social, economic, political, and cultural advancement movements. It explores the contributions of women to the manifestation of Black Nationalism, Black Internationalism, and Universal Humanism, through such movements as Garveyism, Pan-Africanism, the New Negro Renaissance, and Négritude. The chapter focuses on the works and philosophies of Zora Neale Hurston, Jane Nardal, Paulette Nardal, and Amy Jacques-Garvey, while making references to activist women such as Maria Stewart, Ida B. Wells-Barnett, and Anna Julia Cooper. While chapter 5 pays particular attention to Du Bois and Garvey's divergent and convergent viewpoints, it focuses mainly on community economic self-reliance and political consciousness, as they are outlined and achieved in Du Bois' and Garvey's respective philosophies and activism. The chapter also examines Du Bois' and Garvey's engagement in the New Negro Renaissance. Moreover, it demonstrates the extent to which Garvey's activism and Du Bois's literary and politial thoughts helped shape the political content of the literary and cultural movements of the Francophone world and Hispanic America: Négritude, Negrismo, and Afrocriollo. Chapter 6 engages a discussion on the preservation of African heritage, the principles of race valorization and revitalization, as they are formulated in the writings of Jean Price-Mars; namely, *La vocation de l'élite* and *Ainsi parla l'oncle*. The discussion is pursued through the scrutiny of the precepts of responsibility and leadership, to elaborate the premise of Price-Mars' work. That is, the role the elite must play in the socioeconomic sustenance of the masses. Interwoven in the analysis on preservation and valorization, within the context of Haiti and the black Diaspora, are the writings of Jacques Roumain on matters of class and power struggles. Furthermore, the chapter links the national preoccupations of the Indigéniste movement to the international interests of the Négritude movement, to frame the foundational connections between the two movements. Chapter 7 explores the tragedy of neocolonialism in Césaire's triumvirate plays: *La Tragédie du Roi Christophe* (1963), *Une tempête* (1968), and *Une Saison au Congo* (1973). Didactically, each play exposes the complexities of self-governance in newly freed black nations. In so doing, the chapter probes the notion of nominal independence to analyze the political, economic, and social obstacles various nations encountered following *de jure* independence. Chapter 8 examines the ideological paradoxes of Negrista writings in relation to the subsequent rise of the Afrocriollo Movement. The chapter further analyzes a few of the works of the Afro-Cuban poet Nicolás Guillén, in dialogue with the poems of the Afro-American poet Langston Hughes and the Haitian poet/novelist/essayist Jacques Roumain. The chapter evaluates the significance of the Afrocriollo movement within the general Hispanic culture and within the world community. Chapter 9 studies the emergence of independent African nations, starting with Ghana, as well as the continuing liberation and equality struggles for blacks in the United States. The chapter deciphers the works of Kwame Nkrumah and Malcolm X by placing the two activists within the ideological context of their predecessors and contemporaries, particularly George Padmore and Patrice Lumumba, as well as with their successors, such as the proponents of the Black Power Movement in the United States.

The book concludes with an examination of the trajectory of black activism starting from the eighteenth century onward and its relevance to today's society. It discusses the contribution black intellectuals and activists should continue to make within the Afro-diasporic community and the greater world, given that the intrinsic aspect of the human struggle and the black struggle, more specifically, lies in *evolution* and *continuity*. The appendix offers a biographical overview of the life of each leader—for the convenience of the reader. It comprises a listing of their place of birth and childhood, their educational training—both formal and informal—their political careers and writings. The objective is to present the personal background and intellectual writings of each leader, in order to provide a framework for understanding their thoughts and actions. Readers may opt to read the appendix before the chapters. Lastly, the manifestoes, poems, addresses, and articles are included in the original languages, in order to present the unaltered message of each author and avoid differing interpretations. The translations of all French and Spanish writings are, however, inserted for the convenience of the reader who cannot access the original languages. Translations are mine except for the plays and poems: Aimé Césaire's plays and poem, Jacques Roumain's and Nicolás Guillén's poems.

Notes

1. Raphaël F. Berrou, Pradel Pompilus, *Histoire de la Littérature Haïtienne, Tome III* (Port-au-Prince: Editions Caraïbes, 1977) 734.

2. Kwame Nkrumah, *Ghana: The Autobiography of Kwame Nkrumah.* 1957. (New York: International Publishers, 1976) 45.

3. Among such works one would note: George Shepperson, "Notes on Negro American Influences on the Emergence of African Nationalism" (1960); Robert W. July, "Nineteenth-Century Negritude: Edward W. Blyden" (1964); Hollis R. Lynch, "Edward W. Blyden: Pioneer West African Nationalist" (1965); Tony Martin, *Race First* (1976).

4. Such historical and interpretive approaches include the following: Georges Ngal, *Aimé Césaire: Un Homme à la Recherche d'une Patrie* (1975); Michel Fabre, *From Harlem to Paris: Black American Writers in France, 1840–1980* (1991).

5. These notable texts include Abiola Irele, "Negritude or Black Nationalism" (1965); Olisanwuche P. Esedebe, *Pan-Africanism: The Idea and the Movement, 1776–1963* (1972); Albert Owusu-Sarpong, *Le Temps Historique dans l'Œuvre Théâtrale d'Aimé Césaire* (1986); Têtêvi Godwin Tété-Adjalogo, *Marcus Garvey: Père de l'Unité Africaine des Races, Garveyisme et Panafricanisme* (Tome I and II, 1995); Brent Hayes Edwards, *The Practice of Diaspora* (2003).

6. Kwame Nkrumah, *Consciencism: Philosophy and Ideology for Decolonization and Development with Particular Reference to the African Revolution* (New York: Monthly Review Press, 1964) 56.

7. Ibid., 78–79.

8. Tony Martin, *Race First: The Ideological and Organizational Struggles of Marcus Garvey and the Universal Negro Improvement Association* (Dover: The Majority Press, 1976) 90.

1

Interpreting the Concepts of Black Nationalism, Black Internationalism, Pan-Africanism, and Universal Humanism within the Diaspora

Nationalism is first and foremost a state of mind, an act of consciousness, which since the French Revolution has become more and more common to mankind. The mental life of a man is as much dominated by an ego-consciousness as it is by a group-consciousness.

—Hans Kohn[1]

Nationhood is the only means by which modern civilization can completely protect itself. Independence of nationality, independence of government, is the means of protecting not only the individual, but the group. Nationhood is the highest ideal of all peoples. . . . We of the Negro Race are moving from one state of organization to another, and we shall so continue until we have thoroughly lifted ourselves into the organization of government.

—Marcus Garvey[2]

Our political philosophy will be black nationalism. Our economic and social philosophy will be black nationalism. Our cultural emphasis will be black nationalism. . . . The political philosophy of black nationalism means: we must control the politics and the politicians of our community. They must no longer take orders from outside forces. We will organize, and sweep out of office all Negro politicians who are puppets of outside forces.

—Malcolm X[3]

Bᴇғᴏʀᴇ ᴇɴɢᴀɢɪɴɢ ɪɴ ᴀɴ ᴇxᴀᴍɪɴᴀᴛɪᴏɴ of the sociopolitical and literary movements of the black Diaspora and its inherent principles, it is
important to probe and interpret certain concepts relating to government
and civil participation of blacks within national barriers and abroad. Because
the concepts of Black Nationalism, Pan-Africanism, Black Internationalism, and Universal Humanism have, for decades, engendered definition and
interpretation debates among scholars, I provide a definition framework
within which ideological variants are examined both synchronously and diachronically. In scrutinizing the philosophical background of evolving ideas,
as well as their significance to various race leaders, one would note that the
multi-dimensional movements of the black world addressed—on manifold
levels—national, international, and universal issues and questions concerning
the sociopolitical and cultural interests of black folk as a nation, and as a race,
in the midst of other nations and races.[4] It is essential to immediately point
out—though this argument is closely examined throughout the chapter—that
the concept of Black Nationalism, whether it is envisioned as *a* black nation
geographically assembled in Africa, or black nations dispersed throughout
the globe, held different meanings for leaders.[5] However, notwithstanding
the geographic variation and epochal interval within the notion of Black Nationalism, its perennial aim has been the re-evaluation of the black condition
and the rehabilitation of the race. Thus, the primary focus of Black Nationalism has remained on the political, economic, sociocultural, and intellectual
development for blacks.

Within the definition framework of Black Nationalism, the study of the
philosophies and actions of Toussaint Louverture and Marcus Garvey are
consequential. Louverture and Garvey are world leaders who articulated
seminal beliefs at critical historical junctures; each undertook unprecedented
actions that changed the destiny of blacks, both symbolically and tangibly.
Toussaint Louverture, along with Jean-Jacques Dessalines, Henry Christophe,
and the rank and file of his army, liberated the Africans of Saint-Domingue
from slavery and established the first free black nation of the New World.
In the twentieth century Marcus Garvey led the grand—of an incomparable
magnitude thus far—mass Diaspora movement of the black world, which
continues to influence today's intellectuals, as well as grass root world activists. In a cross-generational and cross-geographic exchange, Toussaint
Louverture's Black Nationalist philosophy affected leaders such as Frederick
Douglass, Edward Blyden, Martin Delany, W. E. B. Du Bois, and Marcus
Garvey, just as Garvey influenced successors such as Kwame Nkrumah and
Malcolm X.[6] Hence, the *symbolism* behind Louverture's and Garvey's ideolo-
gies and activism have been, for decades, and remain of irrefutable relevance

to Black Studies, particularly in the realms of the sociocultural and political history of the black world.[7]

The Concepts of Nationalism and Black Nationalism

In general the concept of nationalism requires, first and foremost, the acknowledgment of nationhood. In other words, the principles of nationalism serve as the psychological disposition and expression of nationhood. Thus, to analyze nationalism, it is essential to first understand the components that constitute a nation. In *The Politics of Nationalism and Ethnicity*, James G. Kellas offers a succinct definition of "nation" and "nationalism" which runs parallel to the elemental definition of black nationhood and nationalism. Kellas reminds us that nations are founded, variably, on "objective" elements such as language, territory, religion, or common descent, as well as "subjective" sentiments which are "essentially a people's awareness of its nationality and affection for it." Kellas continues to specify that "the term nation is also commonly applied to states, as in the United Nations, consisting of the 'nations' of the world. While many states share features of nations, and can be called 'nation-states,' there are also nations within states, and such states are correctly called 'multinational states.'"[8]

If nation is a community based on a common ancestry, history, and culture, or a common territory, language, or religion, the notion of black nationhood, as viewed by race leaders, is warrantable. From the nineteenth century up to the 1960s race leaders conceived Black Nationhood as a community of people anchored in a specific historical and ancestral past and unified by their political and social agenda. The sentiment of Black Nationalism which accompanied black nationhood was expressed through multidimensional ideologies based on political, economic, and social needs of the nation, as well as its cultural expression and preservation. Hence, nationalism, as an articulated and behavioral sentiment, "seeks to defend and promote the interests of the nation. The political aspect of nationalism is seen most clearly in the demand for 'national self-determination,' or 'home rule.'"[9] It is within the distinctive principles of nation-building through self-determination and governance that one can examine the different types of Black Nationalism from the eighteenth century onward. While one cannot attribute—with certainty—the first sentiments of Black Nationalism to any one man, for it is clearly impossible to arrive at such conclusion, this chapter analyzes the notion of Black Nationalism, starting with its first successful manifestation, namely the Haitian Revolution. It further traces Black

Nationalist actions from the 1790s through the Black Power Movement of the 1960s and 1970s.

Toward the end to the eighteenth century, following the French Revolution in 1789 and the *Cérémonie du Bois Caïman* in 1791, Toussaint Louverture became the chief leader of the military expeditions and battles for independence. After Louverture was cunningly arrested by French officers in 1802, and was incarcerated in Fort de Joux until his death in 1803, Jean-Jacques Dessalines commanded the last military battle of liberation on November 18, 1803, in *Vertières*.[10] Succeeding military victory, Dessalines renamed Saint-Domingue, *Haïti*, and Boirond-Tonnerre drafted the Act of Independence. For Dessalines the appellation "Saint-Domingue" was reminiscent of the slavery era, while "Haïti" was the island's pre-Columbian and pre-slavery name. Hence, the name "Haïti" marked the beginning of a new independent nation. The new nation that was proclaimed on January 1, 1804, was based on the common ancestry, history, and territory of blacks (of pure African and mixed blood), who became known as Haitians. Though the blacks who were transported to Saint-Domingue belonged to different African ethnic groups, spoke different languages, and worshiped different gods and spirits, they nonetheless shared a general African ancestry; they experienced the horrendous tragedy of the slave trade as well as endless toil on the plantations of the colonies.[11] Thenceforth, their common goal became the emancipation and the formation of a free black nation in Saint-Domingue.

There is what I would categorize as four distinct conceptual definitions of Black Nationalism, based on four social and historical contexts. The first example is that of a Black Nationalism within a predominantly black nation or republic. The case of a black nation in Haiti serves as an example of this first category. The second example is that of a Black Nationalism within a greater white society. Blacks of the United States fit within the second example, for they have also struggled for emancipation and the formation of a black nation, though within the United States. The third example is that of a diasporic Black Nationalism which is synonymous to Black Internationalism in that the goal is to have a foundation that is based on political, economic, and sociocultural dialogues among blacks, while maintaining a clear understanding and respect toward the various geographic and national identities within the Diaspora. Lastly, the fourth example—is an archaic view which dates back to the nineteenth century—is that of a Black Nationalism which entails the assemblage of diasporic blacks for the formation of a black nation in Africa. The particular ideology of repatriation embedded in the broader Black Nationalist concept was envisaged by Paul Cuffee in 1815. It was advocated by Edward Blyden in the second half of the nineteenth century; it was later reiterated, modified, and emphasized by Marcus Garvey during the first half of the twentieth century.

At the end of the American Revolution and the Declaration of Independence in 1776, blacks in the United States realized that the principles of the American Revolution, which postulated liberty, justice, and citizenry, were drafted for the protection of whites and excluded people of African ancestry. Instead, they were maintained in the most inhuman slavery system known to men. The reign of maltreatment and the destruction of families, the dismantlement of the concept of humanness (through the daily toil that led to barbarous deaths), the exceedingly high number of rapes and lynchings, were all parts of the experience blacks continued to endure in America. Disenchanted and discouraged about their condition in the United States, a return to their ancestral land became the primary consideration. In 1787, the committee of the African Lodge headed by Prince Hall sent a petition to the Legislative Assembly of Massachusetts to ask for financial assistance for blacks who wished to return to Africa.[12] The Legislative Assembly disregarded the request of the African Lodge, and as a response Prince Hall turned his attention to civil liberties for blacks within the United States. With the "Three-Fifths Compromise" which further reinforced the treatment of slaves as property—where five slaves were counted as three people for the purpose of Southern states' representation in the House and for taxation in both the North and the South—free blacks re-launched the idea of a return to Africa where they would be regarded as full citizens. It was at the juncture of post-revolution America and the desire of "free" and enslaved blacks to go back to Africa that Paul Cuffee's leadership heightened.

Paul Cuffee was a black merchant in Boston and a Quaker who had struggled for the rights of blacks in Massachusetts. When his efforts proved unsuccessful, he began to promote the repatriation of blacks in Africa, especially to Sierra Leone. Cuffee wanted to halt the slave trade and develop an African economy in Africa, based on local products. In 1808, Cuffee obtained the support of the African Institution, and finally visited Sierra Leone in 1811.[13] By 1815, Paul Cuffee had become a successful merchant, land and shipowner. His financial capabilities enabled him to finance the first trip to Africa on his own ship, the *Traveller,* which accommodated thirty-eight volunteer black settlers to Liberia. The trip marked an unforgettable historic moment for it realized the first move of blacks from America to Africa, as a response to slavery.[14] Equally important, Cuffee's ideology and gesture had an effect on the most prominent black leaders of his time and would later influence younger generation leaders—if we are to think of Marcus Garvey's endeavors with the Black Star Line. As Cuffee's political influence grew, he succeeded in assembling prominent black leaders under the umbrella of the African Institution. He brought together Reverend Daniel Cocker of Baltimore, Reverend Peter Williams of New York, Bishop Richard Allen, Reverend Absalom Jones, and

James Forten of Philadelphia. One of the main goals of the African Institution was to lead America's black population back to Africa in order to create an independent black nation on their land of origin. They believed that in America blacks would never prosper as a race, for the American system was structured to generate and maintain the accumulation of white wealth and power.

As the representative of the African Institution, James Forten wrote to Cuffee in 1817 and affirmed their common belief that "Negroes will never become a people until they come out from amongst the white."[15] However, six months after an emphatic call for black exodus out of the United States, members of the African Institution vowed to stay in the New World. The reason for such a drastic change in position resulted from the creation of the American Colonization Society. In February 1817, powerful slaveholders whose agenda was to reinforce slavery in order to bolster the accretion of America's growing capital, formed the American Colonization Society. The society was to finance the repatriation of "free" blacks to Africa. During the time of negotiation, the African Institution calculated that if the most radical and vigorous free blacks departed from the United States, whites would seize the opportunity to maintain remaining blacks in the most inescapable form of bondage and exploitation. In 1830, Peter Williams, pastor of St. Phillips Episcopal Church in New York, delivered a speech in which he voiced the belief—which was shared by other members of the African Institution—that America wanted to get rid of those who were most active in the struggle for liberation and civil liberties for blacks.[16] The decision by black leaders and their constituents to remain in the United States was one of subliminal defiance, for it meant coping with the power structure and combating slavery. During that period certain leaders were convinced that the migration of free blacks to the ancestral land would not ameliorate the situation for those who would remain in bondage under white domination. Thus, as they conceived it, the re-evaluation of an exodus and the final decision to stay was, in 1817, the option most beneficial to black slaves in the United States. In the 1830s, the continuous struggle of black leaders—particularly James Forten and Bishop Richard Allen—and their constituents against slavery and colonization, became a propelling force to the abolitionist movement. Unlike the first three categories of Black Nationalism, which have been functioning throughout the black world, the vision of a Black Nationalism which called for repatriation of blacks in Africa never came into fruition, at least not to the magnitude its proponents intended.

In the first two categories, the dynamic of Black Nationalism in the United States was different from that of Haiti. Though U.S. blacks harbored the same desire for liberation and valorization of self, they could only go as far as imagining the establishment of a nation within a nation, given the national systemic structure of the United States. More complicatedly, within the borders of the United States considerable dissension in political perspectives amidst black leaders muddied the water. A number of black leaders, such as Martin Delany and W. E. B. Du Bois—whose positions consistently varied throughout the years—hoped to see black folk fully integrated within the nation of the United States; consequently, they discouraged and fought against the notion of a nation within a nation, to advocate an eventually integrated and equal society. And so, placing the situation of blacks in eighteenth-century Saint-Domingue and, later, nineteenth-century Haiti in comparison to their U.S. counterparts, there is on the one hand the formation of a black republic within specific geographic barriers, and on the other hand there is the establishment of a black nation within a greater nation. The advocacy of a black nation within the greater United States became increasingly more pronounced throughout the 1960s with proponents of the Black Power movement. It is worth pointing out, however, that while it remains important to discern the variations of Black Nationalism, it is crucial to acknowledge that in all four instances, i.e., with the four categories, the unanimous aim was to form sovereign and autonomous black nations capable of self-guidance, self-governance and prosperity.

More than the sentimentality of Black Nationalism, activists such as Louverture, Blyden, Garvey, Du Bois, Jacques-Garvey, Price-Mars, Césaire, Nkrumah, and Malcolm X, were cognizant of, and understood, the necessary elements that constituted a nation; namely, the political, economic, social, cultural, and intellectual development of each citizen. From the 1790s until his nefarious arrest and deportation in 1802, Louverture and his constituents labored to lay the foundation of nationhood and nationalism. In *The Black Jacobins*, C. L. R. James describes the necessary measures Louverture undertook to begin the establishment of a nation.

> The ultimate guarantee of freedom was the prosperity of agriculture. This was Toussaint's slogan. The danger was that the blacks might slip into the practice of cultivating a small patch of land, producing just sufficient for their needs. . . . He confined the blacks to the plantations under rigid penalties. He was battling with the colossal task of transforming a slave population, after years of licence, into a community of free labourers, and he was doing it in the only way he could see. . . .
>
> He established schools as he could. . . . He erected fine buildings in Le Cap and built a huge monument to commemorate the abolition of slavery. Personal industry, social morality, public education, religious toleration, free trade, civic pride, racial equality, this ex-slave strove according to his lights to lay their foundations in the new state. He sought to lift the people to some understanding of the duties and responsibilities of freedom and citizenship.[17]

With the encouragement of hard work in agriculture and the establishment of schools, Louverture sought to realize the ideology he wanted to permeate the minds of newly freed ex-slaves. His goal was to raise a race and a national consciousness among blacks and to teach them the responsibility of working for one's own advancement. Because enslaved Africans were conditioned to toil under slave drivers' cruel control, emancipation, after years of inhumane travail, signified—for many of them—a break from work altogether. Louverture's monumental task was to teach newly freed ex-slaves the essentiality to work for one's individual progress and the wealth of his/her nation. Through such teachings, he endeavored to spread the principles of nation-building among blacks in Saint-Domingue. After the *Guerre du Sud* in 1799 Toussaint set out to rebuild Saint-Domingue and its economy.[18] Though Louverture was unshakably committed to the liberation struggle, he believed he had to maintain the emphasis on Haiti's natural resource—agriculture—to secure the island's economic prosperity. With his attention on agriculture, he demanded that his citizens work on plantations in order to produce for massive export. However, after liberation from slavery and dusk to dawn toil, most blacks wanted to focus on cultivating smallholdings, enough to provide for their families. The contradictory economic impasse marked the insurmountable difficulty from slavery to black nationhood.

In 1801 Louverture worked harder to expand his nation-building plans after he had annexed the Eastern section of the island (Santo Domingo), which belonged to France since the *traité de Bâle* on July 14, 1795.[19] Aware of the fact that the creation of a nation requires the formation of functional civil and political establishments, Louverture built public schools, divided the island into six departments, created regular courts of law and two courts of appeal—one in the French section of the island and one in the Spanish section—and founded a Supreme Court of Appeal in the capital. In addition to the regular courts, the courts of appeal and the Supreme Court of Appeal, he established special military courts to deal with robberies and crimes on the high road. In 1801, the *gourde* became the monetary unit in Saint-Domingue. It was also in 1801 that Louverture set tax percentages for imported and exported goods in order to expand Saint-Domingue's economy.[20] Above all, blacks participated in government decisions and occupied government positions. During his years as Governor General, Louverture succeeded in raising civic pride as well as racial equality on the island as a whole. And so, before the nominal notion of Black Nationalism Toussaint Louverture's actions effectuated its practice.

Similar to Louverture, though in a different geopolitical and temporal context, Marcus Garvey struggled against all odds to propagate the formation of black nationhood. In his essay "The Plot" Garvey outlines the forces that worked in opposition to his nationhood program. As Tony Martin reemphasizes in *Race First* "the United States government was against him because they considered all black radicals subversive; European governments were against him because he was a threat to the stability of their colonies; the communists were against him because he successfully kept black workers out of their grasp."[21] Certainly the Communist Party, the United States, and the European governments were not the only forces Garvey had to contend with; in addition, the Universal Negro Improvement Association (U.N.I.A.) had to struggle against numerous conspiracies aimed at destroying the association and the Garvey movement. Integrationist organizations were against him because of his conviction that white segregationists represented the general mentality of white America; to counterbalance the prejudice mentality and its ensuing social realities, Garvey upheld black segregation. The reiteration of the forces in opposition, from the outset, is important, for it clarifies the antagonistic environment within which Garvey was working to spread the ideas of Black Nationalism. It is thus reasonable to posit that the Universal Negro Improvement Association's organizational and political potential was stymied, to a considerable degree, by sabotage and adverse criticism.

Garvey's self-preparation as a Black Nationalist leader started in St. Ann's Bay, Jamaica. At the age of sixteen he moved to Kingston to continue his career as a foreman printer, and by the age of eighteen, he began his involvement in the intellectual and political life of Kingston. In 1910, he embarked on a tour to Central and South America, and visited England in 1912. Garvey's sojourn in England was significant for his political career; it was there that he began to notice the difference between the democracy the British maintained in their country and the autocratic system they sustained in their dependent islands.[22] While in England, Garvey had the opportunity to meet with students and black seamen, and was able to observe their hardship just as he had observed the wretched condition of the black masses in Jamaica, and throughout Central and South America. In England Garvey became acquainted with writers of the *African Times and Orient Review*, for which he also wrote. In the circle of the *African Times and Orient Review*'s writers Garvey became more conscious of the vestiges of slavery, the impact of colonialism, and the need for racial solidarity. In the journal, Garvey had also read articles about and written by eminent leaders such as Edward Blyden, Booker T. Washington, W. E. B. Du Bois, John Edward Bruce, and William Ferris.[23] During his sojourn he began to articulate his concept of Black Nationalism, as he became increasingly convinced that in order to advance blacks needed to demonstrate loyalty to their race and focus on their common aim. He understood that before the creation of a nation, the emergence of a group-consciousness was essential.

The Black Nationalism that would precede and bolster the formation of nationhood is first and foremost a state of mind, a group consciousness. "This group consciousness," to refer back to Hans Kohn, "will strive towards creating homogeneity within the group, a conformity and like-mindedness which will lead to and facilitate concerted common action."[24] "Homogeneity" here does not refer to *sameness* within the *varying groups* that constitute *the* group, but *sameness* as in a common ideology to attain a common goal. In the United States Garvey attempted and succeeded, to some degree, to translate his concept of Black Nationalism into the creation of Nationhood.

Garvey spoke for the rights of blacks as a nation; for, the various territorial nationalities they were assigned to were/are a matter of haphazard imposition, given that they were brought from Africa as slaves and never made a choice of one nationality or another.[25] If the construction of nationality in itself (for blacks in particular) was/is only a matter of historical consequences and social circumstances, and not of "natural" law, then it follows that blacks could successfully re-construct and re-form their various territorial nations into a greater black nation. Therefore, he persistently insisted that members of the U.N.I.A were "determined to unite the 400,000,000 Negroes of the world for the purpose of building a civilization of their own. . . . [They were] looking toward political freedom on the continent of Africa, the land of [their] fathers."[26] Garvey did not want to form a government within an already structured government, not because he hated whites but because he believed his approach toward race assertion and determination was the only salvation and means of non-oppositional progress for blacks.

While advocating the ideology of a black nation Garvey was also building black businesses. In addition to the Black Star Line, in 1920 Garvey established the Universal Negro Improvement Association's Negro Factories Corporation. The Negro Factories Corporation managed the U.N.I.A.'s laundries, restaurants, a doll factory, tailoring and millinery establishments and a printing press. Garvey wanted to build black wealth throughout the Diaspora, in preparation for autonomous leadership. In 1923 he emphasized that the U.N.I.A. "did not speak in the language of theology and religion; not in the language of social reform, but the Universal Negro Improvement Association speaks in the language of building a government: of building political power and all that goes with it."[27] "All that goes with it" meant electing government officials, and preparing U.N.I.A. members for civil and political services. He envisaged a social reform which entailed more than small changes and restricted involvement within a largely unequal and unjust society; instead, he was adamant in his conviction that blacks must play a substantial role in nation-building. As Garvey viewed the U.N.I.A. as a microcosmic representation of the African nation he envisioned for the future, while in the United

States he proclaimed himself provisional president of Africa. The U.N.I.A. had its own "Universal Ethiopian Anthem," which became "the anthem of the Negro race." It also had its *Declaration of Rights of the Negro Peoples of the World*, which was adopted at the International Convention of 1920.[28]

Garvey had studied the history of the making of governments throughout the world, particularly of Europe and pre-colonial Africa, before he began to articulate his Black Nationalist ideology. His personal accoutrements and that of his entourage—for which he was ridiculed—revealed both African and European garment traditions that predate the twentieth century. As for the robe he wore on special occasions, he explained, "They called me all kinds of names, for wearing, on demonstrative occasions only, this robe that is commonly worn by their college or university presidents, professors, graduates, church and legal dignitaries and millions of persons of their race, to show collegiate, academic or other distinctions."[29] Comparable to the Governor General Toussaint Louverture, Emperor Jean-Jacques Dessalines, and King Henry Christophe (the first three leaders of the newly freed Black Republic of Haiti), Garvey conferred titles to men and women of his provisional government court. When Garvey was derided for what his contemporaries viewed as buffoonery, he straightforwardly reminded us, "I am accused of creating dukes, barons and knights. Who gave the white man the monopoly on creating social orders?"[30] The trappings of nationhood were of momentous significance because for a nation to be recognized by other nations it must hold certain protocols, it must have certain political and government structures with key officials. With a strategic focus on international organization, Garvey tactically placed representatives of the race in different countries; he sent commissioners to the League of Nations and designated a provisional ambassador to France. In the *Declaration of Rights of Negro Peoples of the World*, he stated, "We call upon the various governments of the world to accept and acknowledge Negro representatives who shall be sent to the said government to represent the general welfare of the Negro peoples of the world."[31] In addition, he wanted a Black House in Washington where black American officials would reside. While the idea of the Black House never came into fruition, the message Garvey was conveying was nonetheless received. The message was: blacks living in the United States should have a government of their own, a government that would address their particular needs and remedy their existing race condition. At that point of Garveyite history, he was calling for the formation of a black nation-state within the greater nation of the United States. His most cogent argument was that in order to have a nation, the *thing*, leaders must simultaneously create the essential elements of nationhood—schools, businesses, publishing companies, and so on—and show the world the external trappings of their nation. Garvey's actions were thus of tremendous symbolism. The black nationhood he worked arduously to establish and for which he was psychologically and structurally preparing blacks throughout the Diaspora, by establishing U.N.I.A branches in countries where blacks resided, is comparable to the black nationhood Toussaint Louverture sought to institutionalize in Saint-Domingue toward the end of the eighteenth century and early nineteenth century.

The U.N.I.A.'s most significant emblem of nationhood was its flag.[32] The Declaration of Rights of 1920 proclaimed the adoption of the red, black, and green flag, as the official colors of the race. Such proclamation was also of paramount importance, for a flag is the ultimate symbol of nationhood. For Garveyites the *red* represented "the color of the blood which men must shed for their redemption and liberty," the black stood for "the color of the noble and distinguished race to which we belong," and the green for "the luxuriant vegetation of our Motherland."[33] Garvey's nationalist gesture went beyond the boundaries of the United States to influence Black Nationalist perspectives throughout the Americas, Europe, and Africa. In 1924, at the charter unveiling ceremony of the U.N.I.A. the Woodstock division in Cape Town, J. G. Gumbs, who was the guest speaker of the event, expressed his appreciation for the new race symbol, i.e., the red, the black, and the green. He viewed the flag as "[their] own."[34] In 1925, the African National Congress of South Africa also adopted a gold, black and green flag, with the gold representing the country's wealth. Analogous to the symbolism of the U.N.I.A.'s flag, the black represents the people, and the green stands for the land. The adoption of the flag by the African National Congress was a clear demonstration of praise toward the Garvey Movement. The flag was proposed by T. D. Mweli Skota, who was an admirer of Garvey's work, and a respected member of the African National Congress (ANC). Martin reminds us that in the 1950s "the red, black and green could be seen in Kenya, this time with a shield, arrow and spear superimposed on it, as the flag of Jomo Kenyatta's nationalist Kenya African Union."[35] Garvey's nationalist trappings, as well as his social and political philosophy, aimed at awakening blacks to a new group consciousness based on race, a common history and destiny. His sociopolitical method opened a space for black participation in political and cultural life, in order to prepare them for closer contacts with other nations and races.

The primary objective of Black Nationalism was to bring black dependency on white to a definite end by establishing (an) autonomous black nation(s).[36] The assertion was that free of white oppression, blacks would advance and become economically, socially, and politically independent, hence would become *man-full, symmetrical, undwarfed*—to use the terms of Bishop Turner in 1895.[37] Once blacks would form an independent nation—either geographically dispersed throughout the globe or assembled in Africa—they would be able to participate in material trade with different nations throughout the world. Thus, the fundamental principle behind Black Nationalism was that before the indispensable interdependence that must exist among nations, blacks must first organize themselves as a nation. For, there can never be interdependence between a dependent faction and an independent entity. There can only be interdependence between two independent entities or two dependent factions, one relying on the other for reasons that would benefit both parties. It follows that it is only as an organized and independent people that black folk can engage in international and reciprocal trades based on respect. Race leaders of the Diaspora were keenly cognizant of the fact that no one nation can or should survive isolated or alienated from the rest of the world. One of Garvey's maxims on nationhood states:

Point me to a weak nation and I will show you a people oppressed, abused, taken advantage of by others.
Show me a weak race and I will show you a people reduced to serfdom, peonage and slavery.
Show me a well organized nation, and I will show you a people and a nation respected by the world.[38]

During the late 1910s Du Bois encouraged blacks to open cooperative stores, and in 1918 he endeavored to form the Negro Cooperative Guild, to set up retail stores, cooperative warehouses, and even banks. In his essay, "W. E. B. Du Bois: Protagonist of the Afro-American Protest," Elliott Rudwick underscores Du Bois' belief that blacks could break out of their "closed economic circle," only if they, "rather than inspiring to be rapacious millionaires, would find it satisfying to be 'consecrated' workers devoted to 'social service' for the race."[39] Du Bois further argued that blacks could "encompass a complex racial manufacturing-distributive system, with profits reinvested in useful race projects like large housing developments. Moreover, the black cooperative system could be extended to race members in far off places like Africa."[40] What Du Bois suggested, as early as the 1910s, was a similar scheme as Garvey's business endeavors. The creation of Garvey's chain of businesses, such as the Black Star Line and the Negro Factories Corporation, were established to generate the economic development of the race, in Africa, the Americas, and Europe. The Negro Cooperative Guild Du Bois hoped to create in the United States and within which he wanted to include the participation of all blacks, the manufacturing-distributive system that he wanted to commence, finally, his agenda to re-invest in the race, all outline his concept of Black Nationalism, both nationally and diasporically. Later, in the 1920s and 1930s, Du Bois' judgment of Garvey's business endeavors as naïve was an expression of Du

Bois' unrealized business ideas within a world of staunch opposition to black development and autonomy. Du Bois' ideas could not materialize partly because of the adverse influence of powerful whites and blacks, who remained preoccupied with being the mighty supervisors of the race.

Black Nationalism and Pan-Africanism

Pan-Africanism is a manifestation of Black Nationalism. As such, the concept of Black Nationalism is broader than that of the movement it fostered. Here, the goal is to probe the different conceptual definitions within Pan-Africanism, as both idea and movement, and to discern any ideological differences that may exist between Pan-Africanism and Black Nationalism. In *Pan-Africanism: The Idea and Movement, 1776–1963*, P. Olisanwuche Esedebe argues that various politicians and writers, from the continent and abroad, have attributed countless definitions to Pan-Africanism. Consequently, "explanations that some African scholars and politicians give often differ from those suggested by African descendants abroad. Sometimes the continental African themselves advance conflicting interpretations."[41] In *Pan-Africanism and Nationalism in West Africa, 1900–1945*, J. Ayodele Langley argues that "although one may, in the absence of concrete evidence, assemble any number of incidents and ideas and call it Pan-Africanism, this method of proceeding tends to obscure the dynamics and complexity of the movement."[42] He further contends that Pan-Africanism cannot and should not be "boxed" or "frozen" into defined epochs and set categories.[43] Rather, according to Langley, "there was not one single Pan-African movement but several, at least up to the close of the 1920s."[44] Examining the complexity of the Pan-African movement in *The Pan-African Movement: A History of Pan-Africanism in America, Europe and Africa*, Imanuel Geiss expresses the difficulty to provide a clear definition of Pan-Africanism. He argues that the challenge to arrive at a definite concept of Pan-Africanism is a "complex problem which can best be approached historically. By looking at its various manifestations we can arrive at simple and comprehensive formulae, compare them with objective reality and modify them continually in the light of modern knowledge."[45] Among the many distinctive views of Pan-Africanism, some leaders, particularly W. E. B. Du Bois, perceived Pan-Africanism as "an intellectual understanding and co-operation among all groups of African descent in order to bring about 'the industrial and spiritual emancipation of the Negro people.'"[46] While leaders such as Du Bois comprehended the need for a synthesis between the spiritual dimension and political actions of the movement, others such as Colin Legum erroneously saw Pan-Africanism from a strictly narrow and simplistic view, i.e., as a movement of ideas and emotions. In his *Pan-Africanism: A Short Political Guide,* Colin Legum describes Pan-Africanism as "essentially a movement of ideas and emotions," which "at times achieves a synthesis; at times it remains at the level of thesis and antithesis."[47] As for the debate between continental and global Pan-African philosophy and movement, Chief Anthony Enahoro viewed Pan-Africanism as a continental affair which aimed at "the economic, social and cultural development of the continent, the avoidance of conflict among African states, the promotion of African unity and influence in world affairs."[48] The Senegalese publicist Alioune Diop, on the other hand, conceived Pan-Africanism as "more or less synonymous with the concept of 'African Personality' or 'Negritude,'"[49] which would be synonymous to global Pan-Africanism.

Formulating an exact definition of Pan-Africanism is a difficult task, for it cannot be indisputably periodized, nor can it be a definitive concept. Therefore, an acceptable concept of Pan-Africanism should offer a list of the major component ideas and a critical analysis of their relation. As Esedebe concludes, the definition of Pan-Africanism is at best a synthesis of various definitions. Namely, "Africa as the homeland of Africans and persons of African origin, solidarity among men of African descent, belief in a distinct African personality, rehabilitation of Africa's past, pride in African culture, Africa for Africans in church and state, the hope for a united and glorious future Africa."[50] Esedebe's outline of the key precepts of Pan-Africanism encompasses continental and global Pan-Africanism, with the awareness that Africa's development and the development of its descendants abroad are equally important and should work relationally. In other words, the valorization of Africa's past, the preservation of African heritage and culture, the affirmation of an African personality, should be recognized by Africans in Africa, as well as by African descendants dispersed throughout the world. Thus, "with some simplification,"

> we can say that Pan-Africanism is a political and cultural phenomenon which regards Africa, Africans and African descendants abroad as a unit. It seeks to regenerate and unify Africa and promote a feeling of oneness among the people of the African world. It glorifies the African past and inculcates pride in African value. Any adequate definition of the phenomenon must include the political and cultural aspects.[51]

This concept of Pan-Africanism is closely related to Black Nationalism. Black Nationalists not only recognized Africa as the ancestral land but also advocated self-governance in Africa and throughout the black Diaspora; moreover, both philosophies expressed the urgency for political and cultural dialogues among black nations. Hence, the argumentation is that similar to

Négritude, Pan-Africanism is a manifestation of, a progeny of Black Nationalism. The core principles of Pan-Africanism that Esedebe underlines are the components figures such as Blyden, Du Bois, Garvey, Jacques-Garvey, Jane Nardal, Paulette Nardal, Césaire, Price-Mars, Nkrumah, and Malcolm X expressed in their ideologies and undertook in their activism, whether under the nomenclature of Indigénisme, Pan-Africanism, Garveyism, and Négritude—to name a few of the black Diaspora's literary and political movements. The distinguishing characteristic I must underline here is if one should define Pan-Africanism solely in terms of continental African unity, independent of diasporic blacks, then there is clearly a considerable qualitative distinction between Pan-Africanism and Black Nationalism. Pan-Africanism, then, would not adhere to the total objective of Black Nationalism, for Black Nationalism does not necessarily or always imply a physical return to Africa, but rather a psychological return, a political dialogue and a socio-cultural relationship with the ancestral land.

The Ideological Link between Black Nationalism, Black Internationalism, and Universal Humanism

The three concepts, Black Nationalism, Black Internationalism, and Universal Humanism, are interwoven, each providing a distinctive dimension to the sociopolitical, cultural, and spiritual facets of the continuing race struggle. The first conceptual distinction between Black Nationalism and Black Internationalism is based on territory. Black Nationalism implies territorial attachment in addition to a common ancestry and a common aim or destiny, while Black Internationalism focuses on ideological aspects based on the history of the race and its destiny. In other words, Black Internationalism is the *group* consciousness of different black nations. Nonetheless, within the philosophies of both Black Nationalism and Internationalism, the race dimension remains of keystone significance on all levels; the commitment to group advancement, through mental liberty and social prosperity, remains constant. Black Internationalism, which became prevalent from the second half of the twentieth century onward, after various black nations had been formed, emphasizes the idea that blacks, though geographically dispersed, must continue their political struggles not only locally and nationally, but as a race. For proponents of Black Internationalism, members of the race are connected through their particular history, their present condition, and their future. Similar to nationalism and Black Nationalism, Black Internationalism is based on psychological disposition and sociopolitical facts. It expresses, at once, political and socioeconomic difficulties as well as psychological, ideological, and cultural thoughts of black folk across the Diaspora.

The liberation struggles of Black Africa, particularly during the 1950s, emerged with a strong Black Nationalist base. In 1956 Léopold Senghor—who was to become the first president of Sénégal 1960–1980—played an important role in the organization of the first Congress of Black Writers and Artists in Paris; in 1966, he sponsored the World Festival of Black Arts in Senegal. As a poet, theoretician, teacher, and statesman, Senghor understood that the Black world's cultural expression through the arts was crucial in inspiring social and political reflection. During the Second Congress of Black Artists and Writers held in Rome in 1959, Frantz Fanon advanced that "the responsibility of the African as regards national culture is also a responsibility with regard to African Negro culture."[52] Fanon's argument was that the liberation of an African country and the valorization of its culture are the liberation and valorization of blacks in general. Each liberation victory helps further the progress of the race, just as intra-racial ethnic prejudice, conflicts, and wars contribute to the regression of the race. Furthermore, the freedom of people of African descent would also lead to the emancipation of the greater world from the plague of cruel injustices and fatal prejudices. Thus, "far from keeping aloof from other nations, therefore, it is national liberation which leads the nation to play its part on the stage of history. It is at the heart of national consciousness that international consciousness lives and grows. And this two-fold emerging is ultimately only the source of all culture."[53] In his reasoning, Fanon outlines the strict correlation that exists between national progress and world advancement, to demonstrate the degree to which the latter depends on the former.

With the vision of forming functional black nations, the aim of each responsible leader was to establish in their respective country a government that would permit and encourage the participation of black officials, by first erecting educational institutions established to prepare independent blacks. Their objective was also to form social structures that would nurture their various African heritages and allow them to express their cultural differences. Comparably, in the 1960s advocates of the Black Power Movement struggled for control over their own community. They requested control of their schools and of the educational system as a whole, they proposed to revise the curriculum for their students, they demanded qualified teachers as well as the intellectual freedom of those teachers, as they also pointed out the necessity for conscientious administrators. Occurring concurrently with the educational demands was the aim for political power and civil rights, as well as for the opportunity to assert economic prosperity that would lead to better living conditions in the black community. Similar to their predecessors, one of the important goals leaders of the Black Power Movement aspired to was the development of successful black communities.

In the formation of prosperous black communities, one of the key elements of consideration is the practice of dialogue among nations of the greater world. In *Le temps historique dans l'œuvre théâtrale d'Aimé Césaire* (*The Historical Time in Aimé Césaire's Theatrical Œuvre*), Albert Owusu-Sarpong under- lines Césaire's conception of humanism. According to Césaire, the Négritude movement helped in the progressive construction of a true humanism by questioning certain existing human conditions in order to generate candid and forthright dialogues. The true sense of dialogue for Césaire is confrontation and acknowledgment.[54] The ideological and dialogical confrontation, which occurs in forthright discussions, should lead to the recognition of each other's words and presence, as well as to mutual respect. Hence, it follows that there cannot be any form of dialogue between an individual and a puppet. Black leaders were convinced that before the race becomes engaged in the dialogue that must exist among humans of different races, blacks must first demand the right to be recognized and respected as *thinking* individuals. In his essay "Discours sur l'art africain" ("Discourse on African Art"), published in 1966, Aimé Césaire posits that humanism cannot exist without its fundamental universal aspect, or with- out dialogue, "car, enfin, il n'y a pas d'humanisme s'il n'est pas universel, il n'y a pas d'humanisme sans dialogue."[55] The Universal Humanism black leaders postulated in their writings went beyond racial, ethnic, religious, and national differences to focus on the common condition and common goals of human beings. Césaire situates Négritude in relation to the essential Universal Huma- nism, and explains, "Notre négritude est un humanisme . . . notre négritude est située dans l'histoire . . . notre négritude est un enracinement. A partir de cela . . . on peut faire n'importe quoi, bien sûr . . . ça n'épuise pas tout . . . c'est comme le mouvement circulatoire du sang . . . c'est comme la vie, à partir de laquelle toutes les végétations sont possibles." ("Our négritude is a humanism . . . our négritude is situated in history . . . our négritude is rootedness. From that . . . one can do whatever, of course . . . this does not exhaust everything . . . it is like the circulatory movement of the blood . . . it is like life, from which all vegetations are possible.")[56] Synthesizing the philosophical works of great thinkers such as Montaigne, Ciceron, and Homer, on the art of dialogue, also, combining the thoughts of Dante, Césaire, and Schiller, on the philosophy of humanism, Owusu-Sarpong defines humanism as the discovery of humanity from within us. Humanism, as Owusu-Sarpong theorizes, is the acknowledge- ment of Man in lieu of men (here, "Man" stands for humanness). It is the awareness that humanness can only exist in its universality.

L'humanisme, c'est la revendication de l'Homme, de tout l'Homme au lieu des hommes, d'une patrie d'Homme. L'humanisme, c'est la découverte de l'humanité qui gît au plus profond de nous, humanité qui n'est riche que dans sa tradition, que dans son universalité, que dans son essence. Malgré les différences individuelles, esthétiques, philosophiques, sociales, raciales et religieuses, l'humanisme atteint l'Homme. Il est un effort total de synthèse et d'unification et est ainsi une véritable philosophie: la Philosophie de l'Homme.[57]

Humanism is the assertion of Man, of the integral Man in lieu of men, a nation of Man. Humanism is the discovery of humanity that lies deep within us, a humanity that is rich only in its tradition, only in its universality, only in its essence. In spite of individual, esthetic, philosophical, racial and religious differences, humanism reaches Man. There is a complete effort of synthesis and unification, and is thus a true philosophy: the Philosophy of Man.

Understanding the need for human collaboration, leaders of the Diaspora often spoke in terms of African descendants' participation within the greater civilization of mankind. As a case in point, Garvey's petition to the League of Nations, the Pan-African Congress' principles (which Du Bois helped draft), Césaire's plays *La Tragédie du Roi Christophe*, and *Une Saison au Congo*, all explore the concepts and manifestations of Black Nationalism, Black Internationalism, and Universal Humanism. Price-Mars' *Ainsi parla l'oncle* and Paulette Nardal's essay "L'Internationalisme Noir" comprise similar arguments. Similarly, during the 1950s and 1960s, Nkrumah's continental and global Pan-Africanism, as well as Malcolm X's various speeches, also stressed the importance of Black Internationalism among black nations, and Universal Humanism among nations of the world. In 1922, in his Principles of the Universal Negro Improvement Association delivered at Liberty Hall, New York City, Garvey underlined the foundational agenda of the Garveyite movement, which simultaneously focused on the establishment of Black Nationalism and Universal Humanism. Garvey explained:

Over five years ago the Universal Negro Improvement Association placed itself before the world as the movement through which the new and rising Negro would give expression of his feelings. This Association adopts an attitude not of hostility of other races and peoples of the world, but an attitude of self-respect, of manhood rights on behalf of 400,000,000 Negroes of the world.

We represent peace, harmony, love, human sympathy, human rights and human justice, and that is why we fight so much Wheresoever human rights are denied to any group, wheresoever justice is denied to any group, there the U.N.I.A. finds a cause. . . .

We are not preaching propaganda of hate against anybody. We love the white man; we love all humanity. . . . The white man is as necessary to the existence of the Negro as the Negro is necessary to his existence. There is a common relationship that we cannot escape. Africa has certain things that Europe wants, and Europe has certain things that African wants. . . . It is impossible for us to escape it. Africa has oil, diamonds, copper, gold and rubber and all the minerals that Europe wants, and there must be some kind of relationship between Africa and Europe for a fair exchange, so we cannot afford to hate anybody.[58]

The Universal Humanism call Garvey underscored in his Black Nationalist speeches and writing was also articulated by eminent leaders of the Diaspora. They understood, unequivocally, that each race and nation must contribute to the continuous development of humanity; for African nations have certain social elements and treasures that European nations need and vice versa. Asia has certain social and political philosophies Africa should incorporate in its sociopolitical structures and vice versa, just as the Americas have certain philosophies and laws that Africa, Europe, and Asia can utilize. In calling for self-sufficiency, black leaders were not advocating black alienation, but were instead spreading the philosophy of independence and interdependence among different nations and races. The relationship they called for was one that would be founded on respect, acceptance, exchange, and mutual help—fundamental principles of their concept of Universal Humanism. It is within the scope of the indissoluble relationship between Black Nationalism, Black Internationalism, and Universal Humanism that we will examine the intellectualism and activism of black leaders of the Diaspora throughout this study.

Notes

1. Hans Kohn, *The Idea of Nationalism* (New York: The Macmillan Company, 1944) 10.
2. Marcus Garvey, *Philosophy and Opinions of Marcus Garvey* (New York: Arno Press and the New York Times, 1968) 6, 7.
3. Malcolm X, *Malcolm X Speaks: Selected Speeches and Statements.* 1965. (New York: Pathfinder Press, 1989) 21.
4. The history and destiny of the race, on which Black Internationalists focused, were based on both feeling and form, i.e., on the emotional connection between blacks as well as organized social and political framework and cultural exchanges through such movements as Pan-Africanism, Indigénisme, Garveyism, Harlem Renaissance, Afrocriollo, and Négritude.
5. On the subject of varying concepts of Black Nationalism, one may consult such works as George Padmore, *Pan-Africanism or Communism? The Coming Struggle for Africa* (1956); Kwame Nkrumah, *Ghana: The Autobiography of Kwame Nkrumah* (1957); C.L.R. James, *The Black Jacobins* (1963); James R. Hooker, *Black Revolutionary: George Padmore's Path from Communism to Pan-Africanism* (1967); Marcus Garvey, *Philosophy and Opinions of Marcus Garvey* (1968); J. Ayodele Langley, *Pan-*

Africanism and Nationalism in West Africa, 1900–1945 (1973); Karl Evanzz, *The Messenger: The Rise and Fall of Elijah Muhammad* (2001).

6. Some of the texts from which one can extract the influential ideas leaders exchanged between one another are Frederick Douglass, *Narrative of the Life of Frederick Douglass, An American Slave, Written by Himself* (1845); James M. Gregory, *Frederick Douglass, the Orator* (1971); Edward W. Blyden, *Christianity, Islam, and the Negro Race* (1967); Martin R. Delany, *The Condition, Elevation, Emigration, and Destiny of the Colored People of the United States* (1852); Jean Price-Mars, *La Vocation de l' Elite* (1919); Marcus A. Garvey, *Philosophy and Opinions of Marcus Garvey* (1968); William Edward Burghardt Du Bois, *Dusk of Dawn* (1940); Aimé Césaire, *Discours sur le Colonialisme* (1953); O. Kwame Nkrumah, *Consciencism: Philosophy and Ideology for Decolonization and Development with Particular Reference to the African Revolution* (1964); Malcolm X, *Malcolm X Speaks* (1965, 1993).

7. One may consult John R. Beard, *The Life of Toussaint L'Ouverture: The Negro Patriot of Hayti* (1853); Robert C. O. Benjamin, *The Life of Toussaint L'Ouverture: Warrior and Statesman, with a Historical Survey of the Island of San Domingo from the Discovery of the Island by Christopher Columbus, 1492 to the Death of Toussaint, in 1803* (1888); Charles C. Mossell, *Toussaint L'Ounverture: The Hero of Saint Domingo, Soldier, Statesman, Martyr* (1890); Michel Vaucaire, *Toussaint Louverture* (1930); Yves Jerome, *Toussaint L'Ouverture* (1978).

8. James G. Kellas, *The Politics of Nationalism and Ethnicity* (New York: St. Martin's Press, 1991) 2–3.

9. Hans Kohn, *The Idea of Nationalism* (1944); Balandier Georges, "Messianism and Nationalism" (1972); E. J. Hobsbawm, *Nations and Nationalism since 1780* (1990); James G. Kellas, *The Politics of Nationalism and Ethnicity* (1991).

10. Frères de l'Instruction Chrétienne, *Histoire D'Haïti* (Port-au-Prince: Saint-Joseph, Archevêque, 1942) 114.

11. See David P. Geggus, "Slavery, War, and Revolution in the Greater Caribbean" (1997); Carolyn E. Fick, "The French Revolution in Saint Domingue: A Triumph or a Failure" (1997); Joan Dayan, *Haiti, History and the Gods* (1995).

12. P. Olisanwuche Esedebe, *Pan-Africanism: The Idea and Movement, 1776–1963* (Washington, D.C.: Howard University Press, 1982) 8.

13. The African Institution, which was regarded as a British humanitarian organization, was dominated by former directors of the Sierra Leone Company.

14. Garvey, *Philosophy*, iii.

15. Ibid., preface.

16. Ibid., iv.

17. C. L. R. James, *The Black Jacobins: Toussaint L'Ouverture and the San Domingo Revolution.* 1963. (New York: Vintage Books, 1989) 241–47.

18. Thomas Madiou, *Histoire D'Haïti*, Tome I, 1492–1799. 1847–1848. (Port-au-Prince: Editions Henri Deschamps, 1987) 406–34.

19. Frères de l'Instruction Chrétienne, *Histoire D'Haïti*, 88.

20. James, *The Black Jacobins*, 244–47.

21. Martin, *Race First*, 13.

22. Ibid., 5–6.

23. Ibid., 6.

24. Kohn, *The Idea of Nationalism*, 11.

25. In her central argument of the transatlantic slave trade and the phenomenon of transshipment, Gwendolyn Midlo Hall's text *Slavery and African Ethnicities in the Americas* demonstrates the degree to which the African origins of diasporic blacks in the Americas are intertwined. During the trade era enslaved Africans of common stocks were debarked on different ports and transshipped to various areas.

26. Garvey, *Philosophy*, 93.

27. Garvey, *The Negro World*, February 24, 1923.

28. Garvey, *Philosophy*, 135.

29. Ibid., 353.

30. Marcus Garvey, *Marcus Garvey: Toward Black Nationhood* (Princeton: Films for the Humanities, 1983). Following the invasion of Ethiopia, Garvey witnessed Italian fascists appoint a Duke of Addis Ababa. He underlined the world's acceptance of a Duke of Addis Ababa in comparison to the ridicule of his nomination of John E. Bruce as Duke of the Nile in 1924 (see *Black Man*, July-August 1936, p. 18).

31. Garvey, *Philosophy*, 141.

32. In 1900 two Caucasians, William A. Heelan and J. Fred Helf, wrote the song "Every Race Has a Flag but the Coon." The song explicitly lists races and nations with their respective flag and motto, except for the black race and black nations. The content of the song was clearly meant to insult the black race. During the second decade of the 1900s Bishop A. Lennox proposed a flag: red, white, blue, and purple. The color symbolism was based on religion and the "the loyalty of the Negro to the United States." Focusing on the race, diasporically, in 1920 Garvey adopted emblematic colors that represent Africa and African descendants.

33. Martin, *Race First*, 45.

34. Ibid., 44.

35. Ibid., 45.

36. *Black Separatism*, which was the term used in the United States during the 1960s, signified a black nation functioning independently from a dominating white nation. In other words, black separatist leaders advocated a separate black nation which interdependently works and collaborates with the greater world community.

37. Garvey, *Philosophy*, vii.

38. Ibid., 14.

39. Elliot Rudwick, "W. E. B. Du Bois: Protagonist of the Afro-American Protest," *Black Leaders of the Twentieth Century* (Urbana: University of Illinois Press, 1982) 78.

40. Ibid., 78.

41. Esedebe, *Pan-Africanism*, 1.

42. J. Ayodele Langley, *Pan-Africanism and Nationalism in West Africa, 1900–1945* (Oxford: Clarendon Press, 1973) viii.

43. Ibid., viii.

44. Ibid., 3.

45. Imanuel Geiss, *The Pan-African Movement: A History of Pan-Africanism in America, Europe and Africa.* 1968. (New York: Africana Publishing, 1974) 3.

46. W.E.B. Du Bois, *The Crisis*, November 1933.

47. Colin Legum, *Pan-Africanism: A Short Political Guide* (New York: Frederick A. Praeger, 1965) 14.

48. Esedebe, *Pan-Africanism*, 1.

49. Ibid., 2.

50. Ibid., 3.

51. Ibid., 3.

52. Frantz Fanon, *The Wretched of the Earth*, trans. Constance Farrington (New York: Grove Press, Inc., 1963) 198.

53. Ibid., 199.

54. Albert Owusu-Sarpong, *Le Temps Historique dans L'Œuvre Théâtrale d'Aimé Césaire* (Paris: L'Harmattan, 2002) 197.

55. Ibid., 192.

56. Aimé Césaire, *Aimé Césaire: A Voice for History* (San Francisco: California Newsreel, 1994) Part II.

57. Owusu-Sarpong, *Le Temps*, 201.

58. Garvey, *Philosophy*, 93–100.

2

Toussaint Louverture: The Educational and Sociopolitical Legacy of a Leader

En me renversant, on n'a abattu à Saint-Domingue que le tronc de l'arbre de la Liberté des noirs; il repoussera par les racines parce qu'elles sont profondes et nombreuses.

By overthrowing me, they only cut down the trunk of the tree of Liberty of blacks; it will re-grow through the roots, for they are profound and numerous.

—Toussaint Louverture[1]

Be assured that I planted well the seed of Negro or black nationalism which cannot be destroyed even by the foul play that has been meted out to me.

—Marcus Garvey[2]

IN EXAMINING THE PRECEPTS OF Black Nationalism as well as the literary and social movements that grew out of and in turn expanded its principles, it is important to situate the black Diaspora's first recognized leader at the core. The relevance of an examination of Toussaint Louverture's educational and political accomplishments in a study that examines the literary and sociopolitical writings of the nineteenth and twentieth century black Diaspora is twofold. First, the intellectual abilities he acquired through self-education, along with his innate intelligence, placed him in a leadership position for all blacks. As a result, in time he came to epitomize the principles of Black Nationalism within the Diaspora. Second, his activism helped generate a nascent black political thought which cross-geographically fomented many slave rebellions and revolutions of the nineteenth century. The growing black political thought of the nineteenth century led to the emergence of movements—in trans-generational lessons and legacy—such as Indigénisme, Pan-Africanism, Garveyism, New Negro Renaissance, Négritude, and Afrocriollo. As a case in point, in 1822 Denmark Vesey recalled the actions of blacks in Saint-Domingue, during the revolution period on the island, to mobilize his followers in North Carolina. In 1893 Frederick Douglass, who served as the United States Minister Resident and Consul General to Haiti between 1889 and 1891, was appointed commissioner of the Haytian Pavillion by President Florvil Hyppolite.[3] On January 1st of 1893 Douglass delivered a speech in which he gave homage to Toussaint Louverture and blacks in Haiti for their unprecedented accomplishments. In his various speeches and writings during the 1920s and 1930s Marcus Garvey lauded Louverture for his examplary leadership. In *Cahier d'un retour au pays natal* (*Notebook of a Return to the Native Land*), published in 1939, Aimé Césaire extolled Toussaint Louverture's achievement in the black struggle for liberty, equality, race organization, and advancement.

Louverture and the Challenges of Nation-Building

Born into slavery, Toussaint Louverture lived forty-five years as a slave before he began to undertake an active role in the struggle against the slavery system. In *The Life of Toussaint Louverture: The Negro Patriot of Hayti*, John R. Beard informs us that Toussaint Louverture was born on May 20, 1743 of parents from Arada in West Africa. He also reports that Toussaint Louverture, born François-Dominique Toussaint, descended from a royal lineage, where his grandfather was the king of the Arada people. His father Gaou-Guinou was captured by a neighboring group during a plundering expedition, and was sold to slave-dealers who brought him to the island of Saint-Domingue.[4] In *Toussaint Louverture* Michel Vaucaire notes that in 1795 François-Dominique Toussaint, from the Bréda plantation, was nicknamed l'Ouverture by a French commissioner after his distinguished victories as the general of his military squads. "Ce sale noir fait l'Ouverture partout"[5] ("This dirty/lousy Negro opens the path everywhere"), exclaimed the French commissioner. The commissioner's observation reveals a conspicuously ambivalent compliment, which nonetheless outlines his acknowledgment of Louverture's abilities as a leader. Toussaint adopted the name "l'Ouverture," which, as a modification, he writes without the apostrophe and became known as Toussaint Louverture, the man who would *open* and pave the way to liberty for all blacks.

During his younger years, Louverture's father taught him the use of medicinal leaves; with that knowledge he became a veterinarian and treated the horses on the Bréda plantation. His godfather, Pierre-Baptiste, taught him to read; in addition to his native African language, Louverture acquired the knowledge of French from his godfather and he also became acquainted with Latin.[6] Building on the foundational reading skill acquired from Jean-Baptiste, Louverture continued to progress in reading, writing, and drawing, and later began to read Abbé Raynal's major work, *Histoire philosophique et politique des établissements et du commerce des Européens dans les Deux Indes* (1780) (*Philosophical and Political History of European Settlements and Commerce in the Indies*); a text which would later prove to be one of the catalytic forces behind the acceptance of his role as the liberator of blacks. According to C.L.R. James' account,

> in addition to his practical education, [Louverture] had, as we have seen, been able to read a little. He had read Caesar's Commentaries, which had given him some idea of politics and the military art and the connection between them. Having read and re-read the long volume by the Abbé Raynal on the East and West Indies, he had a thorough grounding in the economics and politics, not only of San Domingo, but of all the great empires of Europe which were engaged in colonial expansion and trade.[7]

From the scholarship that studies the epoch of the revolution, including C. L. R. James' valuable work, it is evident that Louverture was an autodidact par excellence.[8] He had prepared himself both intellectually and physically for the great leadership responsibility that awaited him. During his childhood years Louverture was weak and sickly to the extent that his parents doubted he would live past childhood.[9] However, as he approached adolescence, he began to strengthen his frame by "the severest labours and the most violent exercises."[10] By the age of twelve Louverture went beyond the physical capacities of his peers "who so swift in hunting? who so clever to swim across a foaming torrent? who so skillful to back a horse in full speed, and direct him at his will? The spirit of the man was already working in the boy."[11] In adulthood, he increasingly became an influential and respected personality in Saint-Domingue, as both blacks and whites showed trust in his moral standard, his political abilities, and physical strength. Louverture is described as a man of natural strength of character who was impenetrable, taciturn, yet compassionate. Characteristically, the sagacious leader was accustomed to think more than he spoke, a trait that helped him master unshakable self-control, focused reflection, and the ability of succinct speech.[12]

The intellectual and intelligent abilities Toussaint Louverture possessed as an ex-slave, as early as the eighteenth century, led blacks and mulattoes to view him as an ingenious leader who could reform the existing social and political structure in Saint-Domingue to a more equitable society. During his years as a slave, Louverture learned the military craft and came to possess the diplomatic acumen necessary to become a capable leader. Throughout the years he acquired various experiences in administration, politics, military art, economics, as well as national and foreign affairs. With his knowledge of world economics and politics Louverture was able to negotiate with European powers in world affairs, during an era when blacks were only regarded and treated as sub-humans. The leadership and control he demonstrated over his soldiers, his ingenuity in political matters, and his extraordinary bravery, gained him the confidence of his followers, even in the most difficult or seemingly impossible military situations. One could argue that Louverture's actions—given the slavery system and his position within it—remained incomparable to any leader thus far. His strategies and actions in international politics made him the exemplary leader for his successors within the black Diaspora.

In *Black Intellectuals* William Banks offers a definition of black intellectualism that is relevant to the conceptual framework of this analysis. Banks' concept of intellectualism "focuses on individuals who are reflective and critical, who act self-consciously to transmit, modify, and create ideas and culture."[13] The emphasis on self-conscious deeds, the modification and transmission of knowledge and wisdom, and the creation of ideas and culture is significant for it creates a broader space where enslaved ancestors are acknowledged for their contribution to contemporary black thought. Such spectrum does not negate the importance of ancestors who never had the opportunity to learn to read or write, but have been invaluable soldiers in the fight for freedom. The enslaved Africans who brought, maintained, and modified such roles as that of warriors, cultivators, priests and priestesses, medicine men and women, as well as *griots* in the Americas, are undeniable sources of knowledge for the black Diaspora. The intellectuals and activists whom are examined throughout this text include not only formally educated individuals such as Dr. W. E. B. Du Bois, Dr. Jean Price-Mars, and Dr. Anna Julia Cooper, but also autodidacts such as Toussaint Louverture, Marcus Garvey, and Malcolm X. The intellect and intelligence of those figures made their social and political endeavors conceivable and considerably successful. In *Black Intellectuals* Banks uses Richard Hofstadter's definition of the intellect and intelligence— from Hofstadter's *Anti-intellectualism in American Life* (1963)—to support his view on black leaders' social and political achievements: "Intellect is the critical, creative, and contemplative side of mind. Whereas intelligence seeks to grasp, manipulate, re-order, adjust, intellect examines, ponders, wonders, theorizes, imagines. Intelligence will seize the immediate meaning in a situation and evaluate it. Intellect evaluates, and looks for the meaning of situations as a whole."[14]

Taking into consideration the different texts Louverture read, among which *Caesar's Commentaries,* it is worth emphasizing that Abbé Raynal's text, *Histoire philosophique et politique des établissements et du commerce des Européens dans les Deux Indes,* outlined the basic principles of human freedom and dignity that Louverture would later strive to apply in Saint-Domingue. Here, I would underline that Louverture, along with the majority of blacks in Saint-Domingue and elsewhere, recognized the importance of freedom and knew the value of human dignity as they endured degradation and dehumanization. Given that the need for freedom is instinctual to all Men, the slaves must have pondered on philosophies similar to those expressed by Abbé Raynal, although as slaves they were forcefully prohibited from writing, and therefore lacked the skills necessary to publish their own observations and ideologies. In his thorough analysis of the slave system and the condition of blacks within that destructive machine, Abbé Raynal wrote, and Toussaint Louverture attentively read:

Liberty is everyone's own property. There are three kinds of liberty—*natural liberty, civil liberty, political liberty;* that is to say, the liberty of the man, the liberty of the citizen, and the liberty of the community. Natural liberty is the right which nature has given to every one to dispose of himself according to his own will. Civil liberty is the right which society ought to guarantee to every citizen to do all that is not contrary to the laws. Political liberty is the condition of a people which has not alienated its own sovereignty, and which makes its own laws, or which is in part associated in its legislation.

Mild and loving Jesus! Could you have foreseen that your benign maxims would be employed to justify so much horror? If the Christian religion thus authorized avarice in governments, it would be necessary for ever to proscribe its dogmas. In order to overturn the edifice of slavery, to what tribunal shall we carry the cause of humanity? Kings, refuse the seal of your authority to the infamous traffic which converts men into beasts. But what do I say? Let us look somewhere else. If self-interest alone prevails with nations and their masters, there is another power. Nature speaks in louder tones than philosophy or self-interest. Already are there established two colonies of fugitive negroes, whom treaties and power protect from assault. Those lightnings announce the thunder. *A courageous chief is only wanted. Where is he? That great man whom Nature owes to her vexed, oppressed, and tormented children. Where is he? He will appear, doubt it not; he will come forth, and raise the sacred standard of liberty.* This venerable signal will gather around him the companions of his misfortune. More impetuous than the torrents, they will everywhere leave the indelible traces of their just resentment. *Everywhere people will bless the name of the hero, who shall have re-established the rights of the human race; everywhere will they raise trophies in his honour.* (Emphasis added)[15]

Abbé Raynal's observation and analysis brought forth the basic principles of humanity during a time when barbarity toward blacks prevailed in all the colonies. He shed light on the colonists' meditated misinterpretation of the Bible for deliberate misuse of the teachings of Christianity. He denounced the commerce in humans, which he believed was based, foremost, on economic greed, and subsequently on race, custom, and religious prejudices. As early as 1780, in the midst of the slave trade, Abbé Raynal's text is permeated with the cry for liberty and equality among humans. He advocated the need for natural, civil, and political liberties, which are the elements that distinguish humans from animals and objects. For, "without liberty, or the possession of one's own body and the enjoyment of one's own mind, there is neither husband, father, relation nor friend; we have no country, no fellow-citizen, no God."[16] Moreover, the text presaged the coming of a liberator who would free members of the race from their state of stark dehumanization. Toussaint observed the social condition in Saint-Domingue as he read and re-read the words of Abbé Raynal. In time he realized he had the responsibility to lead his people to freedom; wholeheartedly, he accepted that he was "the great man who Nature owes to her vexed, oppressed, and tormented children," the man "who shall have re-established the rights of the human race." Responding to his call, Toussaint Louverture began the journey to re-establish freedom and dignity among the race in order to give black folk their proper place within the human community.

As the "*général en chef*," the chief general, to the government of Saint-Domingue, and later, in 1801, as the "*Gouverneur Général à vie*," Governor General for life in Saint-Domingue, Louverture started to apply the laws of natural, civil, and political liberties for blacks in the colony. By 1801 Toussaint Louverture began to build civil and governmental buildings throughout Saint-Domingue, and for the first time since the inception of the Atlantic Slave Trade, blacks in Saint-Domingue started to experience natural liberty. Out of bondage, the ex-slaves began to see themselves as humans once again; they were allowed to receive an education, to occupy governmental positions, to engage in trades, and finally, to practice the religion of their choice. Although Toussaint Louverture was himself Catholic—the religion adopted from his former masters—and encouraged blacks to adhere to Catholicism, he nonetheless accepted their Vodouist faith. The Black Nationalism which was burgeoning in Saint-Domingue would later reach the rest of the Americas as well as the African continent. In *The Black Jacobins* C. L. R. James writes,

Black men who had been slaves were deputies in the French Parliament, black men who had been slaves negotiated with the French and foreign governments. Black men who had been slaves filled the highest positions in the colony. There was Toussaint, the former slave, incredibly grand and powerful and incomparably the greatest man in San Domingo. There was no need to be ashamed of being black. The revolution had awakened them, had given them the possibility of achievement, confidence and pride. That psychological weakness, that feeling of inferiority with which imperialists poison colonial peoples everywhere, these were gone . . . Sure of himself, Toussaint reorganized the administration with boldness and skill.[17]

The *Cérémonie du Bois Caïman* of 1791 laid the foundational premise of the Black Nationalism which continued into the nineteenth century and onward: possession of self, political autonomy, and economic advancement. At the end of the practice of slavery in 1794 and at the dawn of the formation of the black republic in 1801, blacks no longer felt debased; the atmosphere of degradation and dishonor that reigned among blacks in Saint-Domingue was replaced with racial pride and a spirit of accomplishment.[18] Hence, the revolution had revived them from the mechanized and zombified state of slavery. The confidence that was growing within the black community in Saint-Domingue and the general faith in the race became the ingredients of race consciousness. Following Louverture's governance, leaders such as Jean-Jacques Dessalines, Henry Christophe, and their constituents, fought for and won the independence of Haiti in 1804.

In preparation for nationhood Louverture's preoccupation with education went beyond his personal accomplishment to set goals for the black youth of Saint-Domingue. Louverture initiated his plan to send young black and mulatto children to France in order to receive the education necessary to later govern. The plan did not come into fruition, given the continuous upheavals between blacks in Saint-Domingue and the French government. More importantly, analyzing Louverture's educational agenda post factum, from a twenty-first century perspective, one could immediately ponder whether or not in the 1800s it was possible for black and mulatto children to receive, in France, an education that would respond to the needs of blacks in Saint-Domingue. We will explore the question of relevant education for black pupils within the Diaspora in subsequent chapters; however at this point, one could justifiably view Louverture's decision as the first step towards educating the black youth, as he faced a number of established obstacles. First, recently liberated from slavery and operating in an illiterate ex-slave community, he did not have many options for educating young blacks; self-education, and education from individual white missionaries and institutions were the scarce sources. Second, in European countries as well as in South and North American countries the Catholic Church has been the foundation of formal education, but the Vatican did not recognize Haiti's independence until the late nineteenth century, with *Le Concordat de 1860* between the *Saint-Siège* and the Haitian government. The caveat remained, however, that neither missionary nor formal Catholic education could philosophically or politically prepare Haitians for leadership of the Black Republic. In retrospect, one can assert that though self-education was instrumental for slaves, ex-slaves, and black leaders dating from the nineteenth century onward, a formal system of appropriate education based on the history and the reality of the newly freed blacks, was essential to the formation of successful nationhood.

Denmark Vesey, Frederick Douglass, and the Path to Emancipation

Through self-education, nonetheless, many blacks in the Americas have made themselves into prominent leaders. Amidst the ex-slaves who stand as commendable leaders, not only for blacks but all humanity, is the orator Frederick Douglass. Comparable to Toussaint Louverture in the eighteenth century, Frederick Douglass was also an autodidact who dedicated his time to extensive reading in preparation for the leadership position that awaited him in the United States. Douglass' self-training gave him the opportunity to thrive as one of the most notable anti-slavery spokespersons of the nineteenth century. At the age of ten he began to read with the aid of a teacher; however, in addition to his teacher's assistance Douglass obtained a spelling book and learned to read with the help of white playmates. At the age of thirteen, he bought a book entitled the *Columbian Orator,* which he paid for with money he earned from blacking boots.[19] Later, his autobiography, *Narrative of the Life of Frederick Douglass: An American Slave, Written by Himself* (published in 1845), narrates his life journey from slavery to freedom and from freedom to leadership. Douglass' autobiography recounts the ways in which a religious man named Lawson foreshadowed his emergence as a leader. The old colored man he referred to as Father Lawson was a spiritual father who influenced his character and destiny. Douglass reveals that "[Father Lawson] threw [his] thoughts into a channel from which they have never entirely diverged. He fanned [his] already intense love of knowledge into a flame, by assuring [him] that [he] was to be a useful man in the world."[20] Father Lawson faithfully believed the Lord had momentous work for Douglass and he must prepare himself to accomplish his duty. Lawson's assertion "made a deep impression" on Douglass' mind.[21] He confesses,

> I verily felt that some such work was before me, though I could not see *how* I should ever engage in its performance. "The good Lord," he said, "would bring

it to pass in his own good time," and that I must go on reading and studying the scriptures. . . . Thus assured, and cheered on, under the inspiration of hope, I worked and prayed with a light heart, believing that my life was under the guidance of a wisdom higher than my own.[22]

Believing the Lord reserved him a great task, Douglass consciously and resolutely initiated his preparation toward self-development. He began to copy letters during his free time at the shipyard where he worked "with playmates as [his] teachers, fences and pavements for [his] copying books, and chalk for [his] pen and ink, [he] learned the art of writing."[23] Having observed and reflected on his personal condition within American society as well as on the condition of fellow blacks, Douglass began to increasingly scrutinize the slavery system within which the miserable and despairing condition of blacks remained stagnant. Through transcriptional exercises from the Bible, Douglass developed not only his ability to write, but also his competence to intimately explore and interpret the Bible. His close readings of the scriptures, away from colonialists' deceitful interpretations and agenda, had a catalytic effect on his decision to combat slavery and liberate the souls of black folk. On September 3, 1838, camouflaged as a sailor and protected by a "Sailor's Protection," Douglass left Baltimore and sailed for New York.[24] After many years of preparation in oratory, he delivered his first acclaimed anti-slavery speech in Nantucket in 1841 to an audience of powerful abolitionists among whom was Mr. William Lloyd Garrison. "So great was the impression made upon the audience by his eloquent words, that it was the means of opening to him that field in which he has won so many laurels as a platform speaker and orator. Not long after this he was appointed a lecturing agent of the Anti-Slavery Society."[25] Few years after his 1841 speech in Nantucket, and as the Anti-Slavery Society's lecturing agent, Douglass had the opportunity to travel to England, Scotland, and Ireland, where he met remarkable intellectuals and prominent politicians who endorsed and supported him as the Anti-Slavery agent and spokesperson of those still in bondage.

Following the publication of his narrative in 1845 and his travels throughout Europe, in 1847 Douglass founded the *North Star*, which would later be called the *Frederick Douglass' Paper*. The *North Star*, along with a printing press, with Martin R. Delany as the coeditor, was the first paper to be under the complete control of blacks. With blacks in managerial positions, the *North Star* functioned as the anti-slavery organ for abolitionists in particular, as it educated its general readers on various subjects. As a lecturer, agent of the anti-slavery movement, and the founder of the *North Star*, Douglass became known as an eminent leader and educator. "In the midst of all his duties," writes James Gregory, "he also found time to act as conductor of the

Underground Railroad. It was his business to receive fugitive slaves, secrete them, raise means, and send them on to Canada."[26] Douglass demonstrated a character and intelligence akin to his ideological precursor, Louverture. With unwavering conviction, they assumed the responsibility to educate themselves in preparation to their call to liberate black folk and lead them to social progress. Douglass' training gave him the ability and opportunity to become one of the most eloquent and respected orators, as well as one of the most reflective thinkers of the second half of the nineteenth century. During an epoch when the idea of free blacks, and more so, the idea of educated blacks, was unfathomable in every colony and plantation, Louverture, and later Douglass, imagined not only freedom, but also black-controlled businesses, black educators, politicians, and professionals.

A number of black leaders emerging in nineteenth century United States saw a direct connection between Louverture's accomplishments in Saint-Domingue and their own endeavors to educate and liberate slaves. In 1841, when Frederick Douglass officially became the Anti-Slavery Society's agent he did not neglect to show admiration for remarkable personalities such as Abraham Lincoln, Toussaint L'Ouverture, and Florvil Hyppolite (president of Haiti during Douglass' appointment as commissioner for the Haitian government). Though each of these men influenced Douglass as a leader, Louverture was for him an eminent and highly esteemed world leader, incomparable to any other. On January 1, 1893 (Haiti's 89th independence day), during the World's Columbian Exposition in Chicago, Douglass delivered a speech in which he situated Louverture and the liberty of Haitians within the greater context of world leaders and revolutions.[27] The Haitian pavilion at the World's Columbian Exposition was not only significant for the recognition of Haiti in world affairs, but it was also a site of pride for blacks throughout the Diaspora. African Americans used the Haitian pavilion to distribute and advertise pamphlets, books, and various artworks produced in the community.[28] Excerpts from Douglass' speech are evidence of the reverence he showed Louverture and the significance he placed on Haiti's independence.

> In taking possession of and dedicating this pavilion to the important purposes for which it has been erected, Charles A. Preston and myself, commissioners appointed by the government of Hayti to represent that government in all that pertains to such a mission, wish to express our satisfaction with the work thus completed. His Excellency, General Hyppolite, has been the supreme motive power and the mainspring by which this pavilion has found a place in these magnificent grounds. . . .
>
> We meet to-day on the anniversary of the independence of Hayti, and it would be an unpardonable omission not to remember that fact with all honor at this time and in this place. Considering what the environments of Hayti were

ninety years ago; considering the peculiar antecedents of its people, both at home and in Africa; considering the long enforced ignorance, their poverty and weakness, and their want of military training; considering their destitution of the munitions of war, and measuring the tremendous moral and material forces that confronted and opposed them, the achievement of their independence is one of the most remarkable and one of the most wonderful events in the history of this eventful country, and I may almost say in the history of mankind. . . .

They were slaves accustomed to stand and tremble in the presence of haughty masters. Their education was obedience to the will of others, and their religion was patience and resignation to the rule of pride and cruelty. As a race they stood before the world as the most abject, helpless, and degraded of mankind. Yet from these men of the Negro race came brave men; men who loved liberty more than life. Wise men, statesmen, warriors, patriots, and heroes. . . .

History will be searched in vain for a warrior more humane, more free from the spirit of revenge, more disposed to protect his enemies, and less disposed to practice retaliation for acts of cruelty than was Toussaint L'Ouverture. His motto from the beginning of the war to the end of his participation in it was protection to the white colonists and no retaliation of injuries. No man in the island had been more loyal to France, to the French republic and to Bonaparte; but when he was compelled to believe by overwhelming evidence that Bonaparte was fitting out a large fleet and was about to send a large and powerful army to Hayti to conquer and reduce his people to slavery, he, like a true patriot, and a true man, determined to defeat this infernal intention by preparing for effective defense.[29]

Douglass' homage to Louverture and the blacks in Saint-Domingue, who fought for their freedom against powerful English, French, and Spanish armies, stressed the effect of the black struggle for liberty in one nation on other blacks in the Diaspora. He further emphasized the wretched social situation from which the slaves and freedmen of Saint-Domingue arose to fight for their freedom. "Considering their destitution of the munitions of war, and measuring the tremendous moral and material forces that confronted and opposed them," Douglass underlined, "the achievement of their independence is one of the most remarkable and one of the most wonderful events in the history of this eventful country, and I may say in the history of mankind."[30] Frederick Douglass who was born a slave—albeit, similar to Toussaint Louverture, was fortunate to receive more human treatment than most slaves—understood the staunch oppositional forces that stood in the way of freedom for blacks. Given the French military power under Napoleon Bonaparte in the late eighteenth and early nineteenth century, in order to achieve independence in 1804 the slaves and freedmen who were familiar with the strategies of war had to train and lead soldiers during the thirteen-year revolution.

Earlier in the nineteenth century, before the emergence of Frederick Douglass as an agent of the anti-slavery movement, Denmark Vesey of Charleston,

South Carolina, also viewed black officers and soldiers of Saint-Domingue as symbolic for the liberation of slaves in the United States. In psychological preparation for the 1822 conspiracy, which was aborted before the rebellion began, Denmark Vesey sought to assemble Africans born in Africa and the New World under the race umbrella for a common cause. However, once whites became aware of Vesey's conspiracy, he and his followers were arrested and brought to trial. Some were hanged, others were deported to Africa or the Caribbean, and the rest were released. In *Exchanging Our Country Marks*, Michael A. Gomez points out that many of the prosecution witnesses, both slaves and free blacks, testified to "Vesey's unique vision of deliverance from bondage, a vision that involved blacks not only from North America but also from Africa and the Caribbean."[31] A witness conveyed Vesey's message of a unified black struggle by explaining that "Vesey told me that a large army from Santo Domingo and Africa were coming to help us, and we must not stand with our hands in our pockets; he was bitter towards whites."[32] Another witness underlined Vesey's admonition against ethnic factions by urging them to "unite together as the San-Domingo people did"; he earnestly demanded that they "never betray one another; and to die before [they] would tell upon one another."[33] As early as the 1820s, Vesey viewed the battle against slaveocracy as a diasporic struggle that must be strategized beyond geographic and temporal barriers.

The transcendence beyond ethnic barriers toward race became Vesey's ideological nucleus in rallying southern blacks to revolt against slavocracy. To a considerable extent, the Haitian revolution was successful because African and Creole blacks had developed a common language, which was essential for communicating strategies. Moreover, the common language symbolized the establishment of a community, a black community with the vision toward freedom. And so, the notion of race, along with acknowledgement of a common African origin, became prevalent in the struggle for dignity and liberation. Toussaint Louverture and his contemporary, Dessalines, envisioned the revolution as the evolutionary process of slaves into individuals, and as the progress of the race from a dual object-animal way of life to humanness and citizenry. While he principally focused on the emancipation of blacks in Saint-Domingue, Louverture envisioned the eventual freedom of all African descendants. In 1802, upon a manipulated deportation to France and before boarding the ship the "Héros," Louverture spoke his last recorded words to the French. His statement emphasized his black diasporic vision. Louverture prophesied, "En me renversant, on n'a abattu à Saint-Domingue que le tronc de l'arbre de la Liberté des noirs, il repoussera par les racines parce qu'elles sont profondes et nombreuses."[34] Louverture was imprisoned in Fort de Joux in Jura, where he expired in 1803.[35]

In 1925 Garvey wrote from his Atlanta Prison cell, "Be assured that I planted well the seed of Negro or black nationalism which cannot be destroyed even by the foul play that has been meted out to me." He continued,

> If I die in Atlanta my work shall then only begin, but I shall live, in the physical or spiritual to see the day of Africa's glory. When I am dead wrap the mantle of the Red, Black and Green around me, for in the new life I shall rise with God's grace and blessing to lead the millions up the heights of triumph with the colors you well know. Look for me in the whirlwind or the storm, look for me all around you, for, with God's grace, I shall come and bring with me countless millions of black slaves who have died in America and West Indies and the millions in Africa to aid you in the fight for Liberty, Freedom and Life.[36]

The comparable tone and content between Louverture's prophecy and Garvey's message is transparent. Toussaint Louverture's metaphoric prophecy maintained an effective diasporic ideology for many successive leaders. Garvey's reproduction of that metaphor demonstrates his life-long zeal as a student of world history. The image of the tree is significant on two levels. One, the "trunk" represents Toussaint Louverture along with other blacks that Europeans killed in order to abort any rebellion against the slavery system. Following the same symbolism, Africans who were transported from Africa to the New World would later be referred to as *bois-d'ébène, ebony-tree*. Second, the image of the *roots* Toussaint depicted in 1801 would be extensively theorized from the late twentieth century onward, with the symbol of the rhizome and that of the submarine connection between people of African descent, if we think of the works of such scholars as Edouard Glissant's *Le discours antillais* (*Caribbean Discourse*), Edward Kamau Brathwaite's *Ancestors*, and James Clifford's *Routes: Travel and Translation in the Late Twentieth Century*.[37] Louverture's image of the deep-rooted tree of Liberty, and its numerous roots (*racines*), metonymically signify the ancestral "origin" of black folk and the current "Diaspora"—made of various black nations, otherwise formulated as Black Internationalism. Stated differently, *the tree of Liberty for blacks* represents the common genesis and destiny they confront as a race; the tree of Liberty is, thus, what holds and unites the *roots*, the *nations*. Above all, his prophecy of the regenerating tree emphasizes the notion of continuum in the black struggle. Garvey's message also contains the idea of continuum: "In the new life I shall rise," "look for me in the whirlwind," "I shall come back and bring with me."[38] While Louverture's metaphor of the tree was earth-based, Garvey's message also included a metaphysical dimension, which leads to the world of spirits. His metaphor invokes the spirits of the countless slaves who died in Africa, at the bottom of the sea, or in the New World. For Garvey, these *spirits* remain participants of the struggle as they joined forces with the *living.* Moreover, the spirits do not manifest within boundaries; they travel from Africa to the Americas to Europe, in order to participate in the fight for black liberty and dignity.

Notes

1. Frères de l'Intruction Chrétienne, *Histoire D'Haïti*, 100.
2. Garvey, *Philosophy*, 237–38.
3. James M. Gregory, *Frederick Douglass: The Orator* (New York: Thomas Y. Crowell Company, 1971) 19.
4. John R. Beard, *The Life of Toussaint Louverture: The Negro Patriot of Hayti* (London: Ingram, Cooke, and Co., 1853) 24.
5. Michel Vaucaire, *Toussaint Louverture* (Paris: Firmin-Didot et Cie, 1930) 19.
6. Beard, *The Life of Toussaint Louverture,* 36.
7. James, *The Black Jacobins,* 91.
8. Charles C. Mossell, *Toussaint L'Ouverture: The Hero of Saint Domingo* (1896); Thomas O. Ott, *The Haitian Revolution 1789–1804* (1973); Jerome Yves J., *Toussaint L'Ouverture* (1978); Wenda Parkinson, *"The Gilded African" Toussaint L'Ouverture* (1980); and David P. Geggus, *A Turbulent Time: The French Revolution and the Greater Caribbean* (1997).
9. Beard, *The Life of Toussaint Louverture,* 26.
10. Ibid., 27.
11. Ibid., 27.
12. Ibid., 28.
13. William Banks, *Black Intellectuals: Race and Responsibility in American Life* (New York: W.W. Norton & Company, 1996) xvi.
14. Ibid., 25.
15. Beard, *The Life of Toussaint L'Ouverture,* 30, 35–36.
* Beard notes that the sections that express uninhibited revenge have been softened or omitted in the translation of Abbé Raynal's original text, *Histoire Philosophique et Politique des Etablissements et du Commerce des Européens dans les Deux Indes.* Vol. III. 193–205.
16. Ibid., 31.
17. Ibid., 244.
18. Ibid., 88.
19. Gregory, *Frederick Douglass,* 19.
20. Frederick Douglass, *Narrative of the Life of Frederick Douglass: An American Slave, Written by Himself.* 1845. (New York: Literary Classics of the United States, 1994) 233.
21. Ibid., 233.
22. Ibid., 233.
23. Ibid., 235.
24. Ibid., 26. The "Sailor's Protection" served as freedom document.

25. Ibid., 28.

26. Gregory, *Frederick Douglass*, 33.

27. Mossell, *Toussaint Louverture*, 474–75.

The World's Columbian Exposition assembled various nations that came to display and represent their culture. Haiti was invited as the "first country in the New World to make an assertion in the interest of liberty and universal suffrage."

28. Ida B. Wells-Barnett, *Crusade for Justice: The Autobiography of Ida B. Wells*, ed. Alfreda M. Duster (Chicago: The University of Chicago Press, 1970) xx.

With the cooperation of Frederick Douglass, Ferdinand L. Barnett, and I. Garland Penn, in July 1893 Ida B. Wells-Barnett wrote a booklet entitled *The Reason Why the Colored American Is Not in the World's Columbian Exposition—The Afro-American's Contribution to Columbian Literature* in which she denounced the exclusion of African Americans in an exposition that took place in the United States.

29. Gregory, *Frederick Douglass*, 191–98.

30. Ibid., 191–98.

31. Michael A. Gomez, *Exchanging Our Country Marks* (Chapel Hill: The University of North Carolina Press, 1998) 2.

32. Ibid., 2.

33. Ibid., 2–3.

34. Frères de l'Instruction Chrétienne, *Histoire D'Haïti*, 100.

35. Ibid., 100.

36. Garvey, *Philosophy*, 239.

37. Kamau Brathwaite, *Ancestors* (1977); Edouard Glissant, *Le discours antillais* (1997); James Clifford, *Routes: Travel and Translation in the Late Twentieth Century* (1997).

38. Garvey, *Philosophy*, 239.

3

Edward Blyden, Martin Delany: Perspectives on Education and Religion

It cannot be denied that the wisest plan of education for any people should take cognizance of past and present environment, should note the forces against which they must contend, or in unison with which they must labor in the civilization of which they form a part. It should not be ignored, further, that the colored man in America, because of his marked appearance and his unique history, will for a long time need peculiar equipment for the intense, the unrelenting struggle for survival amid which he finds himself in the America of today.

—Anna Julia Cooper[1]

THE GROWING NUMBER OF BLACK Studies programs and departments in the United States is the outcome of centuries-long championing for the implementation of relevant education for blacks. The call for an education that would transform race condition has been articulated by scholars and activists living in Africa, the Caribbean, Europe, and the United States—from the eighteenth century to the present day. In the United States, the particular emergence of Black Studies toward the end of the 1960s and early 1970s is the result of militant conviction of Black Power advocates. The educational philosophy that undergirds and propels the Black Power principles, however, is longstanding; it germinated from the intellectual and activist deeds, which dates back to the late eighteenth century. The works of Edward Blyden and Martin Delany offer critical reflection on self-respect, self-reliance, self-preservation, self-elevation, and advancement, through appropriate education. *Christianity, Islam and the Negro Race* was published in 1887, after an active life in Liberia, while The *Selected Letters of Edward Wilmot Blyden* and *Christianity* were posthumously published as a compilation.[2] Delany's *The Condition, Elevation, Emigration, and Destiny of the Colored Peoples of the United States,* was published in 1852, and *Blake; or the Huts of America,* was published in its entirety in 1861.

Until his death in 1912, Blyden maintained three major aims: the religious re-education of blacks, the general education of blacks in African history, language, and culture, and the unification of Africa for the social and political progress of Africans and those of African ancestry living throughout the world. Embedded in his agenda for [re]education, are two concepts Blyden postulated and worked arduously to translate into practice: the "revolution of mentalities" and the "African Personality." The implication within the "revolution of mentalities" was broad, for it covered a large spectrum regarding the transformation of social and political life for blacks. It principally impressed upon Africans the necessity to reject the subservient roles Europeans assigned to them through slavery and the colonial system. To eradicate the mentality of subordination Blyden called for the [re]education of black Africa both secularly and religiously.[3] Within the secular sphere Africans would push for the re-education of pupils in African social and political sciences, namely history, literature, and languages. Within the religious realm, they would break barriers of sectarianism amongst themselves—physically, mentally, ideologically—in order to work for the advancement of Africa, as a collective force. The mental revolution also underlined the need for Africans to retain their cultural identity or "African Personality" and to resist the pressures of becoming simulated or assimilated Europeans. In the foreword to *Selected Letters of Edward Wilmot Blyden*—entitled "Edward Wilmot Blyden, Precursor of Negritude"—Léopold S. Senghor wrote of Blyden and his effort to galvanize the ideas of a "revolution of mentalities" and an "African Personality." Senghor explains:

> I speak then of a dual effort, social and cultural. Since he was both a minister and a professor, it was natural for Blyden to emphasize the school as the major instrument of culture, and also religion, as the highest and most complete expression of this same culture . . . It was thus that he adapted the programs of Alexander School to African realities—to the language, the history, and the customs of Africa, while at the same time encouraging the study of the languages, sciences, the technology—the whole range of cultural processes—of Europe.[4]

Blyden was certain that Africa would only be able to advocate and retain its cultural identity as well as the integrity and self-respect of its citizenry when its institutions are within the control of Africans. The simultaneous economic prosperity, political autonomy, and sociocultural affirmation were the objective of the Pan-African movement. In 1872, Blyden founded and edited *The Negro*, a weekly paper geared toward diffusing his views on the necessary strategies and steps for the advancement of the race. Comparable to Blyden, Crummell and Delany centered the Pan-African movement within the social, cultural, political, and economic matters of the race; they maintained the conviction that the salvation of the race lies in education, which would lead to consciousness, self-pride, and self-respect. Conscientious leadership and organization, cultivated through knowledge of self, would in turn lead to political efficacy and economic growth. Alexander Crummell posited that "the primal need of the Negro is absorption in civilization, in all its lines, as a preparation for civil functions and the use of political power. Just now he is the puppet and the tool of white demagogues and black sycophants."[5] For Crummell, an effective educational system would prepare blacks for a wide range of professions in both technical and intellectual spheres. The assessment was that the race was in need of groups equipped with multifarious abilities that would enable movement toward economic and political prosperity. While the cognizance for immediate educational reform was established, the challenge remained in the implementation and practice. On January 5, 1881, Blyden delivered his Inaugural Address as President of Liberia College at Monrovia. The speech, entitled "The Aims and Methods of a Liberal Education for Africans," addressed the importance of a relevant education for Africans living in Africa. While the address was written specifically for Liberia College, its message is pertinent to the purpose of vocational and academic institutions as a whole.

> The college is only a machine, an instrument to assist in carrying forward our regular work—devised not only for intellectual ends, but for social purposes, for religious duty, for patriotic aims, for social development; and when as an instrument, as a means, it fails, for any reason whatever, to fulfill its legitimate functions, it is the duty of the country, as well as the interest of the country, to see that it is stimulated into healthful activity; or, if this is impossible, to see that it is set aside as a pernicious obstruction. . . .
>
> We are arriving at the principles necessary for our guidance, through experience, through difficulties, through failures. The process is slow and sometimes discouraging, but, after a while, we shall reach the methods of growth that are adapted to our wants. The work of a college like ours, and among a people like our people, must be at first generative. It must create a sentiment favourable to its existence. It must generate the intellectual and moral state in the community which will give it not only a congenial atmosphere in which to thrive, but food and nutriment for its enlargement and growth; and out of this will naturally come the material conditions of success.[6]

Given that education—vocational and intellectual—is central to our mundane life, the educational system of a nation should be theorized and organized according to the nature as well as the needs of its people. Following that reasoning Blyden argued that because each race has its own distinctive characteristics and history, the education its members receive ought to be in harmony with their race's personality, their past and present condition. He contended that it is only when each group is educated in the proper context that its members can contribute to the advancement of the world. To steer a group or a race toward mimicry is to restrain its creative abilities. Blyden thought of Liberia College and black institutions in general, as a *machine* or an *instrument* modeled to assist in carrying forward works of intellectual ends, of encouraging religious duty and patriotic aims, of serving social purposes and racial development. His use of the term "machine" immediately triggers attention to the influences his educational theories had on leaders such as Booker T. Washington and his creation of the Tuskegee Institute—which became known as the Tuskegee Machine because of its structural rigidity—and W. E. B. Du Bois and his advocacy of the Talented Tenth.[7] I should point out in passing, but in close relation to Blyden theories, that his concept of education was in greater accordance with Du Bois' philosophy than with Washington's Tuskegee Institute. The educational machine Blyden envisaged emphasized both intellectual and agricultural [or manual] development for Africans while Washington's Tuskegee Institute focused on industrial development for African Americans. In the late nineteenth century and early twentieth century Washington enforced an accommodationist practice among blacks, where they were strongly discouraged, if not prohibited, to aim for integration within the intellectual and political spheres of the United States. Instead, Washington encouraged blacks to acquire vocational skills and contribute to the development of the country through manual labor. Contrary to Washington, while Du Bois advocated the need for the Talented Tenth, who would serve as the intellectual and political leaders of the race, he also believed in the vocational need of the race. He was convinced that agricultural, intellectual, and industrial knowledge were all essential skills to the growth and improvement of black folk. In an unpublished essay written in the early 1940s, Du Bois penned a long reflection on "The Meaning of Education." The essay expounded his consistent view on the individual, national, and global benefits of well-trained minds, in all dimensions of human life—in the humanities, natural sciences, social sciences, and technology.

> Technical training is of immense importance. It characterizes civilization. But it is of secondary importance as compared with the people who are being civilized and who are enjoying civilization or who ought to enjoy it. Manifestly the civilized people of the world have got to be characterized by certain things; *they must know this world, its history and the laws of its development. They must also*

be able to reason carefully and accurately. Attention must be paid to human feel-ings and emotions which determine and guide this knowledge, and reason and action must follow a certain pattern of taste. These things: knowledge, reason, feeling and taste make up something which we designate as Character and this Character it is which makes the human being for which the world of technique is to be arranged and by whom it is to be guided. *Technique without character is chaos and war. Character without technique is labor and want.* But when you have human beings who know the world and can grasp it; who have feelings guided by ideals; then using technique at their hands they can get rid of the four great evils of human life. These four evils are ignorance, poverty, disease and crime. . . . No dexterity in technical manipulation can for a moment in school or in life become a substitute for the trained and disciplined mind which knows the world. (Emphasis added)[8]

Du Bois' philosophy on education is partly rooted in the influential writings of Blyden and Alexander Crummell, who believed in the multi-dimensions of the human mind and society as a whole. During an inauguration event in Washington, D.C., Crummell presented his views on the importance of education for civil functions and political power. He maintained that a race was civilized only when it produced "letters, literature, science, philosophy, poetry, sculpture, architecture . . . all the arts. . . . No purblind philanthropy is to be allowed to make 'Industrial Training' a substitute for it."[9] In 1895, Du Bois had the opportunity to hear Crummell's speech delivered at a meeting held at Wilberforce University. From the speech Du Bois adopted the idea that a "natural aristocracy of talent" should lead the black race. By their edu-cation the "aristocracy of talent" should "know the world, its history and law of its development," and "must be able to reason carefully and accurately."[10] Crummell's conception of the responsibility and the leading role of the black aristocracy later encouraged Du Bois' articulation of the "Talented Tenth." The Talented Tenth was not meant to be the ultimate thinkers of the race, but rather was meant to inspire, guide, and help cultivate the intellectual capabili-ties of black folk.

Following David Walker's 1829 plea for education in *David Walker's Appeal,* and continuing the debate on black intellectualism, in 1831 Maria Stewart published *Religion and the Pure Principles of Morality, the Sure Foundation on Which We Must Build.* As early as 1831, Stewart argues the urgency for "head-work" in the black community.[11] She was convinced that blacks would only acquire equality when they are spiritually, morally, and intellectually prepared. Similarly, in "On Education" written in the 1930s, Anna Julia Cooper explained that "the old education made [the Negro] a 'hand,' solely and simply." Cooper further reasoned that blacks have had manual education throughout their lives as slaves, and so to counterbalance the manual education they received through slavery and the continuing reconstruction period, Cooper advanced that they must be taught subjects which would train them to think critically. Since manual education "sought to deliberately suppress and ignore the soul," the opportunity to develop their mental and intellectual capabilities "will give them the power of appreciation and make them righteous."[12] Similarly, with the endeavor to combine intellectual development and industrial training, in the latter half of the nineteenth century Blyden proposed his "Methods of Liberal Education for Africans." It was with the same rationale that Blyden recommended the relocation of Liberia College in the interior of Liberia in 1881; a proposal Crummell had put forth in the 1850s, but which was rejected. Instead, the college was erected in Monrovia. Both leaders were certain that in the hinterland, synchronous with their intellectual training, students would be able to dedicate a portion of their time "to manual labour in the cultivation of the fertile lands which will be accessible, and thus assist in procuring from the soil the means for meeting a large part of the necessary expenses; and where access to the institution will be convenient to aborigines."[13] In the hinterland the work of students would be *generative*, for they would be in contact with the indigenous and agriculturist population, and would themselves be involved in the cultivation of lands.

Equally important, Blyden wanted to prepare leaders who would later participate in the unification of Africa. Without an intellectual base and economic means Africa would be continuously threatened by imposing cultures and ideologies as well as foreign political governance, whether directly or indirectly. Hence, Europeans would continue to rule Europe and Africa while Africans remain subordinates on their own land. If in the future Africans are to control their own land, achieve social and political success, and be regarded as full citizens, their children must first receive a relevant education. Furthermore, incapacitated at home, Africans cannot intervene when those of African descent of the Diaspora are in need. Blyden pointed out the incapability of Africa to come forth and mediate the unjust imposition of foreign power in Haiti in 1861, just as Africans and those of African descent were incapable of offering substantial help when the same powers attempted to control Liberia.[14] Blyden associated the political impotence to the dispersion of blacks throughout the world and to a politically disunited Africa. Armed with the confidence that united Africans would stand stronger against the caprices of foreign powers, he sought to dissipate destructive particularism and territorial dissention within the continent. One of the urgent solutions, as Blyden conceived it, was the restructuring of Liberia College, where students would be taught by Africans who have the capability to raise black consciousness and a sense of pride and character in their pupils. He did

not oppose the teaching of European subjects altogether, for he believed that
certain periods of European history and intellectualism offer universal values
and teachings. On the other hand, he remained mindful of the periods imbued with scientific and ideological racism as poisonous to the mind of the
black student. These texts only create a deeply rooted complex of inferiority
in the student's mind, which in turn forces him/her to depreciate him/her
self, disparage the race, and imitate—to neurosis—everything European, or
simply not black. In *Christianity, Islam and the Negro Race* Blyden reasons:

> We shall devote attention principally, both for mental discipline and informa-
> tion, to the earlier epochs of the world's history. It is decided that there are five
> or six leading epochs in the history of civilization. I am following Mr. Frederic
> Harrison's classification. *First*, there was the great permanent, stationary system
> of human society, held together by a religious belief, or by social custom growing
> out of that belief. This has been called the Theocratic state of society. The *second*
> great type was the Greek Age of intellectual activity and civic freedom. *Next* came
> the Roman type of civilization, an age of empire, of conquest, of consolidation of
> nations, of law and government. The *fourth* great system was the phase of civi-
> lization which prevailed from the fall of the Roman Empire until comparatively
> modern times, and was called the Medieval Age, when the Church and Feudal-
> ism existed side by side. The *fifth* phase of history was that which began with the
> breaking-up of the power of the Church on the one side, and of feudalism on
> the other—foundation of modern history, or the Modern Age. That system has
> continued down to the present; but, if sub-divided, it would form the *sixth* type,
> which is the Age since the French Revolution—the Age of social and popular
> development, of modern science and industry. (Emphasis added)[15]

The immediate point of contention is Blyden's assertion: "there has not
been a period of history more full of suggestive energy, both physical and
intellectual, than those epochs."[16] However, Given the restricted range of
education blacks received from the period of enslavement well into the late
twentieth century, also considering that Cheikh Anta Diop's first trailblaz-
ing works on African culture and civilization were not published until 1955
and 1967 (*Nations Nègres et Culture* 1955, *Antériorité des Civilizations Nègres,*
1967), Blyden's acceptance of Harrison's classification (in 1887) is not astonishing.[17] Notwithstanding the accepted exclusion of the Phoraonic Egyptian
civilization—essentially a Negro civilization—from Harrison's classification,
Blyden's intellectual preoccupation focused on the development of the Negro
mind. He cautiously suggested that the college excludes epochs *five* and *six*, or
at least postpones those periods until the later college years, when the student
has developed a more critical mind. He rated the works that were written
during the *fifth* epoch (which was the era of the breaking-up of the Church,

the era of feudalism and emergence of modern history, or the Modern Age)
and the *sixth* epoch (i.e., the period of the French Revolution, the age of social
and popular development, of modern science and industry), as corrupting
works, on which the mind of the youthful African should not be trained.[18]
Blyden further explained that it was during the *sixth* period the Transatlantic
Slave Trade began; consequently, it was also during that period European
scholars began to invent theological, social, and political theories that would
for centuries proscribe and degrade the black race. Blyden maintained that
the *sixth* epoch

> continues to this day, and has an abundant literature and a prolific authorship.
> It has produced that whole tribe of declamatory Negrophobists, whose views,
> in spite of their emptiness and impertinence, are having their effect upon the
> ephemeral literature of the day—a literature which is shaping the life of the
> Negro in Christian lands. His whole theory of life, quite contrary to what his
> nature intends, is being influenced, *consciously* and *unconsciously*, by the general
> conception of his race entertained by the manufacturers of this literature—a
> great portion of which, made for to-day, will not survive the next generation.[19]
> (Emphasis added)[19]

To reverse the existing conscious and unconscious self-disdain, Blyden
proposed a curriculum that: one, would create a corpus of capable and responsible blacks, who would be able to give a "healthy tone" to society, and,
two, to rear and nurture a black nation that would not view its race with
disparagement, but which would be strengthened by self-confidence, self-
respect, and efficiency in work. Anticipating the new Liberia College as the
exemplar of black institutions, Blyden endeavored to dismantle programs
where students were filled with "*formulas* of thought and expressions," simply
to boast their level of European "education" and "civilization" to their compatriots.[20] Blyden's most consequential message was that each race has its own
idiosyncrasies or personality, which implied neither superiority nor inferiority. Thus, to wholly participate in the development of the world, members
of the race should receive an education that is in harmony with their way of
thinking and conceiving the world. In *Christianity, Islam and the Negro Race*,
Blyden underlines that

> it is true that culture is one, and the general effects of true culture are the same;
> but the native capacities of mankind differ, and their work and destiny differ, so
> that the road by which one man may attain to the highest efficiency, is not that
> which would conduce to the success of another. The special road which has led
> to the success and elevation of the Anglo-Saxon is not that which would lead to
> the success and elevation of the Negro, though we shall resort to the same means

of general culture which enabled the Anglo-Saxon to find out for himself the way in which he ought to go.[21]

He recommended the study of the classics and mathematics because these subjects contain universal principles and serve as intellectual nourishment for pupils, while subjects such as catechism, history, and science, as taught by missionaries, contain poisonous formulae irreparably damaging to the black student's intellect. Simply put, if the purpose of education is to secure personal growth and societal efficiency, then the African must be educated accordingly.

Blyden's Religious Thoughts

Concurrent with the call for secular education was the advocacy for religious education among Africans. In *Christianity, Islam and the Negro Race* Blyden introduces and analyzes the origins of Semitism, Christianity, and Islam as three religions deriving from one source, but which has each adopted a different social manifestation. The timing of Blyden's reflection on religion and education was significant, for after his longstanding ministry in the Christian church in Liberia, his involvement in the Muslim community in Sierra Leone, his readings on Semitism, and his professorial career among Christians and Muslims, he was able to offer a critical examination in regard to each religion's economic, political, and social impact on African and African descendants. In his chapter "Islam and Race Distinctions" he explains,

It is remarkable that the eight distinct religions of which history gives account all had their origin in Asia, and the three highest religions—the Jewish, the Christian, the Mohammedan—took their rise among Semitic peoples. And it is equally remarkable that since Christianity left the place of its birth it has seemed to be the property exclusively of the European branch of the human family. And, so far as it has become the possession of the Western Aryans, it has shared the fate of that other great religion which rose among the Eastern branch of the Indo-European family, viz., Buddhism, as being for the most part confined to one or two races. . . .

They [Christians] aimed at securing material aggrandisement at any cost. Indian and Negro must be made willing or unwilling tools in the prosecution of their design. The human soul—the immaterial—was of secondary importance. The Semitic mind, on the other hand, destitute, it has been alleged, of the scientific instinct, looks upon man—every man—as standing in direct relation to God, who has not ceased His communications with His creatures, still speaking to them at times in dreams and visions, and at other times by the ordinary events of life. . . . The Shemite lays most stress, in religion, upon prayer; the Aryan upon preaching. . . .

The Mohammedan religion, on the other hand, an offshoot from the Semitic mind, disregarding all adventitious circumstances, seeks for the real man, neglects the accidental for the essential, the adventitious for the integral. Hence it extinguishes all distinctions founded upon race, colour, or nationality. "I admonish you to fear God," said Mohammed to his follower, "and yield obedience to my successor, although he may be a black slave." And, therefore, throughout the history of Islam, in all countries, race or "previous condition" has been no barrier to elevation. . . .

The religion of Jesus, after eighteen hundred years, nowhere furnishes such practical evidence of cosmopolitan adaptation and power. "Christianity is not to blame for this," to use the suggestive words of Mr. Bosworth Smith, "but Christian nations are."[22]

For Blyden, in their primal teachings, Christianity, Islam, and Semitism, placed the human soul first, by encouraging a direct relation between God and each human being. In its evolution, Christianity, or rather, Christian nations began to focus more on preaching than prayer, more on the accumulation of material goods through the conquest of weaker nations than on the well being of humanity. It is an established knowledge that preaching played a fundamental part in territorial aggrandizement endeavors, for it was through preaching and conversion that Christian nations succeeded in annexing various countries in Africa and Asia. However, in his comparison of Christianity and Mohammedanism, Blyden focuses generally on the institutions and evil deeds of self-proclaimed Christians, who enslaved and assassinated Africans in the name of the Bible; he opted not to mention the negative deeds of Arab nations, which for centuries have also rationalized their form of slavery in the name of Islam. Nonetheless, if Blyden viewed Mohammedanism as more befitting for blacks it was undoubtedly because Mohammedanists did not institutionalize the Transatlantic Slave Trade and the plantation system which dehumanized, and destroyed blacks at an innumerable rate. Though Blyden was himself a Christian, he perceived Mohammedan doctrine of fraternity more fitting for Africa than "missionary-Christianity."[23] Blyden vehemently criticized white missionaries who came to Africa to teach submission while other missionaries were teaching the same lessons to blacks throughout the Americas. With the same rigor he also condemned black African Christians who, as "black missionaries," had learned and were eager to pass on to their fellow colonial subjects the lessons of submission.[24] He delivered a speech in Lagos which called for the formation of an African Church independent of European dominance. Though Nigerians embraced the idea it never came into realization. While the proposed African Church never went beyond the mental picture, Blyden's vision, nonetheless, "inspired the foundation of the small United Native African Church. Thus, he takes his place in the history of African separatist and independent Church movements."[25] Throughout his activist years Blyden strove to eradicate the many pernicious beliefs Europeans planted in Africa. In *Christianity, Islam and the Negro Race*, he postulates that

> generations descending from Huguenot and Puritan ancestry were trained to believe that God had endowed them with the right to enslave the African forever. And upon those Africans who became members of the Christian Church, the idea was impressed that it was their duty to submit, in everything, to their masters. Christian divines of all shades of opinion, in the South, taught this doctrine, and embodied it in books prepared specially for the instruction of the slaves—their "oral instruction," for they were not allowed to learn to read.[26]

Because of his formal education in missionary schools in Liberia, Blyden was also taught the doctrine of white supremacy and the belief that Europeans had the responsibility to civilize Africa. However, his knowledge of Greek, Latin, and Hebrew, his familiarity with the history of the ancient world, and his ability to critically analyze the Bible, made it possible to contest notions of white superiority and black inferiority, and to introduce the fundamental teachings of the Scriptures. To prepare for the educator role of both Muslim and Christian Africans, as well as for the struggle of African unification, Blyden taught himself Arabic. He held the belief that Muslims would play a significant role in the formation of an African State or States; moreover, as Lynch argues, Blyden had been "deeply impressed by the Islamic intellectual religious movements which since the eighteen century had been taking place in West Africa."[27] He was also aware of the prejudice that Christians held against Muslims. And so, to dismantle the prejudice that existed on the African Continent, in 1871 Blyden started to write and lecture on the role of Islam. His general argument was that,

> Islam had had a highly salutary effect on West African Negroes: it had removed retrogressive and barbaric pagan customs without destroying the wholesome fabric of West African society; it had acted as a unifying factor "binding tribes together in one strong religious fraternity"; it discouraged racial prejudice and fostered egalitarianism; it had given rise to a corpus of Muslim Negro scholars and was responsible for whatever learning there was in West Central Africa; finally, it had encouraged industry which had reflected itself in large towns and cities.[28]

Blyden saw a direct connection between the religious principles taught to a people and their social and political progress. Christianity, as was taught by white missionaries to their black pupils, encouraged and nurtured acquiescence, imitation as well as self-disparagement, while it avoided and prohibited what Blyden calls the *training, strengthening,* and *disciplining* of the mind.[29] Hence Christianity, according to Blyden, kept Africans in a stagnant position by depriving them of the mental and intellectual trainings that are essential to move forward. Islam on the other hand, gave rise to a corpus of responsible black scholars, who contributed to the development of large towns and Muslim cities. From 1874 to 1879 Blyden taught Arabic to Christians and English to Muslims to accomplish his goal of establishing communication and cooperation between West Africans of different religions for the progress of Africa as a whole. Between 1880 and 1884, as president of Liberia College, Blyden added the study of Arabic to the curriculum and often hosted Muslim *ulamas* and their students.[30] Blyden stayed in Sierra Leone between 1887 and 1895, where he was allowed to teach English and Western subjects to young Muslims, and he also taught Arabic to Anglophone Africans.

It is worth noting that Blyden's greatest philosophical ambiguity lies in his relation with Christianity and Islam. Throughout his life he ideologically vacillated between the two religions while remaining a Christian. One could also argue, however, that Blyden's oscillating behavior between the two doctrines underscores his belief that, in lieu of condemning or neglecting a particular religion or culture, it is feasible to learn and adopt the best from different religions and cultures. And so the question is posed! Where does Blyden position traditional Negro African religion within his religious scheme?

From 1906 to 1907 Blyden wrote numerous articles on Africa's traditional life in the *Sierra Leone News.* In 1908 the articles were assembled in a book form and published under the title *African Life and Customs.* In *African Life and Customs* Blyden pays particular attention to African spiritualism and religious mores to explain that in African society there is no clear separation between the secular and the religious, as the latter permeates all levels of Africa's social structure. He begins his analysis with a definition of religion, and the distinction between religion and theology, to challenge stereotypical theories on Africa's religious backwardness. He notes,

Religion, as we said at the outset, is that which binds us to a higher Power, and is practised by men of all climes and countries. Theology is our conception of and our attempt to describe the Being worshipped, Who has no name. What He is to one race, He is not in every respect to another. "I am that I am," or "I shall be that I shall be," is His own definition of Himself. Religion is the ocean, theology the river. All rivers flow into the ocean, but the ocean is not the river, and the river not the ocean. The African does not attempt to formulate a theology. He says, as the Psalmist did, "Such knowledge is too wonderful for me; I cannot attain unto it." . . . They [the Africans] believe that the divine powers inhabit stones, trees, springs, and animals; and we find traces of this kind of worship in the Bible and the early history of the Greeks. We find, for example, a sacred stone at Bethel called the House of God. There is a sacred oracular tree at a place called Sichem.[31]

Blyden further underlines the inculcation of Europe's concept of the Being in the African's mindset as unnecessary; moreover, such intrusion helped destabilize African society as a whole. "From our standpoint," he asserts, "we do not believe that Africa needed the theological interference of Europe, for the Theology of Europe is derived from the conceptions of Roman, Celt and Teuton, which have modified Semitic ideas promulgated in the Bible."[32] When the theology, which influences the religious customs of a people, is not in harmony with their way of life, their conception of the self and their social construct are also affected. Thus, Blyden emphasizes and concludes the following:

> The African Religion is a matter that affects all classes of the people—men, women, and children. As a Pagan, the women assist in the functions of Religion, which are the functions of the State. They visit the sacred groves. The Bundo and Porroh rites act conjointly with the State in training the youths of both sexes to morality and patriotism. As in other matters, the Religion is communistic. When this system is recklessly and indiscriminately interfered with, the result is what we are witnessing everywhere in West Africa, as in Uganda—dislocations, degeneracy, death.[33]

Ultimately, taking into consideration the coexistence and social impact of the various religions in Africa during his lifetime—traditional African Religion, Christianity, and Islam—Blyden sought to focus on the development of the continent while advocating the preservation of its people's *personality* as well as its fundamental customs.

Martin Delany: The Antidote to Race Debasement

Delany's *The Condition, Elevation, Emigration, and Destiny of the Colored People of the United States* is the manifesto of the economic, political, and social predicament of blacks in the United States. At the time Delany wrote and published *The Condition* (1852), he was against any idea of emigration, particularly to Africa, but postulated the idea of self-help within the United States. In his call for self-help, he encouraged blacks to stay in the United States to eventually acquire their freedom and prosper as Americans. The analysis of *The Condition* reflects on the dangers of the teachings of an appropriated Christianity, which was geared to deliberately miseducate blacks through the misuse of the Scriptures. Because Delany viewed organized religion as well as the secular social and political establishments in the United States as ruinous and oppressive forces that hindered the psychological freedom of blacks, he earnestly urged blacks to question the biblical lessons whites were teaching. Instead, he encouraged them to develop an intimate relationship with the Supreme Being, through the nurturing of their spirituality. *The Condition* outlines the principles the black community must understand and follow. In these principles he introduced and examined the three laws of human life: the Spiritual, Moral, and Physical Laws.

> They are *three*—and like God himself, represented in the three persons in the God-head—the *Spiritual, Moral* and *Physical* Laws. That which is Spiritual, can only be accomplished through the medium of the Spiritual law; that which is Moral, through the medium of the Moral law; and that which is Physical, through the medium of the Physical law. Otherwise than this, it is useless to expect anything. Does a person want a spiritual blessing, he must apply through the medium of the spiritual law—*pray* for it in order to obtain it. If they desire to do a moral good, they must apply through the medium of the moral law—exercise their sense and feeling of *right* and *justice*, in order to effect it. Do they want to attain a physical end, they can only do so through the medium of the physical law—go to work with muscles, hands, limbs, might and strength, and this, and nothing else will attain it.
>
> The argument that man must pray for what he receives, is a mistake, and one that is doing the colored people especially, incalculable injury. That man must pray in order to get to Heaven, every Christian will admit—but a great truth we have yet got to learn, that he can live on earth whether he is religious or not, so that he conforms to the great law of God, regulating the things of earth; the great physical laws.[34]

These laws, which may appear evident to the twenty-first century sensibility, were usually not practiced by the enslaved. And so, the principal point Delany consistently reiterated during his various assemblies and in his texts, particularly in *The Condition* and *Blake*, is the idea that it is in the best interest of black folk to distinguish between spiritual and physical matters, between the Scriptures and the Law, between religion and politics. Nonetheless, Delany also recognized the difficulty to set religion apart from politics because for centuries societies around the globe have created an intertwined union between the two. Therein lies the lesson Delany sought to teach, which was that the great majority of white missionaries, who also worked with and are products of secular establishments, were utilizing a custom-built—so to speak—or appropriated version of religion, designed to keep blacks in subordination. As a result, black slaves, and later black citizens, came to attach their social and political conditions to the belief of belonging to a chosen suffering race which will have its chance to attain relief and happiness in

Heaven. The message was that, while it was undoubtedly important for blacks to nourish their spirits and strengthen their relationship with God, it was also crucial for them to recognize the need to gain control over earthly matters through persistent revolutionary and evolutionary actions, through *training, strengthening,* and *disciplining* of the mind—to use Blyden's terms. Delany rationalized that "God sendeth rain upon the just and unjust," and the fact that all men have had good and bad experiences on earth, regardless of their deeds, "should be sufficient to convince us that our success in life, does not depend upon our religious character, but that the physical laws governing all earthly and temporary affairs, benefit equally the just and the unjust."[35] Delany further explained that the greatest misconception among blacks was the belief their degradation and oppression were deserved punishments for their unfaithfulness to God. However, the logic is basic: if poverty, oppression, and degradation were punishments allocated only to the wicked, then European enslavers would have been a materially destitute group in lieu of a prosperous one. With that understanding, Delany impressed blacks to ignore any interpretation their oppressors give to the word of God "for the purpose of deluding [them] to the more easy subjugation," but should gain confidence as "freemen, comprising some of the first minds of intelligence and rudimental qualifications, in the country."[36]

In his *Autobiography,* Malcolm X also denounced the hypnotic lesson of the *pie-in-the-sky* that was taught to blacks. Comparing his family's economic situation—during his childhood—to other blacks in his town, Malcolm X explained that the Little family was better off than the town blacks "who would shout, as my father preached, for the pie-in-the-sky and their heaven in the hereafter while the white man had his here on earth."[37] Malcolm's father was a Garveyite who believed in hard work but never subscribed to the politic of subordination. With the same admonition against looking toward the sky for what one can accomplish on earth, in 1893 Anna Julia Cooper particularly cautioned black women on their "simple faith" and advised them to seek education and self-empowerment. In "The Intellectual Progress of the Colored Women in the United States since the Emancipation Proclamation: A Response to Fannie Barrier Williams" written in 1893, Cooper observed, "we had remaining at least a simple faith that a just God is on the throne of the universe, and that somehow—we could not see, nor did we bother our heads to try to tell how—he would in his own good time make all right that seemed most wrong."[38] Challenging the physical and, most importantly, the psychological bondage of blacks, Delany sought to discredit the notion of a maledictory race. The solution he envisioned necessitated the commitment of blacks to practice various means of elevation, principally, education and emigration. Delany's proposed actions meant that blacks would assume control of their

own destiny by educating themselves in both vocational and intellectual matters. Progressively they would come to build and manage their own establishments. In his chapter entitled *Means of Elevation,* he explicates that

> moral theories have long been resorted to by us, as a means of effecting the re-
> demption of our brethen in bonds, and the elevation of the free colored people
> in this country. Experience has taught us, speculations are not enough; that the
> *practical* application of principles adduced, the thing carried out, is the only true
> and proper course to pursue.
>
> White men are producers—we are consumers. They build houses, and we
> rent them. They raise produce, and we consume it. They manufacture clothes
> and wares, and we garnish ourselves with them. They build coaches, vessels, cars,
> hotels, salons, and other vehicles and places of accommodation, and we deliber-
> ately wait until they have got them in readiness, then walk in, and contend with
> as much assurance for a "right," as tough the whole thing was bought by, paid
> for, and belonged to us. By their literary attainments, they are the contributors
> to, authors and teachers of, literature, science, religion, law, medicine, and all
> other useful attainments that the world now makes use of. We have no refer-
> ence to ancient times—we speak of modern things. Our elevation must be the
> result of *self-efforts*, and work of our *own hands*. No other human power can ac-
> complish it . . . These are the proper and only means of elevating ourselves and
> attaining equality in this country or any other, and it is useless, utterly futile, to
> think about going any where, except we are determined to use these as the neces-
> sary means of developing our manhood.[39]

His advocacy for black businesses is an enterprise for which Blyden,
and later generation leaders such as Garvey, Du Bois, and Malcolm X also
championed. As Delany observed, by neglecting to invest in their own community, blacks were contributing to the prosperity of their oppressors, while
aggravating their existing impecunious condition. The education of the black
community in its entirety was the antidote; that is, the education of black
youths, of women, and of adult males. As a starting point Delany founded
Avery College, which trained women in reading, writing, arithmetic, and various domestic skills. The education and respect of the woman, as he viewed it,
signify the respect of her progeny; the elevation and advancement of the race
depended on the education of black women.

In *Blake; or the Huts of America,* Delany translated his philosophy into
literary form. He reasserted his perspective on religion and politics, through
his protagonist Henry who later emerged as Blake, at the heights of his Black
Nationalist journey. Henry traveled to Canada, Cuba, and the U.S.-South,
heralding the message of a "revolution of mentalities," which entailed the re-
education of black folk, the re-interpretation of the Bible, and the unification
of diasporic blacks for a successful rebellion against the slavery system. The

novel is permeated with conversations on religion and education that Henry/
Blake holds with slaves and fugitives. In chapter 6, Delany depicts a debate
between "Mammy," her husband "Daddy Joe," and Henry. The two elders
represent the psychological disposition of the older slave generation, while
Henry represents the emerging revolutionary voice.

> *Mammy:* Henry, wat de mauttah wid yeh? I neveh heah yeh talk so fo'—yeh
> sin in de sight ub God; yeh gone clean back, I reckon. De good Book tell us, a
> tousan' yeahs wid man, am but a day wid de Laud. Boy, yeh got wait de Laud
> own pinted time.

> *Henry:* Well, mamy, it is useless for me to stand here and have the same gospel
> preached into my ears by you, that I have all my life time heard from my enslav-
> ers. My mind is made up, my course is laid out, and if life last, I'll carry it out.
> I'll go out to the place today, and let them know I have returned.[40]

> *Mammy:* Dah now! Dah now! See wat dis gwine back done foh yeh! Bettah put
> yo' trus' in de Laud! Henry, yeh gone clean back t' de wuhl ghin, yeh knows it!

> *Henry:* you're mistaken, Mammy; I do trust the Lord as much as ever, but I now
> understand him better than I use to, that's all. I don't intend to be a fool of any
> longer by false preaching.

> *Daddy Joe:* Henry! Yeh gwine lose all yo' 'ligion? Wat yeh mean, boy!

> *Henry:* Religion! That's always the cry with black people. Tell me nothing about
> religion when the very man who hand you the bread at communion has sold
> your daughter away from you![41]

Throughout *Blake*, Henry avowed to no longer be duped by false teaching.
By refusing the teaching of missionaries, Henry does not negate the existence
of the Supreme Being, as *Mammy* concludes, but seeks to "understand [God]
better than [he] used to." While *Mammy*, who symbolizes the older slave generation, is concerned with abstract ideas of religion, Henry works to apply the
teachings of liberation to the struggle of liberating black folk, both psychologically and physically. Although Delany did not advocate a return to Africa
in his novel, he nonetheless postulated the principles of Black Nationalism,
by proposing the idea of a strong black nation in Cuba. He believed that a
strong black nation in Cuba would be beneficial to blacks of the United States
as it would help in dismantling slavery and generating self-pride for all blacks.
Henry, as the radical voice of the novel, expresses Delany's own philosophy
not only on religion but also on education and Black Nationalism. Henry's
first step toward liberation was his cognizance of the missionaries' detrimental preaching. Aware that whites were interpreting the Bible to their advantage, he urges blacks to study the Bible on their own and to give it meanings
of liberation rather than of subordination. James H. Cone's theoretical text,

A Black Theology of Liberation (published in 1970), corresponds with the philosophies held by Delany—as well as Marcus Garvey and Malcolm X. Cone
ponders the distinction between knowledge, the praise of God, and the politics of religion. Cone explains that

> the oppressed and the oppressors cannot possibly mean the same thing when
> they speak of God. The God of the oppressed is a God of revolution who breaks
> the chains of slavery. The oppressors' God is a God of slavery and must be de-
> stroyed along with the oppressors. The question then, as Black Theology sees
> it, is not whether black people believe in God, but whose God? . . . Here it is
> important to note that every significant black liberation movement has had its
> religious dimensions. Black liberation as a movement began with the pre-Civil
> War black churches who recognized Christian freedom grounded in Jesus Christ
> was inseparable from civil freedom. . . . To try to separate black liberation from
> black religion is a mistake, because black religion is authentic only when it is
> identified with the struggle for black freedom. The influences of Marcus Garvey,
> Elijah Muhammed, Malcolm X, and Martin Luther King, Jr., demonstrate the
> role of religion in the black community.[42]

The Bible of the oppressor cannot be the Bible of the oppressed. "That every
significant black liberation movement has had its religious dimensions" also
supports the idea that every religion—whether Buddhism, Christianity, Islam,
Semitism, or Vodun—has its rudimentary liberation dimension. Cone's main
argument is that in its genesis, Christianity is a religion of liberation, which has
been deliberately mis-used in order to perpetuate slavery and maintain blacks
in wretched poverty, even long after the abolition of slavery. In Cone's argument the word *Bible* means the *interpretation of the Bible*. Hence, given that the
Bible of the oppressor postulates the belief of a natural *submission* of blacks, the
Bible of blacks ought to teach *revolution* and *liberation*, here on earth. Within
the context of misinterpretation *language* is crucial. For, "the legitimacy of any
language, religious or otherwise, is determined by its usability in the struggle
of liberation."[43] Stated differently, the legitimacy and power of the oppressors'
God only exist through their interpretive words. Early in the twentieth century,
in his various addresses and writings, Marcus Garvey expressed the belief that
each race, ethnicity, and individual identifies with, constructs, and interprets
the Supreme Being based on each group's societal ideology, historical specificity, cultural and earthly agenda. In *Philosophy* Garvey wrote, "If the white man
has the idea of a white God, let him worship his God as he desires. If the yellow
man's God is of his race let him worship his God as he sees fit. We, as Negroes,
have found a new ideal. Whilst our God has no color, yet it is human to see
everything through one's own spectacles, and since the white people have seen
their God through their white spectacles, we have only now started out to see
our God through our own spectacles."[44]

In light of Delany's general effort for race advancement and, taking into consideration his journeys throughout the United States, Africa, and Cuba, both in his literary work and his actual life, it is worth pondering Delany's oscillating political positions. Delany epitomizes political inconsistency both in views and actions—even in comparison to W. E. B. Du Bois. Du Bois' sociopolitical evolutionary thought occurred over a long period of an activist career, where with the natural process of time and changing political climates, one is expected to carefully observe one's environment in order to rethink and rearticulate a position. However, Delany's shift from one position to the next took place in relatively short periods of time—on an average of four to eight years—and with the prospect of personal opportunities. From his campaign to maintain blacks in the United States (in the early 1850s) to his advocacy for an eventual settlement in Central and South America (towards the end of the 1850s to early 1860s); from his condemnation of the Republic of Liberia as an illegitimate country during the 1850s to his subsequent visit and attempt to establish a black nation in Abbeokuta; from his focus on the Civil War (during mid to the end of the 1860s) to another back-to-Africa period in 1878 (after he had lost his power in the United States), Delany's inconsistency in ideology and political actions is conspicuous. Inspired by Delany's infectious slogan "Africa for Africans, and black men to rule them," Crummell came back to the United States with Delany to raise money and disseminate the goal of rehabilitating Africa.[45] But, with the postwar and the secession of the Southern states from the Union, Delany decided to stay in the United States to fight for the freedom and citizenship of blacks. In 1878, following the disillusionment of the post-emancipation and Reconstruction era, once again, Delany called for the migration of African Americans to Africa. More than the changing geopolitical positions, when in 1867 Wendell Phillips suggested the nomination of a black man as vice-president of the Republican Party, Delany opposed. "Neither whites nor blacks were ready for a black vice-president, he argued, resting his rationale largely upon a gradualist philosophy which stressed familiar nineteenth-century homilies: education, moral rectitude and economic self-sufficiency."[46]

Within the context of elevation, Delany's stand against blacks aspiring to political posts is striking. In a psychoanalytic observation one could view Delany's 1867 opposition to the qualified black man Wendell Phillips proposed for vice-president as indicative of the leader's unconscious mental disposition. Delany's actions reflected the fact that he was a product of the same white educational system he at times vigorously condemned. Because Delany was internally conflicted, he had his own reservations—consciously and/or unconsciously—about the competence of blacks in the political sphere. In this regard, Delany is an example of the theory of the educational dilemma

Blyden developed in *Christianity, Islam and the Negro Race.* Briefly stated, Blyden explained that a great majority of blacks schooled within the European educational system will inevitably hold certain complexes of race inferiority against their own race; thus, his philosophy of appropriate education for blacks. Notwithstanding Delany's ambivalence in action and ideology, he has unquestionably made invaluable philosphical contributions to black thought and advancement. His works contain observations and reflections that remain pertinent to human life, and the progress of today's black folk.

Notes

1. Anna Julia Cooper, "On Education," *The Voice of Anna Julia Cooper: Including A Voice from the South, and Other Important Essays, Papers, and Letters,* ed. Charles Lemert and Esme Bhan (New York: Rowman & Littlefield Publishers, Inc., 1998) 250.

2. *Christianity, Islam and the Negro Race* is a compilation of speeches and articles published during the second half of the 1870s.

3. I specify black Africa [here] to stay in consonance with Blyden's concept of Pan-Africanism, which was synonymous to "Pan-Negroism." In *Selected Letters of Edward Wilmot Blyden,* Hollis R. Lynch footnotes the following statement: "In my biography of Blyden, I used the term 'Pan-Negro' because I thought then, and still do, that it was more faithful to Blyden's own ideas. He was foremost in his time in trying to capitalize and dignify the term 'Negro.' *And, unlike other interpretations, his 'Pan-Africanism' had a strict and exclusive racial basis.* I have used the term 'Pan-African' in these volumes out of deference to the widespread current revulsion among black people to the use of the term 'Negro'" (emphasis added). See Blyden, *Selected Letters,* 4.

4. Edward Wilmot Blyden, *Selected Letters of Edward Wilmot Blyden,* ed. Hollis R. Lynch (New York: KTO Press, 1978) xx–xxi.

5. David Levering Lewis, *W. E. B. Du Bois—Biography of a Race, 1869–1919* (New York: H. Holt, 1993) 169.

6. Edward Wilmot Blyden, *Christianity, Islam and the Negro Race* (Edinburgh: Edinburgh University Press, 1967) 71–72.

7. Louis R. Harlan, "Booker T. Washington and the Politics of Accommodation," *Black Leaders of the Twentieth Century* (Urbana: University of Illinois Press, 1982) 3–4.

8. W. E. B. Du Bois, *Against Racism: Unpublished Essays, Papers, Addresses, 1887–1961* (Amherst: The University of Massachusetts Press, 1985) 252.

9. Ibid., 170.

10. Lewis, *W. E. B. Du Bois—Biography,* 165.

11. Maria Stewart, "Religion and the Pure Principles of Morality, the Sure Foundation on Which We Must Build," *Classic African American Women's Narratives,* 13.

12. Cooper, "On Education," 249–58.

13. Blyden, *Christianity, Islam and the Negro Race,* 73.

14. Esedebe, *Pan-Africanism*, 40. Quoted from *Liberia's Offering* (New York, 1862) 74–76.

15. Blyden, *Islam, Christianity and the Negro Race*, 81–82.

16. Ibid., 82.

17. Cheikh Anta Diop, *The African Origin of Civilization*, trans. Mercer Cook (Chicago: Lawrence Hill & Co., 1974).

18. Ibid., 82.

19. Ibid., 82–83.

20. Ibid., 75.

21. Blyden, *Christianity, Islam and the Negro Race*, 83.

22. Blyden, *Christianity, Islam and the Negro Race*, 241–49.

23. Ibid., xiv.

24. In *Things Fall Apart* Chinua Achebe depicts the moral destruction and social chaos the intrusion of missionaries introduced in African life.

25. Ibid., xiv.

26. Ibid., 29.

27. Hollis R. Lynch, "Nineteenth-Century Negritude," *Journal of African History* VI, 3, (1965) 380.

28. Ibid., 381.

29. Blyden, *Christianity, Islam and the Negro Race*, 380.

30. Ibid., 381.

31. Edward Blyden, *African Life and Customs* (London: African Publication Society, 1969) 64, 68.

32. Ibid., 63.

33. Ibid., 73.

34. Martin R. Delany, *The Condition, Elevation, Emigration, and Destiny of the Colored People in the United States.* 1852. (Baltimore: Black Classic Press, 1993) 38–39.

35. Delany, *The Condition*, 39–40.

36. Ibid., 40.

37. Malcolm X, *The Autobiography of Malcolm X* (New York: Ballantine, 1999), 6.

38. Cooper, "The Intellectual Progress of the Colored Women in the United States since the Emancipation Proclamation: A Response to Fannie Barrier Williams," *The Voice of Anna Julia Cooper*, 202.

39. Delany, *The Condition*, 41–48.

40. Martin R. Delany, *Blake; or the Huts of America.* 1861. (Boston: Beacon Press, 1970) 16.

41. Ibid., 20.

42. James H. Cone, A *Black Theology of Liberation.* 1970. (New York: Orbis Books, 1990) 112–13.

43. Ibid., 114.

44. Garvey, *Philosophy*, 44.

45. Lewis, *W.E.B. Du Bois—Biography*, 162.

46. Delany, *Blake*, xviii.

4

The Voices of the Foremothers: Race, Gender, and Survival

Les femmes de couleur vivant seules dans la métropole, moins favorisées jusqu'à l'Exposition Coloniale que leurs congénères masculins aux faciles succès ont ressenti bien avant eux le besoin d'une solidarité raciale qui ne serait pas seulement d'ordre matériel; c'est ainsi qu'elles se sont éveillées à la conscience de race.

The women of color living alone in the metropolis, less favored until the Colonial Exposition than their male counterparts, who have had easier access to success, first felt the need for race solidarity which would not soley be of material order; thus, their race consciousness was awaken.

—Paulette Nardal[1]

I N 1846 SOJOURNER TRUTH PUBLISHED the *Narrative of Sojourner Truth* with the help of Olive Gilbert, a northern white woman to whom she dictated her life story.[2] Sojourner Truth was a self-emancipated former slave and preacher, who unlike Toussaint Louverture and Frederick Douglass, was unable to read or write. However, Truth's contribution to the anti-slavery movement surpassed that of both Louverture and Douglass in one major regard. Her sermons and published narrative paid particular attention to the black woman's experience, especially within the United States' slave system. As William L. Andrews explains, it was Truth's "detailed and often heart-rending depiction of slavery's assault on the dignity of black women, especially as mothers, that made the *Narrative of Sojourner Truth* the first woman's slave narrative in the United States."[3] Truth's narrative was crucial to the multidimensional freedom movement in the United States, for while leaders such as David Walker and Frederick Douglass strove for the liberation of black folk, the neglected issues particular to slave mothers and newly freed mothers remained buried beneath the general preoccupation of the race. If in 1846 Truth laid bare the life of a slave mother—Isabella—who powerlessly and hopelessly watched the condescending treatment of her child as chattel and a machine of production, it was partly because she had the rudiments of a literary tradition. The writings of anti-slavery figures such as Maria Stewart and Jarena Lee served as examples of the work to be accomplished in regard to the black woman.

To acknowledge the centuries-long contribution of black women to the race's liberation, and to give resonance to their once muffled and subdued voices, there has been a growing scholarship focusing on their commitment to the literary and sociopolitical movements of the past two centuries.[4] Though considerably less acknowledged, until the latter part of the twentieth century, women of the black Diaspora have played a significant role in the articulation and manifestation of Black Nationalist principles, in their literary works and activism, both in the private and public spheres. Well before their voices began to gain currency, and in spite of restriction from the intellectual realm, women in the United States and the black Diaspora unremittingly strove for the advancement of African descendants, in their homes as well as in their local, regional, national, and international communities. To be sure, while the argument has been that the majority of black males excluded their female counterparts from their leadership fold, it is worth acknowledging, with fairness, that a number of male leaders valued the contribution of black women in the crusade to solve the race problem; for example, Martin Delany, Alexander Crummell, Edward Blyden, and Marcus Garvey. In spite of the long-standing condescending tradition in regard to the leadership of women, men like Garvey helped carve a public space within which black women were able to navigate and progressively participate in social, political, and intellectual movements of the Diaspora. Such visionary men correctly believed and, more importantly, predicted that the education and participation of women would be of consequential importance to the development of the black community as a whole. In 1852, Delany explained that

no people are elevated above the condition of their *females*; hence, the condition of the *mother* determines the condition of the child. To know the position of a people, it is only necessary to know the condition of their females; and despite themselves, they cannot rise above their level. Then what is our condition? Our *best ladies* being washerwomen, chamber-maids.[5]

As expounded in *The Condition,* and expressed in various speeches, Delany consistently drew the connection between the advancement of a people and their females. In 1886 Anna Julia Cooper developed a similar argument. In "Womanhood: A Vital Element in the Regeneration and Progress of a Race," Cooper maintained that "now the fundamental agency under God in the regeneration, the retraining of the race, as well as the ground work and starting point of its progress upward, must be the *black woman.*"[6] She argued that "with all the wrongs and neglects of her past, with all the weakness, the debasement, the moral thralldom of her present,"[7] the black woman has the grand task of elevating the race. Metaphorically reiterating Delany's 1852 axiom that "no people are elevated above the condition of their *females,*" in 1886 Cooper added that "a stream cannot rise higher than its source. The atmosphere of homes is no rarer and purer and sweeter than are the mothers in those homes. A race is but a total of families. The nation is the aggregate of its homes. As the whole is sum of all its parts, so the character of the parts will determine the characteristics of the whole." The involvement of women in the social and political arenas did not translate into the neglect of their homes; for their works in the community and the home were/are complementary, just as each man was responsible for his home and the betterment of his community. She used metaphors and adages to elucidate the idea that it is not only women who have the responsibility to elevate the race—though she believed that women have a special role—but each member of the race is also accountable. In a collective whole, the character of each individual contributes to the general character of the race. For while as the pillar "only the black woman can say: when and where I enter . . . the whole *Negro race enters with me,*" the struggle requires multitudinous and collaborative efforts.[8]

In *Africa and America: Addresses and Discourses,* Crummell devoted a chapter to the condition of black women entitled "The Black Woman of the South: Her Neglects and Her Needs." The paper, which was presented to the "Freedman's Aid Society" on August 15, 1883, depicted the predicament of black women in the South. Though the paper focused on the situation of black women of the U.S. South, the problems Crummell brought forth were common to all black women of the slavery system and post-emancipation era. They were all women who struggled to protect their families against the horrors of slavery, and who fought to diminish the impact of psychological slavery after juridical abolition. The black woman's lot from the slave market to the plantation, from the slave era to post-emancipation, was that of physical maltreatment, psychological abuse, and dispossession of herself. Crummell acknowledged that the black woman "had to fight like a tigress for the ownership and possession of her own person . . . she mated as the stock of the plantation were mated, *not* to be the companion of a loved and chosen husband, but to be the breeder of human cattle, for the field or the auction block . . . She was a hewer of wood and a drawer of water."[9]

By the end of the nineteenth century, Crummell advocated the idea that recently freed black women of the Reconstruction era had to be educated in order to help in the transformation of black life in the South. He believed the rights and progress of black women were necessary for the advancement of the race. In other words, Crummell was certain that without the proper training of women, blacks would never attain a stable family life, a cooperative community, social and political progress; for, mothers played a fundamental role in the preparation of the youth and, by extension, future leaders. Similar to Delany's Avery College, Crummell proposed the creation of an "Industrial School" in every Southern state, for the education of black girls. The school would train girls in reading, writing, arithmetic, and geography. It would also teach girls all domestic work and garden cultivation, as well as the trades of dressmaking, millinery, straw-platting, and tailoring for men.[10] Although the industrial school Crummell envisaged did not entail advanced intellectual work for women, it was nonetheless a critical step in transitioning from the situation that existed during slavery and the Reconstruction period. Cognizant of the fact that the educational work philanthropists had undertaken since emancipation was geared toward males, Crummell recommended a school that would meet the needs of young black women. Furthermore, in his sermon entitled "Common sense in common schooling," Crummell posits that "the end of all true education is to learn to do duty in life and to secure an honorable support and sustenance."[11] He continued to explain that parents have the responsibility to train their children—boys and girls—for their current lives and future. "You are accountable to God," he maintained, "for the soul, the life, the character, and the conduct of your child. Hence duty and responsibility are the two paramount considerations which are to be allied with the entire training of your children, whether at home or in their school life."[12] The reward of proper training is that the girl who becomes a woman will hold a strong commitment to the family and the community; she would have had the opportunities necessary to acquire the indispensable social tools to be an effective and productive citizen. Such tools are to be found in education, not solely in basic subjects such as arithmetic, reading, writing, and geography, but also in household duties.

In 1881, two years prior to the delivering of Crummell's speech to the "Freedman's Aid Society" in 1883, Blyden had also discussed the educational needs of black women during his inaugural address as president of Liberia College. However, unlike Crummell, Blyden stressed the need for the intellectual education of women. He viewed their intellectual development as complementary to their industrial training—which meant work in the home and gardens. As mentioned in chapter 3, Blyden was a relentless advocate of both intellectualism and agriculturism for all Africans, as he understood that the development of Africa depended equally on both realms. In his speech he asked that girls be allowed to benefit from the advantages of the college for "[he] cannot see why our sisters should not receive exactly the same general culture as [the men] do."[13] He continued his thought with the following proclamation:

> I think that the progress of the country will be more rapid and permanent when the girls receive the same general training as the boys; and our women, besides being able to appreciate the intellectual labours of their husbands and brothers, will be able also to share in the pleasures of intellectual pursuits. We need not fear that they will be less graceful, less natural, or less womanly; but we may be sure that they will make wiser mothers, more appreciative wives, and more affectionate sisters.[14]

As early as 1831 Maria Stewart had also proposed the creation of institutions that would service the educational needs of the "daughters of Africa."[15] Given that during the nineteenth century white philanthropists and the majority of freed black men, did not view black women as fit and capable of intellectualism, Stewart proposed the creation of institutions of higher learning *by* black women and *for* black women, so that they would no longer be "compelled to bury their minds and talents beneath a load of iron pots and kettles."[16] "Let every female heart become united, and let us raise a fund ourselves," she urged, "and at the end of one year and a half, we might be able to lay the corner-stone for the building of a High School, that the higher branches of knowledge be enjoyed by us."[17] From these convictions, the extent to which leaders and scholars such as Edward Blyden, Maria Stewart, Alexander Crummell, and Anna Julia Cooper anticipated the intellectual role black women would later play in the Black Nationalist movement is notable.

From the 1890s until her death in 1931, Ida B. Wells-Barnett was known as the most outspoken protest race leader of her time, as "the champion of the turn-of-the-century anti-lynching crusade."[18] The lone and resolute crusader remained at the forefront of the anti-lynching movement, particularly during and immediately after World War I, when black soldiers returning from Europe were publicly debased and massacred. In the forward to *Crusade for Justice: The Autobiography of Ida B. Wells*, John Hope Franklin pays tribute to one of the most courageous women in the liberation struggle against injustice. He writes,

> Her zeal and energy were matched by her uncompromising and unequivocal stand on every cause that she espoused. She did not hesitate to criticize southern

whites, even before she left the South, or northern white liberals, or members of her own race when she was convinced that their positions were not in the best interests of all mankind. She did not hesitate to go to the scene of racial disturbances, including riots and lynchings, in order to get an accurate picture of what actually occurred. She did not hesitate to summon to the cause of human dignity anybody and everybody who she believed could serve that cause.[19]

From the dawn of the twentieth century onward, black women continued the work of their foremothers in order to help establish an independent and progressive black race. During the Garvey era, one began to notice an overt and increasing participation of black women in the literary and political realms. Working with Amy Ashwood (whom Garvey married in 1919) and Amy Jacques (whom he married in 1922 until his death), were the numerous U.N.I.A. women fighting for the liberation of the race. Among these women were the Universal African Black Cross Nurses (a ladies division that Amy Ashwood organized in Jamaica at the inception of the U.N.I.A, and which later became known as the Universal African Black Cross Nurses in the United States) and the Universal African Motor Corps, which was a paramilitary female organization.[20]

In the section "Women's Leadership of and Participation in the UNIA" of her essay "Women and the Garvey Movement in Jamaica," Honor Ford-Smith reminds us that in 1914 Amy Ashwood was co-founder of the U.N.I.A. in Kingston. Ford-Smith also points out that as a young woman Amy Ashwood viewed the practice of social work as an effective venue for black women; a place where women can gain agency and help remedy the multifaceted problems black folk face daily. To translate her belief into action, Ashwood initiated the U.N.I.A.'s social work activities in Jamaica.[21] Since the very beginning of the U.N.I.A. in Kingston, Ashwood influenced the organization to pay attention to issues regarding women. As a case in point, in 1914 the U.N.I.A. debated the question, "Is the intellect of a woman as highly developed as that of a man?" After her stay in Panama from 1916–1918, in the spring of 1918 Ashwood moved to the United States and continued her work for the U.N.I.A. It was during that year, the summer of 1918 that the organization became incorporated in New York. Ashwood worked as an editor for the U.N.I.A.'s *Negro World* until the demise of her marriage to Marcus Garvey. Later, Amy Jacques-Garvey became the editor of the paper and one of the hardest working members of the Garvey movement and, later, of Pan-Africanism. In addition to Garvey's wives, other women also held significant leadership positions at the local level as well as the executive level of the organization. For example, "Henrietta Vinton Davis," whom Garvey's biographer (Tony Martin) describes as "an orator, an associate to Frederick Douglass, and a Shakespearean actress," was at one time President General and International Organizer of the U.N.I.A. and was part of a delegation to Liberia while Garvey was incarcerated. Later Madame de Mena replaced her in her post as International Organizer.[22]

The U.N.I.A. women were just as involved in the cultural and literary spheres of the movement as they were in its social and political dimensions. Martin reveals that "women writers and artists were given special encouragement at these conventions [International Conventions of the Negro Peoples of the World]. Women's Day at the 1921 convention featured exhibits on art, music, antiques, needle work and literature."[23] Many women poets published in the *Negro World*, and the most prolific of the Negro poets was a woman U.N.I.A. member known as Ethel Trew Dunlap.[24] Dunlap was very dedicated to the liberation and advancement movement; her poems along with her activism reflected her commitment. In her poem "Black Bards" published in 1921, Dunlap wrote,

> And then, dark bard, if thou canst patient be-
> If it will not be to thy soul distress,
> While others wear the laurels, to confine
> Thine appetite to flavor of success-
> Dip pen in ink and loose the prisoned thoughts
> That shall go forth to set a nation free-
> Burn evil's rubbish piles with virtue's torch-
> And thou indeed a noble bard shall be!

Dunlap was committed to the U.N.I.A.'s program and avoided white patronage, which she believed could have had a stifling effect on her poems. This section of her poem speaks against the temptation of financial success—by publishing in white-controlled publishing houses—and for the sacrifice of race freedom. White-controlled publishing houses, according to Dunlap, had the agenda and the power to monitor the black poet's thoughts, and thus imprison his/her spirit. Consequently, such imprisonment hinders the poet's ability to fully and critically contribute to the development of political ideas.

Amidst the prominent Harlem Renaissance women poets who published in the *Negro World*, was the well-known and controversial Zora Neale Hurston. Even though Hurston published three poems in the *Negro World* in 1922, she was not, by any stretch of the imagination, a Garveyite. In fact, in 1924 she wrote an ill-humored satire on Garvey entitled "The Emperor Effaces Himself," which she sent to Carl Van Vechten, one of the well-known white patrons of the Harlem Renaissance.[25] Hurston was an ambiguous figure for both Harlem Renaissance writers and Garveyites. Unlike Ethel Dunlap, Hurston's poems of the early 1920s were viewed as both asocial and apolitical; consequently, her peers vehemently criticized her distance from current sociopolitical issues. Many of Hurston's contemporary critics speculated that her "race-less" writings were the result of her association with white patrons and philanthropists who helped publish her works. In *Literary Garveyism* Tony Martin observes that "people like Hurston reflected the price the artists of the Harlem Renaissance too often had to pay for entry into the mainstream of white acceptance."[26] Notwithstanding the debates encircling Hurston's writings of the early 1920s, which admittedly lacked the racial and historicist dimensions that were vital to the race movement of the time, the analysis of her later writings are consequential to the examination of black culture, particulary literature and philosophy. While one could question Hurston's initial position within Harlem's writers' enclave, one could also concede that as she matured as an intellectual and a woman "who has been to the horizon and back," she made an indelible contribution to the preservation and appreciation of African-America folklore.

Zora Neale Hurston: The Significance of African-American Folklore in Black Cultural Thought

By 1925 Hurston's social observation and political criticism became an integral part of her writings. For example, the play *Color Struck* (1925) depicts the tragedy of colorism within American society; moreover, her 1955 letter published in the *Orlando Sentinel*, "Court Order Can't Make the Races Mix," is a forthright disapprobation of the 1954 Supreme Court ruling in the Brown V. Board of Education case. The publication of *Mules and Men* in 1935 marks the beginning of Hurston's most important works in the black literary canon. Under the tutelage of Professor Boas in the 1930s, and with her familiarity with African-American folklore, Hurston became—in the words of Ernest Hemingway—"probably the most informed person today on Western Negro folk-lore."[27] By the time *Mules and Men* appeared, if Hurston was not the most knowledgeable scholar on "Western Negro folk-lore" in the general sense, she was certainly the most cultivated scholar in African-American folklore and its relation to Africa. By the 1930s Jean Price-Mars had already conducted his research on Haitian folklore and its African provenance, which led to the publication of *Ainsi parla l'Oncle* in 1928. As Robert E. Hemenway points out in the 1978 introduction to *Mules and Men*, "the twentieth century saw an increasing interest in black folkways, but generally speaking, Afro-American folklore between 1850 and 1930 was almost always collected by whites and usually preselected to conform to either collector's romantic notion of black people or racist stereotypes."[28] These stereotypes always revolved around and were developed from the characterization of the "Sambo" type, i.e. black folk as submissive, God-fearing to a level of mental and societal paralysis, inferior and simple-minded. It must be remembered that while *Mules and Men* was accepted by some, it also received reproving criticism from others. In 1936 Sterling Brown lauded the text for its "simplicity, raciness, earthiness, and plausibility"; at the same time Brown attacked what he viewed as a "lack of political awareness among Hurston's storytellers."[29] Brown's criticism of *Mules and Men* as apolitical indicates a misreading of the text. For, while there is not an articulated theoretical framework of the social plight and political predicament of the time, the stories told depict the complexity of black life within American society. The tales express the injustice and tyranny of that society. Furthermore, the significance of her work lies in its affirmation and valorization of black folklore, through the recording and preservation of the tales. Without such preservation through literary works, the unwritten and unpublished black folklore, according to Hurston, "would be a tremendous loss to the Negro race and to America . . . for the unlettered Negro has given the Negro's best contribution to America's culture."[30] As Hemenway succinctly notes, *Mules and Men* does not only signify a milestone for its publication in 1935, it remains today "one of the most important collections of Afro-American folklore ever to be published."[31]

The many fables that are recounted in *Mules and Men* are fundamentally the existential and philosophical reflections of black folk of the South. Stories such as "Why Negroes Are Black," "Why Women Always Take Advantage of Men," "De Reason Niggers Is Working so Hard," "Why the Sister in Black Works Hardest," are indicative of an effort to comprehend the world around them. For centuries human beings have questioned and pondered the mysteries of their world, and their condition within it. They have observed and conjectured; a number of them have become known as world-renowned philosophers because of their thoughts. The storytellers in *Mules and Men* have, too, pondered the human condition, but their humanness as they knew it had been made *one* with enslavement and destitution, as their concept of humanity had been shaped within the slavery system. Thus, their interpretation and reasoning are often outlandish conjectures, for the enslaved and their progeny lacked the historical content of their own situation, i.e., the motives and history of slavery, the politics behind the plantation system, and the ensuing unremitting poverty of black folk. In fact, the narrators refer to the tales they recount to the anthropologist Zora as "lies." The choice of such a word implies their awareness that the explanations they offer are suggestions and not conclusions nor serious theories. Yet, the human need to make sense out of his/her situation is the force that compelled them to imagine and create tales. Thus, it is not surprising that in their stories they try to grasp the reasons why "Negroes Are Black," "Women Always Take Advantage of Men," "The Sister

in Black Works the Hardest," "De Reason Niggers Is Working so Hard," and
"How the Negroes Got their Freedom."[32] Moreover, the stories often present
a level of comical absurdity that emphasizes Hurston's societal criticism.

Because of the stereotypical content and surmise embedded in the stories,
as well as the argot used to convey the message, Locke and other proponents
of the New Negro Renaissance viewed *Mules and Men* as embarrassing
and compromising to the race advancement agenda. One can grant them
the criticism against the text. However, the alternative argument is that
Hurston's approach was intended to lead to individual and communal reflection, social investigation, and conversations on the matters presented. In
addition to the situation lessons of each story, the general lesson of *Mules
and Men* is that the lack of knowledge of one's history leads to outlandish conjectures and degrading stereotypes, which the enslaved not only
internalizes but passes on. Unknowingly and unconsciously, he/she serves
to perpetuate the enslaver's dehumanizing ideals and categorization. Consequently, the lack of a sound theoretical analysis of their condition—for
which Hurston was reproached—*was* the reality of the storytellers. It is
precisely the presentation of the realities of the time that renders Hurston's
text sociopolitical. The criticism is embedded within the stories told, and
the role of the reader is to decipher the meaning behind each story. Through
the unaltered presentation of the words uttered, as well as the depiction of
the complex characters, readers are able to assess the social atmosphere of
the time, and arrive at their own critical analyses and understanding. I share
Robert Hemenway's analytical perspective of Hurston's text, which is that
the writer's approach is "presentational" and the "folklore was expected to
speak for itself."[33] In chapter 7 one of the characters, Larkins, makes a point
which relates both to the opaque dictums that pervade the stories and Zora's
narrative voice on the framework of the book.

> "Ole coon for cunnin', young coon for runnin'," and "Ah can't dance, but Ah
> know good moves." They all got a hidden meanin', jus' like de Bible. Everybody
> can't understand what they mean. Most people is thin-brained. They's born wid
> they feet under de moon. Some folks is born wid they feet on de sun and they
> kin seek out de inside meanin' of words.[34]

In essence, what Hurston delivers is a heuristic reading where one can
extract cultural perspectives and one's own sociopolitical interpretation.
However, her contextual structures and narration (sometimes imbued with
sarcasm) along with the spatial environments she depicts, all reveal her intention. That is the exposure of the social condition. In *Mules and Men* the story
"Big Talk," of chapter 5, recounts a conversation between two slaves who

boast to each other their supposedly taboo behaviors toward "Ole Massa." The emphasis is on *supposedly*, because the ambivalence of the story is that it is founded on the *double entendre* Hurston often uses in the stories she presents.

> *Slave 1.* Ole Massa made me so mad yistiddy till Ah give 'im uh good cussin' out. Man, Ah called 'im everything wid uh handle on it.
>
> *Slave 2.* You didn't cuss *Ole Massa*, didja? Good God! Whut did he do tuh you?
>
> *Slave 1.* He didn't do *nothin'*, an' man, Ah laid one cussin' on 'im! Ah'm uh man lak dis, Ah won't stan' no hunchin'. Ah betcha he won't bother *me* no mo'.

After hearing about his friend's "affront" toward the master and his "triumph" over him, slave number two used the alleged defiance as encouragement; he went ahead and cursed the master, who beat him nearly to death, as punishment. When he confronts his friend about his unexpected experience, slave number one replies:

> *Slave 1.* Man you didn't go cuss' im tuh his face, didja?
>
> *Slave 2.* Sho Ah did. Ain't dat whut you tole me you done?
>
> *Slave 1.* Naw, Ah didn't say Ah cussed 'im tuh his face. You sho is crazy. Ah thought you had mo' sense than dat. When Ah cussed Ole Massa he wuz settin' on de front porch an' Ah wuz down at the big gate.

Later on, slave number two took revenge on his friend with a similar ambiguous story. He recounts that while *Ole Miss* was sitting on the porch, he went and looked up her dress. "Well, whut did she say?" slave number one replies.

> *Slave 2.* Not a numblin' word, an' Ah stopped and looked jus' as long as Ah wanted tuh an' went on 'bout mah business.
>
> *Slave 1.* Well de nex' time Ah see her settin' out on de porch Ah'm goin' tuh look too.

As said, the next time he went and looked up *Ole Miss'* dress while she was sitting on the porch. She screamed at his insolent behavior; as one would expect, such insolence almost cost his life. He went to his friend and said if you looked up *Ole Miss'* dress, why did the master do nothing. Slave number one answers:

> *Slave 1.* Man, when Ah looked under Ole Miss's drawers they wuz hangin' out on the clothes line. You didn't go look up in 'em while she had 'em

on, didja? You sho is uh fool! Ah thought you had mo' sense than dat, Ah claire Ah did. It's uh wonder he didn't kill you dead. Umph, umph, umph. You sho ain't got not sense at atall.[35]

The humor of the story is obvious. With the statement "Ah'm uh man lak dis," one would note the slave's desire for manhood, with the privileges and the rights that maleness holds. The slave is aware that he is not a *man* in the definition of the time and place from where he is speaking, since the story of manhood he is recounting is a false one. His implication is: if he had the privileges and the rights of a man, he would curse the "master," who then, would not be his master in the first place, but simply another man. Hence, the slave lives in the realm of the imaginary. His rebellious act against the societal norm within which he lives, is a rebellion of the mind, not yet realized. This passage offers two readings, which are examples of the *double entendre* approach. In the first reading the story may seem as an affirmation of the social structure which shows the "master's" ultimate power. In the second reading one may view the story as a criticism of society, by demonstrating to *absurdum* the power a human being (Ole Massa) has over another human being (the slave). I would suggest that Hurston intended the second reading even though she maintains her distance as the narrator. To take further the argument that Hurston displays comical absurdity in order to bring forth societal criticism, let us focus on her transcription of the "white man's prayer," in the story "Praying for Rain."

> Lord, first thing, I want you to understand that this isn't no nigger talking to you. This is a white man and I want you to hear me. Pay some attention to me. I don't worry and bother you all the time like these niggers—asking you for a whole heap of things that they don't know what to do with after they git 'em—so when I ask for a favor, I want it granted. Now, Lord, we want some rain . . . I don't mean for you to come in a hell of storm like you did last year—kicking up racket like niggers at a barbecue. I want you to come calm and easy.[36]

The arrogant and demanding tone of the "prayer" is astounding to the point of comedy. It is through the presentation of the seemingly exaggerated and absurd, but *real* to a great extent, that Hurston offers an open text that is simultaneously humorous and heuristic. The stories told in *Mules and Men* not only expose race dynamics in the United States, they also disclose gender conflicts on norms and behaviors. In "Folk Tales," chapter 7, the dispute between Big Sweet and Joe Willard (her man) reveals differing gender perspectives. Joe Willard sees his day off as his opportunity to spend time with his fellows, without their women "dragging" behind them. Big Sweet believes she has the privilege to be wherever Joe is, for "*any* time [she] shack up wid any man [she] gives [herself] de privilege to go wherever he might be, night or day. [She] got de law in [her] mouth."[37] The affirmation "Ah gives myself de privilege" is telling; it demonstrates Big Sweet's acknowledgment of her own power over herself. It further underlines the importance she accords to her conviction, and the human right to express herself. Big Sweet follows the rules she judges befits her life, for she "got de law in [her] mouth." After her physical confrontation with Ella and the white boss who stopped the commotion, Big Sweet's man exclaims, "you wuz uh whole woman and half uh man. You made dat cracker stand offa *you*." Presley quickly adds "Who wouldn't? She got loaded muscles. You notice he don't tackle Big Sweet lak he do de rest round here. Dats cause she ain't got uh bit better sense then tuh make 'im kill her."[38] Joe describes Big Sweet as a whole woman and half of a man, for a woman who behaves in the manner she does is seen as atypical. Big Sweet challenges the order of gender relations and, by so doing, redefines womanness.

Finally, in "Why Women Always Take Advantage of Men," Hurston presents another battle-of-the-sexes type discussion. The fundamental question in the story—or the analysis, one could say—is who holds the ultimate power in gender relations, men or women? The answer is elucidated in a sort of historical account where one learns that initially men were stronger but women received, from God, the three keys to female strengths and male weaknesses, "de key to de do' of de kitchen, and you know a man always favors his stomach . . . de key to de bedroom and he don't like to be shut out from dat neither . . . de key to de cradle and he don't want to be cut off his generations at all."[39] Since then, according to the story, women are the ones who possess the *real* or ultimate power. As one of the women concludes, "you men is still braggin' bout yo' strength and de women is sittin' on de keys and lettin' you blow off till she git ready to put de bridle on you."[40] From the presentation of similar tales of female strength in Hurston's text, Cheryl Wall accurately concluded that the subtext of *Mules and Men* is "the narrative of a successful quest for female empowerment." Furthermore, *Mules and Men* can be viewed as the text that precedes and prepares Hurston's audience for a blatant feminine text, *Their Eyes Were Watching God*. Indisputably, in 1937 *Their Eyes Were Watching God* set another trend in the literary world, with its presentation of the protagonist, Janie Crawford, who articulates and manifests a new definition of black womanness. While *Mules and Men* probes the world of black folk in general, with the subtext of female empowerment, *Their Eyes Were Watching God* focuses on the predicament and the position of black women within a racist and sexist society. In *Their Eyes Were Watching God* Hurston accomplishes her social critique through the experiences and spoken words of Janie Crawford.

In the novel Janie Crawford evolves from a naïve girl to a woman who has "been to the horizon and back."[41] Janie's second husband (Joe Starks), whom she married after she left her first husband while still very young, became the mayor of Eatonville.[42] As a public figure Joe Starks believes his wife should be the epitome of elitism and feminine decorum, according to the standard of the society and the time within which they live. During his opening speech as the mayor and in response to the audience's suggestion that his wife takes the floor, Joe Starks replies, "Thank yuh fuh yo' compliments, but mah wife don't know nothin' bout no speech-makin'. Ah never married her for nothin' lak dat. She's uh woman and her place is in de home." Following the husband's comment, the narrator describes Janie's mental disposition and masked behavioral response as such:

> Janie made her face laugh after a short pause, but it wasn't too easy. She had never thought of making a speech, and didn't know if she cared to make one at all. It must have been the way Joe spoke out without giving her a chance to say anything one way or another that took the bloom off of things. But anyway, she went down the road behind him that night feeling cold. He strode along invested with his new dignity, thought and planned out loud, unconscious of her thoughts.[43]

The representation of the silenced voice and suppressed desires pervade the story. Throughout the novel, however, Janie not only finds her voice gradually, but she uses it publicly. One day, one of the male town-folk observes and tells the mayor, "Yo wife is uh born orator, Starks. Us never knowed dat befo'. She put jus' de right words tuh our thoughts."[44] Again, Joe Starks did not approve of such remarks; he reasserted his belief that Janie's role was to tend his home and store. After two decades of public embarrassment—as she viewed Joe's endless condescending treatment—Janie publicly retaliates. She replies to Joe's chiding remarks of her no longer being a "young gal," and "nobody in heah ain't lookin' for no wife outa [her]. Old as [she] is," by saying:

> Naw, Ah ain't no young gal no mo' but den Ah ain't no old woman neither. Ah reckon Ah looks mah age too. But Ah'm uh woman every inch of me, and Ah know it. Dat's uh whole lot more'n *you* kin say. You big-bellies round here and put out a lot of brag, but 'tain't nothin' to it but yo' big voice. Humph! Talkin' 'bout *me* lookin' old! When you pull down yo' britches, you look lak de change uh life.[45]

In her riposte Janie openly challenges the longstanding discrimination against the aging woman in comparison to the acceptance of her male counterpart. The narrator intervenes to describe the impact of Janie's affront toward Joe.

Then Joe Starks realized all the meanings and his vanity bled like a flood. Janie robbed him of his illusion of irresistible maleness that all men cherish, which was terrible. The thing that Saul's daughter had done to David. But Janie had done worse, she had cast down his empty armor before men and they had laughed, would keep on laughing. . . . Joe Starks didn't know the words for all this, but he knew the feeling. So he struck Janie with all his might and drove her from the store.[46]

The physical blow was Joe's attempt to reclaim his definition of maleness that Janie had publicly destroyed and to silence her once and for all. The day Janie stood up to him and responded to his incessant insults, was the day he disowned her as a wife until his death. Since the day of the open confrontation with Joe Starks in the store, Janie kept her found voice, through self-assertiveness; hence, the subsequent death of Joe Starks symbolized her complete freedom. The night after the burial, she burned all head rags that Joe had forced her to wear in permanence and "went about the house next morning with her hair in one thick braid swinging well below her waist. . . . She would have the rest of her life to do as she pleased."[47]

The stories of female freedom and empowerment that Hurston depicts in both *Mules and Men* and *Their Eyes* cleared the path for later novels; most importantly, they ideologically pioneered the black women's movement of the latter part of the twentieth century, well into the twenty-first century. Her texts paved the way for a new generation of black women writers, and black women representation through their own writings. In *The Character of the Word: The Texts of Zora Neale Hurston*, Karla F. C. Holloway observes that later generations of scholars, black women writers in particular, "look at writers like Hurston within a black aesthetic because she is mother to a tradition and has given voice to a generation of black women's concern that may otherwise have been lost."[48] Through her texts, Hurston became/*is* the griot and orator of black folktales and black female thought. In each of her works, even in the case of *Mules and Men*, which is a transcription of folktales, Hurston creates the context within which each story is told in order to establish a certain critical framework and a particular social and philosophical analysis. Holloway rightly suggests that one can symbolically view Hurston as "both a foremother and a child not yet conceived."[49] The apparent "foremother" attribute is just as pertinent to Hurston as that of a "child not yet conceived," for even though Hurston wrote these texts in the first half of the twentieth century, they did not take full life until the second half of the century, the late 1970s. Their birth or rebirth, as one may call it, did not occur until the new generation of black women writers gave them life. Through her works Hurston gave birth to a generation of black women who in turn will give birth to generations to follow.

In spite of her contemporaries' accusations of lack of racial consciousness and political agenda, and in light of her initial ambiguous sociopolitical
position of the early 1920s, one would concede that Zora Neale Hurston
was conscious of the race movement as well as the women movement. Her
folktales expose the daily black family life and the black community life of
the South. The discussions of the various storytellers include such matters as
religion, relationships, gender relations, and the history of mankind—black
folk in particular. The publication of her folktales *is* the validation of story
telling within the black community, of the oral tradition which dates back
to Africa. Thus, more than a passive consciousness, her writings remain a
legacy in the canons of African-American women writing, African-American
writing, American writing, and world literature in general. As a harbinger of
black folklore and a new tradition of women writing, the merits of Hurston's
contribution to black thought and the preservation of black cultural heritage
remain invaluable.

Jane and Paulette Nardal: The Concept of Black Internationalism

Jane and Paulette Nardal were among the intellectual group of black students living in Paris during the 1920s. Jane, Paulette, and two of their sisters,
belonged to the first generation of Antilleans to study in France. After she
obtained a degree in classics, Jane returned to Martinique to teach music.[50]
Paulette started her higher education in Martinique at the Colonial College
for girls and completed her studies in Paris, where she obtained a degree in
English literature.[51] The research for her thesis on Harriet Beecher Stowe's
Uncle Tom's Cabin helped further her knowledge in American literature.[52]

With her fluency in English and theoretical insights into American culture,
Paulette Nardal possessed the tools necessary to help break the language barrier that existed between many intellectuals of the Diaspora. She served as an
interpreter and liaison between writers living in France and the United States,
principally New Negro Renaissance writers such as Alain Locke, Claude
McKay, and Langston Hughes. As such, she was an example of the intellectualism Blyden, Garvey, Du Bois, and Nkrumah envisaged, in that she made
possible a certain level of communication between black thinkers of different
languages. Moreover, by creating a diasporic intellectual network, she placed
her knowledge of English and French to the use of the struggle for race consciousness and unification. With the *Revue du monde noir* (*Journal of the Black
World*), she labored to create a connection that would allow blacks to develop
a greater knowledge of their common history and culture and to become more
aware of the needs of the race, in order to set a common politico-economic

aim.[53] The *Revue* published the writings of such diasporic writers as Claude McKay, Alain Locke, Langston Hughes, Jean Price-Mars, Félix Eboué, René Maran, and Louis T. Achille.[54] Thus in the 1920s and 1930s Paulette and Jane Nardal practiced what Carol Boyce Davies would later theorize as multilingualism and transnational communication. Boyce Davies views cross-cultural communication, which is indispensable within the Diaspora, as of particular importance among black women. In *Black Women, Writing Identity: Migrations of the Subject*, Boyce Davies argues that

> for the many Black women writers who we read in English, French or Portuguese, a variety of boundary crossings must occur. English or French or Spanish or Portuguese become indispensable for the writer who wants to reach a larger community. And for the women who tell their stories orally and want them told to a world community, boundaries of orality and writing, of geography and space, engender fundamental crossings and re-crossings. For the readers as well, a variety of languages, Creoles, cultural nuances, history has to be learned before the texts can have meaning. Geography is linked deliberately to culture, language, the ability to hear a variety of modes of articulation. It is where one speaks from and who is able to understand, to interpret that gives actuality to one's expression. Many women speak, have spoken, are speaking but are rarely heard. [55]

Today the notion of multilingualism remains critical within the black Diaspora, specifically in terms of dialoguing issues relating to women living in Africa, the Americas, and Europe: gender and sexual oppression, economic marginalization, as well as the lack of social and political agency. In 1928, within a global scope, Jane Nardal published "L'Internationalisme Noir" ("Black Internationalism") in which she advocates the idea that blacks ought to learn the history of their race and the history of their respective countries. Within today's Internationalist agenda, it remains vital that black women continue to raise a general level of black consciousness with a particular attention to black women's concerns around the world. To achieve this level of diasporic awareness as well as to explore and transmit their shared histories/stories, women scholars and writers ought to become familiar with languages beyond the language of their geographic nations. They must remain conscious of the reality that the black movement toward sociopolitical and economic advancement, the black woman movement in particular—which requires communication of ideas—is transnational.

Because of their social involvement and their publications—since the 1920s—on subjects such as race unity, race pride, intellectual and social progress for blacks, Jane and Paulette Nardal viewed themselves as the pioneers of *Négritude*. In "L'Internationalisme Noir" Jane observed that the post-war period created a new dynamic among nations and, as a result, a new atmosphere was in the making. The emergence of a new era also began to affect the black race as many of its members from different nations started to migrate to Europe.[56] Literary movements such as the Harlem Renaissance in New York and Négritude in Paris created a dialogical space for writers of the black Diaspora. While Paulette's "L'Eveil de la Conscience de Race" ("The Awakening of Race Consciousness"), published in 1932, examines and sums up the progress of the race up to the second decade of the 1900s, "L'Internationalisme Noir" outlines a brief trajectory of the emergence of black art and its impact on black advancement from the 1920s onward. For Jane Nardal, black art in all its forms, and the history it teaches, gave the Negro "some originality, some pride in being Negro, in turning back toward Africa, the cradle of Negroes, in remembering a common origin. The Negro would perhaps have his part to play in the concert of the races, where until now, weak and intimidated, he has kept quiet."[57]

It was from similar articles written by the Nardal sisters, the literary and political works written by other blacks of the Diaspora, and through the discussions *de salon* of various Negro art forms that students in France began to articulate the concept of a Négritude *avant la lettre.* In a paper written in 1932, Paulette Nardal writes that black women living alone in Europe first felt the need for race solidarity, for they were regarded less favorably than their male counterparts, and had more difficulty attaining success. In Paulette Nardal's own words, "Les femmes de couleur vivant seules dans la métropole, moins favorisées jusqu'à l'Exposition Coloniale que leurs congénères masculins aux faciles succès, ont ressenti bien avant eux le besoin d'une solidarité raciale qui ne serait pas seulement d'ordre matériel; c'est ainsi qu'elles se sont éveillées à la conscience de race."[58]

"Aux faciles succès" ("of easy success") is perhaps an exaggeration on the part of Paulette Nardal, insofar as black men's access to opportunity in the metropolis during the 1920s and 1930s. Nonetheless, her choice of words underlines that if attaining success was difficult for black males, it was quasi impossible for black women, who were both black and females. Georges Ngal notes Paulette Nardal's disappointment in regard to the lack of acknowledgment she received once the term "Négritude" was coined and the movement was launched. In a letter to Jacques Louis Hymans, she points out that her sister Jane was the promoter of the movement, specifically with the publication of "L'Internationalisme Noir." She explains that Césaire and Senghor adopted the ideas that she and her sister had already introduced, but rearticulated those ideas with more genius. "We were only women," she exclaimed, "true pioneers." "L. S. Senghor et Césaire ont repris ces idées lancées par nous et les ont exprimées avec beaucoup plus d'éclat et de brio. Nous n'étions que des femmes, de véritables pionnières—disons que nous leur avons ouvert la voie" ("L. S. Senghor and Césaire re-articulated the ideas that we launched, and expressed them with more brilliance. We were only women, true pioneers—let us say that we paved the way for them").[59]

In her "L'Eveil de la Conscience de Race," published in the *Revue du monde noir,* Paulette Nardal outlines another aspect of transnationality among blacks. Taking the Antillean—mainly the Martinican and the Guadeloupean—as a case in point,[60] she contends that it is usually away from their native lands and in contact with other blacks, that the Antillean usually develops his/her race consciousness. In *Black Skin, White Masks* Frantz Fanon develops a similar observation, where he psychoanalyzes the Antillean's experience in the metropolis, who, until his/her arrival, did not view himself/herself as black but as Antillean. In his psychoanalysis Fanon diagnoses:

> In what was said there was a lack of awareness that was at the very least paradoxical. Because the Antillean does not think of himself as a black man; he thinks of himself as an Antillean. The Negro lives in Africa. Subjectively, intellectually, the Antillean conducts himself like a white man. But he is a Negro. That he will learn once he goes to Europe; and when he hears Negroes mentioned he will recognize that the world includes himself as well as the Senegalese.[61]

Upon his arrival in Europe the Antillean generally begins to experience deep inner turmoil once he/she is aware of his/her blackness, which usually becomes apparent in relation to whiteness. In the story told in *Black Skin* where the boy—who represents European society—cries "Look, a Negro!" the Antillean becomes aware of the fact that through the lenses of the European he represents an entire race; that he is at once responsible for his body, his race, and his ancestors. It is at such moments that the Antillean usually discovers his/her blackness and ethnic characteristics, as the European conceives them. With the acceptance of a constructed and imposed identity, the Antillean becomes "battered down by tom-toms, cannibalism, intellectual deficiency, fetishism, racial defects, slave ships, and above all else, above all: 'Sho' good eatin.'"[62] The "blackness" the Antillean often sees through the eyes of the European is usually suffused with negativity which quickly develops into a profound sense of inferiority within his/her core. Hence, "intellectual deficiency," "racial defects," "sho' good eatin,'" becomes his/her conception of blackness. For that reason he/she goes to extensive measures to avoid anything black. However, it is only when the Antillean challenges and goes beyond the European's concept of "blackness" that he/she is able to create his/her own black identity; one that is rooted in the history and heritage of the race. The development of positive race consciousness begins.

In "L'Eveil de la Conscience de Race," Paulette Nardal speaks of the positive race consciousness the Antillean develops in the metropolis once he/she comes to terms with and defines his/her blackness. She argues that "the uprooting and the ensuing estrangement they felt in the Metropolis, where Negroes have not always been so favourably received as they have been since the Colonial Exhibition, had given them a real Negro soul, in spite of their Latin education."[63] Nardal expresses her enchantment with the new emergence of race awakening among Francophone African and Antillean students living in France. The new generation of students she refers to, contrary to earlier generations, began to show interest in the literature and history of their native country and that of other black nations. For Paulette Nardal it was finally the emergence of the "New Negro" as opposed to the "Old Negro"—to use nineteenth-century African-American terminology. Maintaining her hopes, Nardal points out:

> We are informed that certain students are preparing memoirs on the American Negro writers and poets, who, in spite of their evident value, had hitherto been left out in the different surveys of American literature published by French university professors. Let us hope that the students coming up for degrees in history and geography will avail themselves of the riches which the black race and the African continent offer to them. Let us hope also that they will give us the opportunity to analyze in this review some masterful doctoral theses.[64]

She viewed the students' interest as an intellectual evolution among thinkers of the race. Similar to her predecessors, she did not perceive such evolution as an attack on, or a rejection of, European culture and philosophy altogether, but as the valorization and revitalization of black culture and philosophy. She contends that she and her contemporaries wanted to go beyond European culture "in order to give [their] brethen, with the help of white scientists and friends of the Negroes, the pride of being the members of a race which is perhaps the oldest in the world."[65] She also asserts that "once they become aware of their past history, they will no longer despair of the future of their own race, part of which seems, at the present time, to be slow in developing. They will give to their slower brothers a helping hand and try to understand and to love them better."[66] Here one would note the re-articulation of the philosophy—of such leaders as Blyden, Crummell, Du Bois, Garvey, Jacques-Garvey, and Malcolm X—that urges educated blacks to assist those in need, and help lead the race.

In her article, Paulette Nardal addresses the question of the emergence and evolution of Black literature within the new awareness of race history and culture. She analyzes the situation of the Antillean in comparison to the black American,[67] to explain that the Antillean—with the exception of the Haitian—took longer to become aware of and address racial prejudice because he/she had had less confrontational experiences with the French than the African American with the European American. From observation and the analysis Friedrich Seiburg develops in his text *Dieu Est-il Français?* (*Is God French?*), Paulette Nardal argues that the non-apparent confrontation between the French and the Antillean was due to the fact that "they [the French] are certain to transform the mind of any coloured man into a truly French one in a comparatively short time."[68] On the other hand, the open scorn with which whites treated blacks in America "incited [blacks] to seek for reasons for social and cultural pride in their African past."[69] The cultural pride in race consciousness that was developed among African Americans, due to racial confrontation in the United States, propelled the creation of an African-American literature which preceded Antillean literature. For Paulette and Jane Nardal, as for writers such as Frantz Fanon and Aimé Césaire, racial confrontation is inevitable in a master/slave relationship, if significant social change is to occur. The confrontation these writers envisaged did not necessarily implicate physical violence but confrontation of ideologies.

In "L'Eveil de la Conscience de Race" Paulette Nardal points out the three stages in the creation of an African-American literature to underline their creative and intellectual growth from the slavery era to the 1920s. First, there was the period of acquisition during which black slaves imported from Africa began to learn the master's language and adapt to the hostile environment. "It was the period of absorption of the white element by the Negroes."[70] The literature of that period was a "docile imitation of their white models." The second stage was during the anti-slavery period, when blacks began to produce a literature that was imbued with controversy and moral protest. As examples, we have Martin R. Delany's *Blake; or the Huts of America* and William W. Brown's *Clotel, or, The President's Daughter*. In the third stage, "the accession of the Negroes to real culture" occurred.[71] In the third stage writers began to write on diverse topics as their writing styles improved due to the fact that education became more accessible to blacks in comparison to the slavery era. In addition, with the industrial revolution grew a multitude of problems and concerns for blacks living both in the North and South of the country. These new dimensions also complicated the content and form of black literature during the third stage. One could argue that throughout the Diaspora the creation of black literature, after the Trans-Atlantic Slave Trade, meant the three inescapable stages of imitation, protest, and creativity—as we will discuss in chapter six in regard to the emergence of Haitian literature.

Amy Jacques-Garvey and the Philosophy of Pan-Africanism

From her initial engagement with the U.N.I.A. to her death on July 25, 1973, Amy Jacques Garvey dedicated her life to the agenda of race uplift.[72] Albeit through seemingly different philosophical and literary approaches, Amy

Jacques-Garvey, Zora Neale Hurston, Jane and Paulette Nardal succeeded in inscribing compelling and indelible ideas to Black Nationalist thought. Many of the social issues Hurston depicted in her novels and expounded in her later essays, the ideologies the Nardal sisters outlined in their works, Amy Jacques-Garvey straightforwardly treated in her speeches and writings during the second half of the twentieth century. Among the topics one would note: the wisdom the black woman often acquires through generational philosophies and activism, her ability to serve as a pillar both at home and in the community, her capabilities as an orator and a leader, the importance of Black Internationalism, and the role of the black woman in its manifestation.[73] Amy Jacques-Garvey is today regarded as the pioneer female leader of the Pan-African movement. Her long life of intellectualism and activism has greatly aided in the fruition and furthering of Black Nationalist and Black Internationalist thoughts. Jacques-Garvey joined the Universal Negro Improvement Association in 1919 and served as a skilled and devoted secretary until the birth of her two sons and the growing motherhood responsibilities that followed. Notwithstanding her domestic responsibilities, Amy Jacques-Garvey continued to render great services to the development of black scholarship. Among her many duties, she made possible the publication of one of the most monumental Black Nationalist texts, *Philosophy and Opinions of Marcus Garvey*. In 1925, while incarcerated in Atlanta, Garvey entrusted her with the important task of editing and publishing *Philosophy*. In October of the same year Jacques-Garvey wrote in response, "I have, at all times, endeavored to serve him who serves and suffers for the race; the compilation of this volume is but a slight effort in that direction. It is an honor and a pleasure to earn the confidence of one who has been, and is, so signally faithful to his sacred trust."[74]

Jacques-Garvey shared Garvey's opinions on the needs of the race, particularly on the importance of unity and education. However, on the question of education, she went further than did Garvey to underscore the necessity for the intellectual and political engagement of black women, both at home and in the public sphere. Similar to her precursor, Blyden, she did not view the intellectual development of black women as a threat to their household responsibilities as both wives and/or mothers. Contrarily, she viewed the involvement in both the private and public spheres as complementary and necessary for the well being of the community. With that understanding, she endeavored to reach black women, not only in the United States, but around the world. Later, during her 1960 visit to Ghana, she acquainted herself with the Women's Division of Nkrumah's Convention People's Party.

Through correspondence with her longtime friend, Evelyn Amarteifio—secretary for the Federation of Women in Accra—she pointed out to Nkrumah the significance of a diasporic black women connection. She explained that it would be "as a link between all Units of the Race—in the West Indies, United States, and Homeland, not only for women's pursuits but as a means of publicizing Africa's national activities to the Western World."[75] The hope behind Jacques-Garvey's undertaking was to forge a collaborative engagement among black women and help them take their place in history as conscientious and dignified leaders of the race. She understood the societal tradition against which race women would contend before their leadership is respected; for, "some men declare that women should remain in the homes and leave professions and legislation to men." In her letter Jacques-Garvey immediately rejected the centuries-long belief that women ought to be restricted to the home to affirm that such idea "has been exploded by woman's competency in these new fields and further by the fact that their homes have not suffered by the division of their time and interest."[76] Ula Taylor's assessment of Amy Jacques-Garvey's ideology and practice is to the point. In a succinct paragraph she indicates that

> in addition to focusing on the need for education, Jacques Garvey's editorials highlighted the interplay between the familial and public lives of women. She instructed black women to be competent mothers and to affirm men in the movement for self-determination. At the same time, she went beyond a relational view of self by anchoring her discourse within the refashioning of gender roles so that women could do their part as political leaders in building the black nation. Although emphasizing their maternal role, Jacques Garvey differed from most of her peers in that she believed that their nurturing traits allowed women to run not only their homes and communities efficiently, but also their respective countries.[77]

Jacques-Garvey certainly practiced what she preached. Throughout her years as an activist and a mother Jacques-Garvey continued to meet the demands of the U.N.I.A. while caring for her two sons.[78] She was Garvey's solid support, and as such she unfailingly attended to his requests, particularly during his incarcerations. Her leadership ability and oratory continued to grow as she matured both as a mother and a political figure. In the 1940s, after Garvey's death, she began to associate with diasporic leaders such as Du Bois, Padmore, Nnamdi Azikiwe (of Nigeria) and, in the 1960s, Nkrumah.[79] Her exemplary relationship with Du Bois was significant, for through their association she urged others to cast away petty prejudices and differences in order to focus on the needs of the race. Her decision to work with Du Bois, the man who once stood in overt opposition to her deceased husband, is a clear example of her commitment to race advancement through solidarity. In 1945, in a long letter written to Du Bois, Jacques-Garvey proposed herself as the co-convener of the *Fifth* Pan-African Congress, which was to be held in Manchester, England. Given that in 1945 women were not yet valued as thinkers and leaders, in her letter Jacques-Garvey sought to underline her intellectual credibility and activist competency at the outset. Taylor informs us that "Jacques Garvey used repetition and long explanations to validate her points so that Du Bois would not dismiss her intellectual contribution. . . . For virtually all her political life, Amy Jacques-Garvey had had firsthand experience with chauvinistic men."[80] To address the gender issue openly so that Du Bois would not hold her biological makeup against her, Jacques-Garvey ended her letter with the following point: "Now dear professor, perhaps you may misunderstand the tone of my letters, as I have been so accustomed to talk with M. G. and take part in Conferences with men, as 'man to man' that I don't think or act, as if I 'were just woman.'"[81] This *a priori* gender discussion was meant to keep Du Bois aware of his possible conscious or unconscious sexist disposition. Jacques-Garvey's statement, "I don't think or act, as if I 'were just woman,'" bears similarity to Paulette Nardal's observation, "we were only women." Both Paulette Nardal's and Amy Jacques-Garvey's gender emphasis underlines their awareness of female marginalization in the public and international arena of sociopolitical movements. Both activists wanted to impress the point that as women they were capable intellectuals, leaders, and pioneers.

Regrettably, in 1945 Jacques-Garvey could not attend the *Fifth* Pan-African Congress because of financial difficulty. Nonetheless, she was an active organizer who made vital contributions in the preparatory stages of the meeting and offered critical suggestions on the issues to be discussed at the meeting. Had Jacques-Garvey been able to afford the trip to England, she would have shared the stage with esteemed leaders such as Du Bois, Paul Robeson (chairman of the Council of African Affairs), Max Yergan (executive director of the Council of African Affairs), and Dr. Harold Moody (president of the League of Colored People and former president of the London Missionary Society).[82] After four decades of speaking, organizing, and acting on behalf of Africa and people of African descent throughout the world, in 1960 Jacques-Garvey made her first trip to the ancestral land. The trip was finally realized when Nnamdi Azikiwe extended an invitation to her to attend his inaugural ceremonies as the first African governor-general and commander-in-chief of the Federation of Nigeria. After her sojourn in Nigeria, she went to Ghana to visit Kwame Nkrumah. Both Azikiwe and Nkrumah "were perceptive enough to acknowledge not only Jacques-Garvey's historic role in the movement, but also her contemporary importance in the next phase of African liberation; hence they took it upon themselves to invite her "home" as a guest of their respective governments."[83] In Ghana, Jacques-Garvey expressed great admiration for Nkrumah and his sacrificing efforts for the independence of the Gold

Coast. She viewed Nkrumah's achievement as a realization of Garvey's dream. In the chapter "Destiny Being Fulfilled," of her text *Garvey and Garveyism*, Jacques-Garvey explained that

"Africa for Africans, at home and abroad," is the slogan of Garveyism, proclaimed by him in 1916 when there were only two independent nations in Africa, but the year 1960 was truly a year of Destiny, when most of the twenty-eight nations emerged from Colonial rule to use their freedom to fight ignorance, poverty and disease, by developing the resources of their territories for the uplift and well-being of all their peoples. Truly, "Nationhood is the highest ideal of all peoples."[84]

For Jacques-Garvey, the independence of numerous African countries marked the beginning of Garvey's dream for Africa. Equally important, the various conferences and organizations—the Conference of Independent African States, the All-African People's Conference, the Community of Independent African States, and the Union of African States—that were established to secure the independence of the countries already liberated, as well as to help those under colonial ruling obtain their freedom, were of significant importance to Jacques-Garvey. For, freedom and collaboration among African countries, and the unity of Africans with African descendants of the Diaspora were Garvey and Jacques-Garvey's undying vision. Elated at the sociopolitical structure of Ghana, Nigeria and Ethiopia, shortly after independence, Jacques-Garvey recounted that "Ghana, Nigeria and Ethiopia Airways have modern, comfortable planes, wholly or partially manned by Africans, also Air Hostesses, efficient and charming. On the seas Ghana has her Black Star Line fleet of ships. . . . City Banks are large and modern, with African Directors, Managers and staff."[85] She was proud of the political and civil participation of Africans in their countries, particularly in businesses and schools. Jacques-Garvey had long awaited the opportunity to visit the African continent. During the Garveyite era she and her husband were denied entry in Africa for fear they would awaken Africans to revolution and disturb the European power structure in Africa. After Garvey's death, her accruing financial difficulty—which started with his arrest on allegation of mail fraud—continued to be a hindrance to leaving the boundaries of Jamaica. Hence, Jacques-Garvey's *at last trip* to the motherland became the apogee of her activist career.

Many Garveyite scholars would concede to Taylor's argument that the philosophy and legacy of Marcus Garvey exist because of the life-long dedication and determination of Amy Jacques-Garvey. Indeed, for decades after Garvey's death his wife signally operated as one of the most influential champions of the Garvey movement. One of her most significant ideological gestures is that in her writings she marries the principles of Garveyism to the precepts of Pan-Africanism.

> She defended attacks against Garvey the man and Garveyism the ideology by rebutting critiques at every turn. The fact that Garveyism is so pronounced today is due primarily to the life-long work of Amy Jacques Garvey. Her efforts resonate in the Rastafarian movement, the Nation of Islam, the Moorish Science Temple, and a variety of political sects that all pay homage to Garveyism. . . . Always forward-looking in her work, and determined to generate an intellectual interest in the black world, Jacques Garvey explored the cross-fertilization of Pan-African ideas in her writings.[86]

During the 1950s and 60s, Amy Jacques-Garvey published numerous essays that perspicuously discussed the state of the black world and the Pan-African philosophy she hoped would unite it. In "The Source and Course of Black Power in America" she maintains that Black Unity is Black Power, "the only power a despised, oppressed minority is capable of attaining."[87] In her essays "The Impact of Marcus Garvey on Africa as Told by Africans," "Marcus Garvey's Impact on Jamaica," and "The power of the Human Spirit," Jacques-Garvey consistently analyzes national struggles in the Caribbean, Africa, and the United States, from a Black Internationalist standpoint. In her diasporic examination, she forthrightly emphasizes the connection between Garveyism and the Nation of Islam in the United States. "Elijah Mohammed was formerly a Corporal in the uniformed ranks of the Chicago division. Malcolm X's father was the Vice-President of the Detroit division; so Malcolm X grew up under the influence of Garveyism." She also underlines the less known facts that "Mrs. M. L. Gordon of the Peace Movement of Ethiopia was formerly an active member of the organization in Chicago. The Ethiopian Federation is also an off-shoot of Garveyism."[88] In her presentation of the interconnectedness between blacks in Africa, the Caribbean, the United States, and Europe, she also points to Malcolm X's Caribbean roots through his mother's lineage. Jacques-Garvey's constant effort to link blacks through their roots and history was an attempt to unite and organize them for a better future.

Amy Jacques-Garvey, Zora Neale Hurston, Jane Nardal, and Paulette Nardal serve as exemplars—from a long list—of black women activists of the twentieth century who helped in creating a dialogical space between nations of the Diaspora. Regrettably, as Brent Hayes Edwards points out in *The Practice of Diaspora,* "there is little scholarship on the transnational work both of radical black women intellectuals such as Amy Jacques-Garvey and more moderate figures including Mary Church Terrell, Adelaide Casely-Hayford, and Fauset." Furthermore, Edwards reminds us that the Fourth Pan-African Congress, which is usually seen as politically least significant, "was almost exclusively organized by black U.S. women such as Mrs. A. W. Hunton and the women of the Circle of Peace and Foreign Relations, who brought in speakers such as the Haitian politician Dantès Bellgarde, the anthropologist Melville Herskovits, Leo Hansberry, and Chief Amoah of the Gold Coast."[89] It is thus in recognizing black women's function within the Black Nationalist agenda that one acknowledges the significant role women activists and intellectuals such as Hurston, Jacques-Garvey, Jane and Paulette Nardal, all played during the twentieth century. Amy Jacques-Garvey's devotion to Garveyism and, later, to Pan-Africanism, played an invaluable part in the teachings of the historical trajectory of the two movements. The Nardal sisters' writings and their *salon*, in which they received numerous diasporic artists, created a cultural space where intellectuals could discuss multifaceted issues of the time: the impact of the war, the history of black folk, their present condition and future. In their own ways Jacques-Garvey, the Nardal sisters, and Hurston labored to realize two main and interrelated philosophies. One, to demonstrate and emphasize the extent to which knowledge of self is fundamental to race progress; two, to reveal the degree to which black women have served as capable scholars and leaders, who will continue to play vital roles in race advancement.

Notes

1. Georges Ngal, *Aimé Césaire: Un Homme à la Recherche d'une Patrie* (Dakar: Présence Africaine, 1975) 55.

2. William L. Andrews, ed., *Classic African American Women's Narratives* (Oxford: Oxford University Press, 2003) xiii.

Sojourner Truth became a traveling preacher in 1843 and by 1850 she was, according to Andrews, "a larger-than-life icon of the antislavery and women's rights struggle in the tumultuous decade before the Civil War."

3. Ibid., xiv.

4. Karla F. C. Holloway, *The Character of the Word* (1987); Cheryl A. Wall, *Women of the Harlem Renaissance* (1995); Ula Yvette Taylor, *The Veiled Garvey* (2002); Denean Sharpley-Whiting, *Negritude Women* (2002); Brent Hayes Edwards, *The Practice of the Diaspora* (2003).

5. Delany, *The Condition*, 199.

6. Anna Julia Cooper, "Womanhood: A Vital Element in the Regeneration and Progress of a Race," *The Voice of Anna Julia Cooper* (New York: Rowman & Littlefield Publishers, Inc.) 62.

7. Ibid., 62.

8. Ibid., 63.

9. Alexander Crummell, *Africa and America: Addresses and Discourses* (Miami: Mnemosyne Publishing Inc., 1969) 64.

10. Crummell, *Africa and America*, 80.

11. Ibid., 337.

12. Ibid., 339.

13. Ibid., 82.

14. Blyden, *Christianity, Islam and the Negro Race*, 89.

15. Maria Stewart, "Religion and the Pure Principles of Morality, the Sure Foundation on Which We Must Build," 12.

16. Ibid., 12–13.

17. Ibid., 12.

18. Thomas C. Holt, "The Lonely Warrior: Ida B. Wells-Barnett and the Struggle for Black Leadership," *Black Leaders of the Twentieth Century* (Chicago: University of Illinois Press, 1982) 40.

19. Ida B. Wells-Barnett, *Crusade for Justice: The Autobiography of Ida B. Wells*, ed. Alfreda M. Duster (Chicago: University of Chicago Press, 1970) x.

20. Honor Ford-Smith, "Women and the Garvey Movement in Jamaica," *Garvey: His Work and Impact*, ed. Rupert Lewis and Patrick Bryan (Trenton: Africa World Press Inc., 1991) 77.

21. Ibid., 77.

22. Martin, "Women in the Garvey Movement," *Garvey: His Work and Impact*, 68.

23. Tony Martin, *Literary Garveyism: Garvey, Black Arts and the Harlem Renaissance* (Dover: The Majority Press, 1983) 31.

24. Ibid., 50.

25. Martin, *Literary*, 75.

26. Ibid., 76.

27. Zora Neale Hurston, *Mules and Men* (New York: Harper Perennial, 1990) xiii. The success of *Mules and Men* helped Hurston obtain the Guggeheim Fellowship to study Vodunism in the Caribbean (namely, in Haiti and Jamaica) and South America, which led to the publication of *Tell My Horse* in 1938.

28. Ibid., xviii.

29. Ibid., xxv.

30. Ibid., xxvii.

31. Ibid., xxviii.

32. Listed are a few of the titles to the folk tales in *Mules and Men*.

33. Ibid., xxvii.

34. Ibid., 134–35.

35. Ibid., 83–85.

36. Ibid., 96.

37. Ibid., 134.

38. Ibid., 162.

39. Ibid., 36.

40. Ibid., 36.

41. Zora Neale Hurston, *Their Eyes Were Watching God*. 1937. (New York: HarperCollins Publishers, 2000) 225.

42. Janie's first marriage was a loveless and convenience marriage arranged by her grandmother. Before her final days, the grandmother wanted to be certain Janie was married and living a respectable life.

43. Ibid., 51.

44. Ibid., 69.

45. Ibid., 94.

46. Ibid., 95.

47. Hurston, *Their Eyes*, 106.

48. Karla F. C. Holloway, *The Character of the Word: The Texts of Zora Neale Hurston* (Westport: Greenwood Press, 1987) 10.

49. Ibid., 16.

50. Brent Hayes Edwards, *The Practice of Diaspora* (Cambridge: Harvard University Press, 2003) 153.

51. Ibid., 154.

52. Ngal, *Aimé Césaire: Un Homme à la Recherche d'une Patrie*, 50.

53. The journal functioned between 1931–1932.

54. Ibid., 50.

55. Carol Boyce Davies, *Black Women, Writing Identity: Migrations of the Subject* (New York: Routledge, 1994) 20.

56. Edwards, *Practice*, 120, 132–33.

57. Ibid. 106.

58. Ngal, *Aimé Césaire*, 55.

59. Ibid., 51.

60. The term *Antillean* refers to the inhabitants of the French Departments d'Outre-Mer, particularly those from Martinique, Guadeloupe, and Guyane Française.

61. Frantz Fanon, *Black Skin, White Masks* (New York: Grove Press, 1967) 148.

62. Ibid., 112.

63. Jacques Louis Hymans, *Léopold Sédar Senghor: An Intellectual Biography by Jacques Hymans* (Edinburg: Edinburg University Press, 1971) 274.

64. Ibid., 277–78.

65. Ibid., 278.

66. Ibid., 278.

67. Here *Antillean* does not include Haitians, for Haiti's literature began to emerge during the second half of the 1830s.

68. Ibid., 274.

69. Ibid., 275.

70. Ibid., 275.

71. Paulette Nardal, "L'Eveil de la Conscience de Race," *Revue du Monde Noir*, April 1932.

72. In this present text I use the hyphen in Jacques-Garvey's name, as it seems to be the spelling both she and Marcus Garvey often used. When using a quotation where the author opts not to hyphen Jacques-Garvey's name, I keep it as it appears in the author's text.

73. Maria Stewart is the first known black woman in the United States to deliver public lectures in Boston in 1830. In *Classic African American Women's Narratives*, William L. Andrews notes that "by delivering in Boston the first of a series of four public lectures, [Stewart's act] directly defied American tradition forbidding women of any color from addressing political issues at a public forum" (ix).

74. Garvey, *Philosophy, volume* II.

75. Ula Yvette Taylor, *The Veiled Garvey: The Life and Times of Amy Jacques Garvey* (Chapel Hill: The University of North Carolina Press, 2002) 217.

76. Ibid., 74.

77. Ibid., 74.

78. Taylor, *The Veiled Garvey*, 236–37.

79. Ibid., 5.

80. Ibid., 168.

81. Ibid., 168.

82. Ibid., 166.

83. Ibid., 216.

84. Amy Jacques Garvey, *Garvey and Garveyism* (Kingston: A. Jacques Garvey, 1963) 284.

85. Ibid., 286.

86. Taylor, *The Veiled Garvey*, 236–37.

87. Amy Jacques-Garvey, *Black Power in America: Marcus Garvey's Impact on Jamaica and Africa* (Kingston: United Printers Ltd., 1968) 11.

88. Ibid., 5.

89. Edwards, *The Practice*, 131–32.

5

Two Personalities, One God, One Aim, One Destiny: W. E. B. Du Bois, Marcus Garvey, and the *New Negro Renaissance*

The Universal Negro Improvement Association has been misrepresented by my enemies. They have tried to make it appear that we are hostile to other races. This is absolutely false. We love all humanity. We are working for the peace of the world, which we believe can only come about when all races are given their due.

—Marcus Garvey[1]

Garvey proved not only an astonishing popular leader, but a master of propaganda. Within a few years, news of his movement, of his promises and plans, reached Europe and Asia, and penetrated every corner of Africa. . . . My first effort was to explain away the Garvey movement and ignore it; but it was a mass movement that could not be ignored.

—W. E. B. Du Bois[2]

THE SCHOLARSHIP ON W. E. B. Du Bois and Marcus Garvey is numerous. The research, thus far, has primarily followed three currents: one, the study of Du Bois' sociopolitical activism and literary accomplishment; two, the study of Garveyism, with an emphasis on Marcus Garvey's political "failure"; and three, the examination of Du Bois' and Garvey's vitriolic political dissention and personality conflict. Building on the three modes of analyses, which are respectively crucial in the study of Du Boisian and Garveyite history, the objective here is to bring to light and accentuate the points of convergence in their Black Nationalist ideology, through an examination of their published works. In so doing, the analysis focuses on Garvey's and Du Bois' complementary roles in championing civil and political rights for blacks, as well as in nurturing and sponsoring artistic development. In that context, one can warrantably state that Du Bois' and Garvey's political activism and social engagement were geared toward one aim: black advancement in thought and action.

Salvaging the Wretched of the Earth:
The Twentieth-Century Crusade

Garvey's and Du Bois' activism and artistic works were fundamentally constructed on the principles of Black Nationalism, expressed through Pan-Africanism and Garveyism. The six *Pan-African Congresses*, which date from 1900 to 1945 with Du Bois as one of the main organizers, underscored the functions of the Pan-African movement, which was both social and political in its basic organizational structure. Garvey's *International Conferences of Negroes* expounded the functions of the Universal Negro Improvement Association; the preoccupations of the conferences were social and cultural, as well as political and economic. One would note that during the twentieth century, Garvey and Du Bois continued the many efforts initiated during the nineteenth century, under the same premise; namely, that Black Nationalism and, by extension, Pan-Africanism and Garveyism, signified economic and political independence for blacks throughout the Diaspora, as it also fostered a "revolution of mentalities" by demanding the freedom and right to express social and cultural idiosyncrasies, through the means of relevant education.

The Pan-African Congresses, ranging from the Pan-African Conference assembled in London in 1900—realized by the Trinidadian Henry Sylvester Williams—to the Fifth Congress, in 1945, addressed a number of social and political issues affecting blacks throughout the world.[3] During the Pan-African Congress of 1919, led by W. E. B. Du Bois in Paris, members representing blacks from different nations drafted their demands to the League of Nations. Section "c" requested considerable amelioration in the matters of land, capital, labor, education, and state in Africa, and black nations in the Western Hemisphere. From the excerpts below, it is noticeable that education, as well as self-governance in political and economic matters, were issues that dominated the Pan-African Congresses throughout the twentieth century. Let us examine, first-hand, some of the requests placed before the League of Nations.

(c) The Negroes of the world demand that hereafter the natives of Africa and the peoples of African descent be governed according to the following principles:

(i)   *The Land.* The land and its natural resources shall be held in trust for the natives and at all times they shall have effective ownership of as much land as they can profitably develop.

(ii) *Capital.* The investment of capital and granting of concessions shall be so regulated as to prevent the exploitation of the natives and the exhaustion of the natural wealth of the country. Concessions shall always be limited in time and subject to state control. The growing social needs of the natives must be regarded and the profits taxed for social and material benefit of the natives.

(iii) *Labour.* Slavery and corporal punishment shall be abolished and forced labour except in punishment of crime; and the general conditions of labour shall be prescribed and regulated by the State.

(iv) *Education.* It shall be the right of every native child to learn to read and write his own language, and the language of the trustee nation, at public expense, and to be given technical instruction in the branch of industry. The State shall also educate as large a number of natives as possible in higher technical and cultural training and maintain a corps of native teachers.

(v)   *The State.* The natives of Africa must have the right to participate in the Government as fast as their development permits, in conformity with the principle that the Government exists for the natives, and not the natives for the Government. They shall at once be allowed to participate in local and tribal government, according to ancient usage, and this participation shall gradually extend, as education and experience proceed to the higher offices of state; to the end that, in time, Africa is ruled by consent of the Africans.[4]

During the Second Pan-African Congress—held in London from August 28 to 29 of 1921—the representatives reiterated the questions of education, the role of Africans in their own affairs and government, as well as their freedom in religion. The leaders present at the Congress—similar to the ideological position of Blyden and Delany—denounced sectarianism in religion in regard to race progress, for they believed that division in systematized religious factions generally hinders the cooperation that is indispensable for advancement. As for education, they advocated intellectual and industrial knowledge as indissoluble components for societal growth. Requests *three, four,* and *five* of the petition, focused on:

(1) Education in self-knowledge, in scientific truth, and in industrial technique, undivorced from the art of beauty.

(2) Freedom in their own religion and social customs and with the right to be different and non-conformist.

(3) Co-operation with the rest of the world in government, industry, and art on the basis of justice, freedom and peace.[5]

The Third Pan-African Congress, which met in London in November 1923, re-stated previous requests that were not answered or seriously taken into consideration by European powers. On behalf of all Africans they demanded once again:

(1) A voice in their own governments. . . .

(4) Free elementary education for all; broad training in modern industrial technique; and higher training for selected talent.

(5) The development of Africa for the benefit of Africans, and not merely for the profit of Europeans.

(6) World disarmament and the abolition of war; but failing this, and as long as white folk bear arms against black folk, the right of blacks to bear arms in their defence.[6]

The Fourth Pan-African Congress, which took place in New York from August 21 to 24 of 1927, insisted with greater determination on the need for African unity in Africa and with peoples of African descent throughout the world. One of the reasons for the growing emphasis on Black Nationalism within Africa and Black Internationalism within the Diaspora was that members of the International African Service Bureau, who were working with the British Communist Party, came to understand the politics of the British communists. The Party did not want to see and were therefore "soft-pedaling" the demands for immediate self-governance in Africa. Aware of the British Communist Party's reluctance to the idea and the reality of a truly independent Africa, members of the International African Service Bureau joined forces with the Pan-African Committee to pursue their goal.[7] It is worth noting here—though chapter 7 discusses Césaire's philosophies and actions more thoroughly—that later, in 1956, with the same logic as the members of the International African Service Bureau, Aimé Césaire would break away from the French Communist Party. In a letter addressed to Maurice Thorez, Secretary General of the French Communist Party, he forthrightly and concisely explained the reasons behind his resignation. One of his many observations of the relationship between blacks and the Communist Party laid bare the conflicting interests between the groups.

I think I have said enough to make it plain that it's neither Marxism nor Communism I repudiate; that the use certain people have made of Marxism and Communism is what I condemn. That what I want is that Marxism and Communism be harnessed into the service of the colored peoples, and not the colored peoples into the service of Marxism and Communism. That the doctrine and the movement be tailored to fit men, not men to fit the movement.[8]

Similar to the British Communist Party, the French Communist Party did not wholeheartedly wish to see the emergence of an autonomous Africa, nor did it wish to see the formation of intellectually and politically independent black nations. Furthermore, Césaire argued that the French Communist Party—European Communist Parties in general—viewed its position to colonial people as one of paternalism, to the extent that their very "anticolonial" stance "bears the stigmata of the colonialism they're combatting."[9]

Pondering the International African Service Bureau's withdrawal from the British Communist Party and its subsequent collaboration with the Pan-African Committee, Padmore contends in *Communism or Pan-Africanism?* that

> the association between Dr. DuBois's Pan-African Congress and the International African Service Bureau was destined to have the most far-reaching consequences in Africa in the years following the Second World War. The link established during the war years stimulated the present revival of Pan-Africanism. By 1945, interest in the future status of Africans and peoples of African descent was sufficiently widespread to bring together for the first time representatives of the newly-formed colonial trade union and labour movements and the emerging nationalist forces in the African territories. It was the largest and most representative Pan-African Congress yet convened.[10]

During the Fourth Pan-African Congress, which assembled after World War I (August 21 to August 24, 1927)—when the great victory of England, France, and the United States brought consistent insurmountable social and political disappointments for blacks throughout the Diaspora—black leaders voiced their demands for civil rights, the eradication of discrimination, and the cessation of unjustified assassination of blacks, particularly through lynching. Their demands included the following goals:

(1) To promote the well-being and unity of African peoples and peoples of African descent throughout the world.
(2) To demand self-determination and independence of African peoples and other subject races from the domination of powers claiming sovereignty and trusteeship over them.

(3) To secure equality of civil rights for African Peoples and the total aboli-
     tion of all forms of racial discrimination.[11]

With the emphasis on equality in civil rights and the abolition of all types
of discrimination, representatives of the Congress sought to address maltreatment not only on the broader scale, but particularly against black soldiers who
fought the European War of 1914–1920. The black soldiers consisted mainly
of American soldiers who were lynched and burned after their military service rendered to the United States in the First World War, and West African
soldiers—also known as *tirailleurs sénégalais*—who fought for France during
the First and Second World Wars.[12]

In the United States, during the period dating from 1917 to 1919, Ida B.
Wells-Barnett decried the escalation in the number of lynching cases in the
South. Wells-Barnett unremittingly conducted her fierce crusade against
lynching in the South and discrimination in the Northern states, as a response to the growing injustice toward blacks during and after the First
World War.[13] The riots of the war period, which grew out of the frustration
of black folk in the face of an unending and acute racism, was the beginning
of the bloody months of 1919 that have been called the "Red Summer." One
of the reasons for such violent racial outbreaks—in addition to increasing
black unemployment, poverty, and various discriminatory assaults based on
race—was that black soldiers who fought the First World War in the name
of democracy, wanted equal rights in their home country, and their rightful
place in society. Hence, black American soldiers, who were treated more
humanely in France than they were treated in the United States, before and
after their military service, joined the battle to change the existing racial
status quo in America. Inspired by a *seeming* non-racial prejudice environment in France, American soldiers began to persistently demand their rights
in the United States.

The non-racial prejudice black Americans observed in France was plainly
artificial. The *tirailleurs sénégalais* who fought for France during the First
and Second World Wars were treated with discrimination akin to the kind
of treatment black soldiers experienced in the United States. During the period immediately following World War II, there were approximately fifteen
recorded uprising incidents, most of which occurred in the south of France
with the exception of an outbreak in Versailles. There was also an incident
in England, at Monshire Camp in Huyton; and in Senegal there was the historic uprising, which took place at the Thiaroye barracks on the outskirts of
Dakar.[14] These uprisings occurred in barracks where African soldiers waited
to be shipped to their respective countries after the war. The insurrections
were fanned by the inferior treatments African soldiers received from the

French with respect to poor housing, clothing, food, and also—perhaps more importantly—because of France's failure to deliver back pay to African soldiers for their military work during the war. While there were a series of protests following the Second World War, the two most serious ones took place at Morlaix and Thiaroye.[15] At Thiaroye hundreds of African soldiers were seriously injured, approximately thirty-five were gravely wounded, and about the same number were murdered by French military men who viewed the Africans' rightful request for pay as an insult and an attempt at seeking social equality. "[The French] fired on the mutineers," described an Ivoirien veteran who witnessed the 1944 massacre."There were many dead that day. We were angry. We thought we might not get back to our villages. We might be killed too. The army fired upon the army—those were the orders. Our regiment wasn't far from them. They brought the bodies to us."[16] In *Colonial Conscripts: The Tirailleurs Sénégalais in French West Africa*, Myron Echenberg reports that in the aftermath of the Thiaroye uprising, with its injuries and deaths, about thirty-four ex-POWs were arrested and tried on charges just below mutiny. All of the men who were tried were convicted and sentenced to prison terms ranging from one to ten years. By 1947, before an amnesty was issued on behalf of the African victims, about five prisoners had died in jail.[17]

In the midst of rampant and ferocious violence against blacks, which includes the Italian invasion in Ethiopia in 1935, the fifth global Pan-African Congress re-emphasized many of the previous concerns that were not yet addressed and the demands that were not yet met. In addition, in Manchester, England, on the 4th of March 1945 members of the fifth global Pan-African Congress observed that

(a) Since the advent of the British, French, Belgian, and other European nations in West Africa, there has been regression instead of progress as a result of systematic exploitation by these alien imperialist powers. The claims of "partnership," "trusteeship," "guardianship," and the "mandate system," do not serve the political wishes of the people of West Africa.

(b) That the democratic nature of the indigenous institutions of the peoples of West Africa have been crushed by obnoxious and oppressive laws and regulations, and replaced by autocratic systems of government which are inimical to the wishes of the peoples of West Africa.

(c) That the introduction of pretentious constitutional reforms in the West African territories are nothing but spurious attempts on the part of alien imperialist powers to continue the political enslavement of the peoples.

(d) That the introduction of Indirect Ruling is not only an instrument of oppression but also an encroachment on the rights of the West African natural rulers.

(e) That the artificial divisions and territorial boundaries created by the imperialist powers are deliberate steps to obstruct the political unity of the West African peoples.[18]

The petition against *indirect ruling* continued to be of relevance to leaders of the mid-1940s, and more so to leaders of the 1950s and 1960s, with the independence of various African nations. The "constitutional reforms in Africa" that Europeans began to advocate in the 1940s, simply meant a new form of control in Africa. The representatives of the Pan-African Congress were able to decipher the European new mode of political ruling and were cognizant of the fact that these reforms did not signify self-governance for Africa. Instead, European powers were placing white and black intermediaries, who were under the commands of metropolitan countries, in control of their businesses on the African continent. As a response, black leaders insistently raised African consciousness on issues of territorial boundaries, which were placed to create and maintain geographical, ideological, and political divisions within Africa.

Garvey and members of the Universal Negro Improvement Association also wrote a number of petitions to the League of Nations to request civil and political rights for blacks throughout the Diaspora. In 1920 the U.N.I.A. drafted and adopted the "Declaration of Rights of the Negro Peoples of the World," which outlined its beliefs and requests on behalf of the race. The excerpt below is inserted to help capture the dynamics of Garvey's movement and the Declaration of Rights in relation to the various Petitions of the Pan-African Congresses.

(1) Be it known to all men that whereas, all men are created equal and entitled to the rights of life, liberty and the pursuit of happiness, and because of this we, the duly elected representatives of the Negro peoples of the world, invoking the aid of the just and Almighty God do declare all men, women, and children of our blood throughout the world free citizens, and do claim them as free citizens of Africa, the Motherland of all Negroes.

(2) That we believe in the supreme authority of our race in all things racial; that all things are created and given to man as a common possession; that there should be an equitable distribution and apportionment of all such things, and in consideration of the fact that as a race we are now deprived of those things that are morally and legally ours,

we believe it right that all such things should be acquired and held by whatsoever means possible.

(3) That we believe the Negro, like any other race, should be governed by the ethics of civilization, and, thereafter, should not be deprived of any of those rights or privileges common to other human beings.

(4) We declare that Negroes, wheresoever they form a community among themselves, should be given the right to elect their own representatives to represent them in legislatures, courts of law, or such institutions as may exercise control over that particular community.

(5) We protest against the atrocious crime of whipping, flogging and overworking of the native tribes of Africa and Negroes everywhere. These are methods that should be abolished, and all means should be taken to prevent a continuance of such brutal practices.

(6) We believe in the doctrine of the freedom of the press, and we therefore emphatically protest against the suppression of Negro newspapers and periodicals in various parts of the world, and call upon Negroes everywhere to employ all available means to prevent such suppression.

(7) We further demand free speech universally for all men.

(8) We believe in the self-determination of all peoples.

(9) We declare for the freedom of religious worship.

(10) With the help of Almighty God, we declare ourselves the sworn protectors of the honor and virtue of our women and children, and pledge our lives for their protection and defense everywhere, and under all circumstances from wrongs and outrages.[19]

Although Du Bois' concept of Pan-Africanism differed from Garveyism, as Padmore points out in *Pan-Africanism or Communism?* there were nonetheless common views and aims between the two leaders. Du Bois' Pan-Africanism, according to Padmore, "differed from Garveyism in that it was never conceived as a Back to Africa Movement, but rather as a dynamic political philosophy and guide to action for Africans in Africa who were laying the foundations of national liberation organizations."[20] While this is true for particular proponents and during certain epochs of the movement (as discussed in chapter 1), we must also note that Blyden, Crummell, and Delany, who are ancestral exponents of Pan-Africanism—albeit *avant la lettre*—also advocated a physical return to Africa. While Du Bois never adhered to the Back-to-Africa philosophy, when comparing his Pan-African Petitions to Garvey's Declaration of Rights of the Negro Peoples of the World one would notice from both documents the repeated demands for basic human rights and privileges that were due to Africans and their descendants. Notably, the call for self-determination and the control of blacks over their communities, the advocacy for religious freedom and freedom of the press, the emphasis on relevant education for blacks, and the demand for citizenship based on true liberty and respect for blacks in Africa and throughout the world.

In November 1922, Garvey addressed the ideological dissentions that existed between the U.N.I.A. and other organizations. In addressing those differences, he was by and large criticizing Du Bois' politics, particularly his, then, integrationist stance. Contrary to Garvey's proposal for an eventual repatriation of blacks in Africa, Du Bois—as mentioned—did not envision an emigration to the ancestral land. Rather, he believed that black folk should remain and struggle for civil rights within their native countries while maintaining international relations with other blacks as well as with other races. Garvey, similar to earlier Pan-Africanists, principally Cuffee, Bishop Turner, and Blyden, did not believe that blacks could ever acquire the same level of citizenship as whites in countries where the substructure has been established by whites. Hence in 1922, during a speech delivered at Liberty Hall in New York, entitled "The Principles of the Universal Negro Improvement Association," Garvey articulated what he viewed as the major difference between his organization and others:

> The difference between the Universal Negro Improvement Association and the other movements of this country, and probably the world, is that the Universal Negro Improvement Association seeks independence of government, while the other organizations seek to make the Negro a secondary part of existing governments. We differ from the organizations in America because they seek to subordinate the Negro as a secondary consideration in a great civilization, knowing that in America the Negro will never reach his highest ambition, knowing that the Negro in America will never get his constitutional rights. All those organizations which are fostering the improvement of Negroes in the British Empire know that the Negro in the British Empire will never reach the height of his constitutional rights. What do I mean by constitutional rights in America? If the black man is to reach the height of his ambition in this country—if the black man is to get all of his constitutional rights in America—then the black man should have the same chance in the nation as any other man to become president, of the nation, or a street cleaner in New York. . . . Are they prepared to give us such political equality?[21]

This became a provocative question which dominated black intellectual thought throughout the twentieth century, well into the twenty-first. Garvey's primary concern was to make clear the rights as well as the position of black folk within human civilization. The practice of blacks as subordinates, or as secondary consideration, was unacceptable to U.N.I.A. members. Garvey's persistent call to freedom in representation reinforced his desire to establish a politically independent black nation where blacks would be able to serve in the highest rank of government. The political independence that would be established would in turn give blacks the freedom to teach their history and culture, to teach and experience a religious life that was in consonance with their African heritage, and to establish their own governmental structure.

While Du Bois and Garvey were emphasizing key differences between the organizations to which they adhered, they were simultaneously advocating Black Internationalism within the United States and abroad. In 1918, before the First Pan-African Congress of 1919, Du Bois proposed the formation of a Negro Cooperative Guild; a cooperative system within which he wanted to include and work with members of the black Diaspora. Du Bois' idea of an international Negro Cooperative Guild did not come into realization. The reason is not clear. It has been argued that Du Bois was not an organizational leader, thus failed to rally the upper and middle classes, along with the masses, to pursue the Negro Cooperative Guild endeavor. In 1940 Du Bois explained that the movement required preparatory "spade work" that was overlooked; black managers and consumers needed to be better educated. During the time Du Bois was planning the Negro Cooperative Guild Garvey was concurrently establishing the Black Star Line and a chain of cooperative grocery stores, laundries, tailoring and millinery companies, a doll factory, restaurants, and a printing press, which would also operate on an international scale.[22] Before his national and international prominence as a leader, in 1897 Du Bois presented a paper entitled "The Conservation of the Races" in which he postulated the doctrine of "Pan-Negroism"; the doctrine Blyden heralded and manifested earlier in the nineteen century. In its ideological content Du Bois' and Blyden's "Pan-Negroism" is essentially Pan-Africanism. The former focuses on the Negro race as the latter emphasizes the geographical provenance of members of the race. Toward the end of the 1910s and early 1920s, the philosophies of Pan-Africanism and Garveyism continued to mobilize blacks on an international level, not solely within the politicoeconomic sphere but also within the sociocultural realm. In 1928, in his Second Petition to the League of Nations, Garvey also expressed the philosophy of "Pan-Negroism" and proclaimed the following:

> As you may observe, the blacks or Negroes belong to no one nationality, in fact, nationality is only a matter of accident, as far as the Negro is concerned, for he had no choice of nationality, hence our petition should not be considered as one in the category of nationals, but one of races, with the right to appeal to the soul and conscience of civilized humanity.[23]

Garvey espoused the philosophy of "Pan-Negroism," or "Pan-Africanism," and viewed blacks as united under one race with the same destiny. The motto of the Universal Negro Improvement Association and the *Negro World*, "One God, One Aim, One Destiny: A Newspaper Devoted Solely to the Interests of the Negro Race," served as a constant reminder of such diasporic view and goal. To take his objective a step closer to realization, the *Negro World* was translated into French and Spanish. Concurrently, Du Bois showed his commitment to the indispensable transnational dialogue that must continue among nations. In the July 1926 issue of the *Crisis* he published an article on education and the importance of teaching foreign languages to black students. His article posited that foreign languages should be considered as an essential subject in education, particularly for blacks, because it is a vital tool of communication and a sociocultural bridge. He viewed foreign languages as an agent without which the Pan-African movement cannot reach its full potential. Du Bois expressed the belief that "no man is educated who cannot speak, read, and understand a foreign language. American Negroes ought to be able to visit Europe and the West Indies and talk to their fellows there. If our schools are not preparing for this, they are not schools."[24] Arguably, Du Bois' statement may be conceived as considerably severe, for one can be relatively educated without the knowledge of a foreign language. However, the quality of education Du Bois proposed is one that is opened to the greater world. In the context of global conversations and exchanges, it can reasonably be argued that an individual who understands another's language is an individual who will also aim—or be opened—to understand and respect the other's culture. Regarding the particularity of the black world, Du Bois argued that the language barrier within the Diaspora adds strength to the existing territorial boundaries. The conclusion to such analysis is that without the dismantling of lingual, intellectual, and territorial barriers, unity and cooperation among black nations will remain difficult, if not impossible, to attain.

Art or Propaganda?

Du Bois and Garvey delivered many addresses and wrote extensively on the issues the Pan-African movement and the Garvey movement were geared to discuss and solve. In addition to their political speeches, and manifestoes, Du Bois and Garvey promulgated Black Nationalism through their involvement in art. Art, as they both viewed it, was one of the most effective vehicles for social consciousness and change. The *Crisis*, which Du Bois founded in 1910, became one of the major organs for the dissemination of Pan-Africanist ideas.

In "W. E. B. Du Bois: Protagonist of the Afro-American Protest," Elliot Rud-wick underlines:

> Calling for a systematic cultivation of all kinds of black art forms, [Du Bois] proudly presented works by young novelists, essayists, painters, and poets, and in the early 1920s he proposed an Institute of Negro Literature and Art. . . . Du Bois' cultural nationalism was intimately related to the stirrings among black intellectuals and artists known as the Harlem Renaissance, but his quasi-socialistic brand of economic nationalism was never widely accepted.[25]

Du Bois understood the inextricable link between the many facets of the social and the political; consequently, he focused on nurturing intellectuals and artists who would contribute to the improvement of the black race, through the development of critical thought and cultural expression. Moreover, he believed the preservation of the Negro spirit was as important as the growth of the Negro market. Art, in all its forms (novel, essay, manifesto, painting, sculpture, music, and theater) offered blacks the opportunity to express their ideas and, by extension, participate in the evolution of black philosophy, for the betterment of their social condition. In the section entitled "The Negro in Art: How Shall He Be Portrayed" of the *Crisis*, various writers monthly offered their opinions on the role of Negro literature in America, and in the black community in particular. The dialogical format was established to allow writers to reply by supporting or refuting the opinions expressed in previous issues. For instance, in April 1926 Langston Hughes wrote the following in response to the question of whether or not there was a real danger in the existing trend where black writers would choose to depict Negro characters of the underworld rather than depicting the truth about their own social class.

> I like this: What's the use of saying anything—the true literary artist is going to write about what he chooses anyway regardless of outside opinions. You write about the intelligent Negroes; Fisher about the unintelligent. Both of you are right. Walpool pictures the better class Englishman; Thomas Burke the sailors in Limehouse. And both are worth reading. It's the way people look at things, not what they look at, that needs to be changed.[26]

In March 1926 Mary W. Ovington wrote, "What publishers, at least the best, want today, is art, not propaganda. They don't want to know what the writer thinks on the Negro question, they want to know about Negroes."[27] In the April 1926 issue J. E. Spingarn refuted Ovington's view and explained that

> the culture of a race must have a beginning, however simple; and imperfect books are infinitely better than a long era of silence. If the white publisher hesitates,

on the ground that it is his business to be a publisher and not a champion of Negro culture, colored brains should create colored periodicals. The world will not close its ears to the voice of a great writer merely because of the imprint on the title-page . . . complex problems of literature cannot magically be solved by a childish formula like that of "art versus propaganda." They must understand that a book may be of high value to a race's culture without being of high rank in the world's literature, just as a man may be a very useful citizen yet a rather mediocre dentist.[28]

Du Bois and Garvey shared the opinion of J. E. Spingarn, in that they both understood the link between artistic work—particularly literature—and activism. They did not subscribe to the philosophy of "art versus propaganda," for they did not equate a socially conscious work with mediocrity. In fact, both leaders published poems that outlined historical facts and analyzed various social conditions. Furthermore, Garvey argued that each race has a corpus of literature that is simultaneously art and propaganda, since propaganda as he defined it, is the dissemination of a people's history, ideology, and culture. In support of Garvey's argument, one would note that European epic literature of war and religion, which had propagandist aim, remains in the canon of great world literature today; for example, Greece's *Iliad* and *Odyssey*, and France's *La Chanson de Roland*.

In the early 1920s Garvey addressed the dilemma of the black artist's relationship with white publishing houses. On one hand many talented black writers were neglected because of their refusal to compromise the race's integrity and agenda through their artistic work. On the other hand, too many writers were creatively and ideologically contained by white patronage and white-controlled publishing houses.[29] In time Garvey came to view the Harlem Renaissance as a fad that was detrimental to black folk's ideological progress. To counterbalance, the U.N.I.A's weekly paper, *Negro World* (which first appeared during the summer of 1918) became a venue for cultural expression. In *Literary Garveyism*, Tony Martin reminds us that in addition to his political philosophy of race consciousness, Garvey had a momentous effect on the literary dimension of the Harlem Renaissance, through the *Negro World's* publication of artistic works. By 1920, two years after the first publication of the *Negro World*, the paper "was already on its way to becoming the focal point of a mass preoccupation with the arts, especially poetry, unequalled by any of the better-known publication of the Harlem Renaissance."[30]

From the peak of the *Negro World's* literary activity—1920–1923—to its last publication in 1933, Garvey consistently allocated publishing space for literary works, including editorials dedicated to literary subjects. Through the commitment of U.N.I.A members, the paper remained "the most highly political of newspapers. Yet it was simultaneously the most literary of newspapers."[31] Many prominent literary figures who published in the *Negro World* also belonged to the greater Harlem literary world. For example, Claude McKay, Zora Neale Hurston, Arthur Schomburg, Eric Walrond, J. A. Rogers, Augusta Savage, Sergeant Lucian B. Watkins, Leonard L. Brathwaite, and T. Thomas Fortune, among others.[32] Garvey used many venues to galvanize people of African descent toward change; in addition to his addresses and manifestoes, as well as the plays and poems he sponsored, he began to publish his own poetry in 1927. Garvey was not an acclaimed poet, he never viewed himself as one; his poetry was another method of communication. Garvey's poems recount the history of the world from ancient time—before the slave trade—to his own time, while envisioning the future of the race. His poem "The Tragedy of White Injustice," published in 1927, is a seventy-stanza long poem which reflects on the history and the lives of blacks from Africa to the Americas and Europe. Let us focus on the transcription of three stanzas of the poem—one on religion, one on mankind, and the last one on education—to capture Garvey's poetic style and historical content.

(9)

With the Bible they go to foreign lands,
Taking Christ and stealth in different hands;
Making of God a mockery on earth,
When of the Holy One there is no dearth:
They say to us: "You, sirs, are the heathen,
"We your brethen—Christian fellowmen,
"We come to tell the story of our God";
when we believe, they give to us the rod.

(45)

Blacks do not hate you because you are white;
We believe in giving to all men right;
Some we do keep for ourselves to protect,
Knowing it as virtue to select.
We are willing to be friends of mankind,
Pulling all together with none behind,
Growing in sane goodness and fellowship,
Choosing but the Almighty to worship.

(62)

Shall there be freedom of liberal thought?
No; the white man has all agencies bought—
Press, pulpit, law and every other thing—
Hence o'er public opinion reigns king.
This is indisputable, glaring fact;

You may find it out with a little tact.
College tutors and presidents are paid,
So that in universities schemes are laid.[33]

His poem "Africa for the Africans," published in 1927—which resonates Delany's 1859-slogan—poetically re-states Garvey's vision of a politically independent Africa. "Hail! United States of Africa," also published in 1927, echoes Blyden's nineteenth century advocacy and Nkrumah's twentieth century philosophy. The poem outlines an African genealogy and envisions the future by depicting the image of a United Africa into nationhood. Poems such as "Mussolini—Scourge of God!" (1935), and "The Devil in Mussolini" (1936), both denounce the Italian invasion in Ethiopia in 1935. His poem "Afric's Love," published in 1934, draws a connection between a return to Africa and death.

Afric's Love
Come sing the song of Afric's love
The love of God so dear,
The Father great in realms above,
The greatest when so near.

The day has come for us to see
The glory of our name,
The hour of our jubilee
Will crown our greatest fame.

The hand of God is showing how
Our princes shall arrive;
Old Egypt's land is throbbing now
With souls that are alive.[34]

Garvey often spoke of his physical and spiritual return to Africa to see the day of Africa's glory. As a symbol of his connection to the black folk who died, those who are alive, and those who will be born, Garvey requested that he is wrapped in the mantle of the Red, Black, and Green, when he expires.[35] In his published poems Du Bois also addressed many historical, social, and political issues of the black Diaspora. In 1962, in his poem "Ghana Calls," dedicated to Kwame Nkrumah, Du Bois drew a similar connection, as did Garvey, between Africa's long-neglected glorious past and future. As Garvey, in his verses Du Bois envisions his death in relation to Africa. Significantly, Du Bois would later die in Ghana, in 1963. He begins "Ghana Calls" with a recount of his travels in England, Scotland, France, and Germany, reflecting on his dreams for the black race.

Anon I woke, but in one corner of my soul
    I stayed asleep.
    Forget I could not,
    But never would I remember
    That hell-hoist ghost
    Of slavery and woe.

I lived and grew, I worked and hoped
    I planned and wandered, gripped and coped
    With every doubt but one that slept
    Yet clamored to awaken.

              * * *

Here at last, I looked back on my Dream;
    I heard the Voice that loosed
    The Long-looked dungeons of my soul
    I sensed that Africa had come
    Not up from Hell, but from the sum of Heaven's glory.

              * * *

From reeking West whose day is done,
    Who stink and stagger in their dung
    Toward Africa, China, India's strand
    Where Kenya and Himalaya stand
    And Nile and Yang-tze-roll:
    Turn every yearning face of man.[36]

This poem illustrates Du Bois' disappointment in American and European powers. After a long career of persistent struggle for human rights and equality in political, economic, and social matters, Du Bois retreated to Africa, disenchanted. In 1951 he was tried in federal court on charges of being an unregistered agent of a foreign power. "Although the judge directed an acquittal, Du Bois became so thoroughly disillusioned about the United States that in 1961 he officially joined the Communist party and moved to Ghana."[37] The height of Du Bois' courtship with the Communist party began in the late 1940s, during his relationship with Shirley Graham, whom he married in February of 1951.

In spite of decades of political opposition and personality conflict, it is important to remember that Du Bois and Garvey acknowledged each other's impact on the continuing sociopolitical struggle. This last point is considerable, for given Du Bois' and Garvey's discord it demonstrates that at a certain point of their activist career they were cognizant of their ideological convergence in regard to the race agenda. In 1915, before departing from Jamaica to the United States, Garvey made a final earnest plea to the Afro-Caribbean of Jamaica, during which he urged:

For God sake, you men and women who have been keeping yourselves away from the people of our own African race, cease the ignorance; unite your hands and hearts with the people Afric. . . . Sons and daughters of Africa, I say to you arise, take on the toga of race pride, and throw off the brand of ignominy which has kept you back for so many centuries. Dash asunder the petty prejudices within your own fold; set at defiance the scornful designation of "nigger" uttered even by yourselves, and be a Negro in the light of Pharaohs of Egypt, Simons of Cyrene, Hannibals of Carthage, L'Ouvertures and Dessalines of Haiti, Blydens, Barclays and Johnsons of Liberia, Lewises of Sierra Leone, and Douglasses and Du Boises of America, who have made, and are making history for the race.[38]

It is questionable whether or not Garvey would have placed Du Bois on his list had he met him first. It is also probable that if Garvey lived as long as Du Bois did he would have perhaps come to publicly acknowledge his opponent as a valuable leader, just as in 1940 Du Bois admitted Garvey's impact on black liberation philosophy and movements. If in 1915 Garvey listed Du Bois among some of the most important leaders of Africa and the black Diaspora, it was because he esteemed him as a capable leader. However, once in the United States, "petty prejudices within their own fold," and personality incompatibility fueled their enmity. In *Dusk of Dawn* Du Bois wrote an ambivalent reflection on Garvey and his approach to the race problem. Such analysis is worth reading at length. He conceded that

after the war he [Garvey] came to America, launched a widely advertised plan for commerce between Negro groups and eventually of Negro domination of Africa. It was a grandiose and bombastic scheme, utterly impracticable as a whole, *but it was sincere and had some practical features; Garvey proved not only an astonishing popular leader, but a master of propaganda. Within a few years, news of his movement, of his promises and plans, reached Europe and Asia, and penetrated every corner of Africa. He actually bought two small boats, summoned huge conventions to New York, and paraded the streets of Harlem with uniformed troops and "Black Cross" nurses.* News of his astonishing plans reached Europe and the various colonial offices, even before my much more modest proposals. Often the Pan-African Congress was confounded with Garvey movement with consequent suspicion and attack. . . . My first effort was to explain away the Garvey movement and ignore it; *but it was a mass movement that could not be ignored.* (Emphasis added)[39]

In 1940, Du Bois brought to light his take on the impact of Garveyism on Black Nationalist philosophy; namely, Garvey's propaganda for race progress reached Europe and Asia, as it permeated Africa and the Americas, even before Du Bois' "much more modest proposals." Garvey's grandiose—audacious, some would say— Black Nationalist plans, particularly his call for commercial exchange and political dialogue between black groups, became the focus of black leaders worldwide. Thus, behind their antagonism, both Garvey and Du Bois aimed for the general advancement of people of African descent. Their conflict remains, however, one of the consequential leadership tragedies of the twentieth century. Though both men made invaluable contributions to black thought, in both social and political realms, one can only imagine the sociopolitical state of black folk of the twenty-first century, if only the two of the black Diaspora's most prominent leaders had been more tolerant of each other's approaches to focus on their aim and the destiny of the race.

Notes

1. Garvey, *Philosophy*, 132.

2. W. E. B. Du Bois, *Dusk of Dawn: An Essay Toward an Autobiography of a Race Concept.* 1940. (New York: Kraus Thomson Organization Limited, 1975) 277–78.

3. In England, toward the end of the nineteenth century, Williams formed the African Association which later became the Pan-African Association.

4. George Padmore, *Pan-Africanism or Communism? The Coming Struggle for Africa* (New York: Roy Publishers, 1956) 119–29.

5. Ibid., 129–36.

6. Ibid., 137–42. The call to defense predates the philosophy of the Black Power movement.

7. Padmore, *Pan-Africanism or Communism?* 148–49.

8. Aimé Césaire, "Letter to Maurice Thorez," *Présence Africaine* nos. 8-9-10 (1956): 9.

9. Ibid., 13.

10. Padmore, *Pan-Africanism or Communism?* 148–49.

11. Ibid., 142–51.

12. Ousmane Sembène, "Camp de Thiaroye," *Monthly Film Review* 56 (1989): 270–71.

13. In 1901 Ida B. Wells-Barnett published an article entitled "Lynching and the Excuse for It" in the journal *The Independent.* In her article Wells-Barnett denounced lynching as the "deepest dyed infamy of the nineteenth century."

14. Myron Echenberg, *Colonial Conscripts: The Tirailleurs Sénégalais in French West Africa, 1857–1960* (Portsmouth: Heinemann Educational Books, Inc., 1991) 100.

15. Ibid., 100–104.

16. Nancy E. Lawler, *Soldiers of Misfortune: Ivorien Tirailleurs of World War Two* (Athens: Ohio University Press, 1992) 272.

17. Echenberg, *Colonial Conscripts*, 101.

18. Padmore, *Pan-Africanism or Communism?* 152–70.

19. Garvey, *Philosophy*, 135–43. The call to defense and protection, by all means, was also emphasized in Garvey's petition.

20. Padmore, *Pan-Africanism or Communism?* 105.

21. Garvey, *Philosophy*, 97–98.

22. Martin, *Race First*, 13.

23. Garvey, *Philosophy*, 135–43.

24. Du Bois, "Foreign Languages," *The Crisis*, July, 1926.

25. Rudwick, "W.E.B. Du Bois: Protagonist of the Afro-American Protest," 77–78.

26. Du Bois, "The Negro in Art: How Shall He Be Portrayed," *The Crisis*, April 1926.

27. Ibid., March 1926.

28. Ibid., April 1926.

29. Martin, *Literary* 157.

30. Ibid., 5.

31. Ibid., 27.

32. Ibid., x, 18.

33. Marcus Garvey, *The Poetical Works of Marcus Garvey* (Dover: The Majority Press, 1983) 3–23.

34. Ibid., 112.

35. Garvey, *Philosophy*, 239.

36. W. E. B. Du Bois, *Selected Poems* (Accra: Ghana University Press, 1964) 38–40.

37. Rudwick, "W. E. B. Du Bois: Protagonist of the Afro-American Protest," 82.

38. Lawrence W. Levine, "Marcus Garvey and the Politics of Revitalization," *Black Leaders of the Twentieth Century* (Urbana: University of Illinois Press, 1982) 111–12.

39. Du Bois, *Dusk of Dawn*, 277–78.

6

Jean Price-Mars: *Indigénisme* and the Formulae of Social Transformation

Si l'éducation est une tentative de modeler l'homme selon un idéal déterminé, il me semble que tout système de pédagogie doit d'abord connaître le tempérament du peuple auquel on se propose de l'appliquer. C'est la première considération, je suis tenté d'affirmer que c'est la considération essentielle qui doit dominer une entreprise d'éducation collective.

If education is an attempt to shape the human based on a well-defined ideal, it seems to me that a pedagogical system must first know the personality of the people that it proposes to educate. That is the first consideration. I am tempted to affirm that it is the essential consideration that must take precedence in a collective educational system.

—Jean Price-Mars[1]

THE CONCEPTS OF THE *Mouvement Indigéniste*, similar to Pan-Africanism and the Harlem Renaissance, were shaped and formulated as a response to particular social conditions, and transformed in time to meet the nuances of Haitian society. On manifold levels, Haitian scholars and activists of the early twentieth century addressed the stages to social reformation. One, the examination of the state of education as it was particularly expounded by Jean Price-Mars; two, the assertion of a literature that is original and particular to the Haitian experience and thought; three, the valorization of African heritage on the island—which included the influence of African philosophy, history, and religion within Haiti's collective consciousness and practice; four, the reconstruction of political structures, and the re-evaluation of policies—with greater consideration for the needs of the masses; and five, the re-thinking and re-negotiating of foreign policies for regulations founded on fairness.

The Indigéniste movement, which emerged in 1925, grew out and evolved from Haiti's literary works of the 1830s. Though the literature of the 1830s were variants of the French literary traditions that were then prevalent, writers gradually sought to introduce a certain level of Haiti's *language* and culture. By the end of the 1830s, the writings of members of the *Cénacle* constituted the first stage of Haitian literature.[2] The Cénacle, which was founded in 1836, included writers such as the Nau brothers and the Ardouin and Lespinasse brothers. For members of the *Cénacle* the national literature of Haiti should reveal certain particularities of the writer's period, as well as the realities of the country. The Nau brothers suggested a Haitian literature that is not limited to the use of standard French, to "le français de la France" ("the French of France"), as Frantz Fanon would later theorize in *Peau noire, masques blancs* (*Black skin, white masks*).[3] Rather, the Haitian writer should incorporate regional French language, with its local and familiar expressions. "Et peut-être" affirms Nau, "La France ne lirait pas sans plaisir sa langue brunie sous les Tropiques" ("And perhaps France would not read with displeasure, its language bronzed in the tropics").[4] Though the literary proposition of the Cénacle announced the formation of a Haitian literature, it is important to bear in mind that the nineteenth-century concept of Haitian literature—as the writers of the *Cénacle* perceived it— remained, by and large, aesthetically French.

Jean Price-Mars termed the literature of the 1830s *bovarysme collectif* to emphasize its lack of originality. The term was invented in the nineteenth century by the philosopher Jules de Gaultier to express the idea of "conceiving one-self other than one is," "à se concevoir autre qu'il n'est."[5] Within Price-Mars' context *bovarysme collectif* was not only a reference to literature, but also an allusion to the lifestyle of the Haitian elite, many of whom were often educated in elitist schools in Haiti and pursued their college education in Europe. As a result of an education based on French intellectualism, these writers gauged their work valuable only if it replicated French culture and evoked a certain *savoir-faire* and *savoir-vivre*.[6] The ensuing impact of an education that was incompatible with the reality of Haitian society was the growing psychological turmoil and social tensions between the elite and the mass of people. To state it differently, the French cultural affirmation of the minority elite class and the mores of the majority masses, which were marked by a pronounced African heritage, were in dissidence. Moreover, there existed cultural contradictions and paradoxes within the elite group whose members variably perceived themselves either as French (depending on the sociocultural situation and/or the politicoeconomic interests), or Haitians of diverse hues. The identity illusion that was pervasive in the elite community was also reflected in the literature of the time. Paradoxically, one could neither classify such literary works as Haitian literature, nor could they be classified as French literature, for the images depicted were simultaneously incongruous to French and Haitian ways of life. In a forty-five page manifesto entitled *Lettre au docteur René Piquion, directeur de l'Ecole Normale Supérieure sur son Manuel de Négritude* (*Letter to doctor René Piquion, director of l'Ecole Normale Supérieure, on his Négritude manual*, 1967), Price-Mars explained the social dilemma of Haitian intellectuals and the effect on their literary works. After his analysis of the state of Haitian literature in the nineteenth century, Price-Mars concluded that indiscriminate imitation led to the *bovarysme* that plagued Haitian culture.

> Evidemment le parti le plus simple pour les révolutionnaires en mal de cohésion nationale était de copier le seul modèle qui s'offrit à leur intelligence. Donc, tant bien que mal, ils insérèrent le nouveau groupement dans le cadre disloqué de la société blanche dispersée, et ce fut ainsi que la communauté nègre d'Haïti revêtit la défroque de la civilisation occidentale au lendemain de 1804. Dès lors, avec une constance qu'aucun échec, aucun sarcasme, aucune perturbation n'a pu fléchir, elle s'évertua à réaliser ce qu'elle crut être son destin supérieur en modelant sa pensée et ses sentiments à se rapprocher de son ancienne métropole, à lui ressembler, à s'identifier à elle. Tâche absurde et grandiose! Tâche difficile, s'il n'en fut jamais! Mais c'est bien cette curieuse démarche que la métaphysique de M. de Gaultier appelle un *bovarysme collectif*, c'est-à-dire la faculté que s'attribue une société de se concevoir autre qu'elle n'est.[7]

> Evidently the easiest decision, for the revolutionaries lacking national cohesion, was to copy the only intellectual model present. Hence, with mediocrity, they inserted the literary group within the framework of the dispersed white society. And so, the day after independence (1804) the Negro of Haiti was dressed in antiquated garment of western civilization. Since then, with a steadfastness that no defeat, no sarcasm, and no perturbation was able to weaken, the elite did her utmost to realize what she believed was her superior destiny, by shaping her thought and her sentiments in order to get closer to her former metropolis, to resemble and identify with it. An absurd and grandiose task! A difficult task, if it were ever realized! It is this strange process that Mr. de Gaultier metaphysically calls *bovarysme collectif*, that is to say, the ability of a society to conceive itself other than it is.

Price-Mars attributed the phenomenon of *bovarysme collectif* to the perception that Europe, France in particular, was for the elite the exemplar of intellectualism. By 1804 (the year of Haiti's independence), France had already established a literary tradition that was read and respected throughout Europe, if not the world. So, the *bovarysme collectif* was for the Haitian elite—who inherited the color prejudice of the slavery era, and has internalized intellectual insecurity vis-à-vis the *metropolis*—a manifestation of an exaggerated admiration for French culture.

In *La vocation de l'élite* (*The vocation of the elite*) published in 1919, Price-Mars argues that after a period of imitation, in the early 1900s Haitian literature began to find its original note in the depth of Haiti's mores as well as in the landscape of the country.[8] Many writers of the 1920s onward reacted against the notion of the *bronzed* French language that members of the *Cénacle* proposed. For writers of the twentieth century the idea of a French *brunie* suggested the presentation of the French language *à la tropicale*.[9] Price-Mars responded to such endeavor by emphasizing that Haitian writers not aim to write as, or become colored French, but write as Haitians born out of specific historical conditions. "Soyons, non pas des Français colorés," he explained, "mais des Haïtiens tout court, c'est-à-dire des hommes nés dans des conditions historiques bien déterminées." ("Let us not be colored French, but Haitians; that is to say, beings born within specific historical conditions").[10] In other words, writers should not only incorporate regional French expressions to create a national literature, their work should also reflect Haiti's customs; the writing must value the traditional lifestyle of the country. The valorization of traditions would allow Haitian artists to explore their African roots and emerge with a literature that is original in form and content. The original literature Price-Mars called for would be neither French nor purely African, but Haitian, with the expression of its African traditions and French influence.

The second stage of the development of Haitian literature started in 1925 with the founding of the *Indigénisme de la Nouvelle Ronde* (*Indigénisme of the New Circle*). Unfortunately, *La Nouvelle Ronde*—which was a monthly journal—disappeared in 1927.[11] In July 1927 members of the *Nouvelle Ronde* coined the *Revue Indigène* from which the word "*Indigénisme*" derived. The *Revue* served as the primary agent in the evolution of Haitian thought and art. Among the members of the circle figured Jacques Roumain, who would later become a revered *Indigéniste* writer and a defender of the peasant class. The founders chose the term "*Mouvement Indigéniste*" in lieu of the proposed "*Ecole Indigéniste*," because the latter implied the notions of fixity and absolutism, while the former suggested the idea of progression, variation, and change.[12] Modification and evolution were indeed the processes that best describe the stages of transformation that were occurring in Haitian thought and art. *Indigénisme* further developed as a literary movement and simultaneously became a sociopolitical movement. The social and political facet of the movement sprung as a response to the American occupation of Haiti, from 1915 to 1934. In 1915 American forces landed on Haitian soil during a period of political turmoil and at a time when European—particularly German—businesses were growing on the island. During a span of two years (from May 4, 1913, to July 27, 1915), four different men ephemerally presided in Haiti—Michel Oreste, Oreste Zamor, Davilmar Théodore, and Vilbrun Guillaume Sam.[13] In July 1915, the Navy ordered Rear Admiral William B. Caperton to go to Haiti to help restore order. The United States forces were sent to Haiti not only to end anarchy but primarily "to prevent any European country, and in particular Germany, from gaining control there."[14] Caperton's first orders were to protect foreign lives and properties. Within a month, however, the American admiral had gained control of the Haitian media and had formalized both civil and military domination over the territory. By November of 1915 "a *modus vivendi* had become the legal basis for U.S. control of five services—customs, finance, the constabulary, public works, and public health."[15] In 1918, a new Haitian constitution was adopted. It granted foreigners the right to own land in Haiti and appointed a Council of State, which was to exercise legislative power until a new legislature was elected.[16] Hence, the intervention became an occupation which lasted until 1934, after president Franklin Delano Roosevelt visited Cap-Haïtien on July 5, 1934. During his visit, Roosevelt announced the complete Haitianization of Haiti's political institutions by August 1, 1934.[17]

During the 1930s, as the atmosphere of the American occupation fueled color dynamics in Haiti, *Indigénisme* sharpened and propagated its Black Nationalist rudiment. In 1938 members of the *Indigéniste* movement such as Carl Brouard, Lorimer Denis, François Duvalier, and Clément Magloire (son) formed the *Griots*.[18] Members of the *Griots* advocated the *Noirisme* philosophy, which denounced social and political prejudice against dark-skinned Haitians.[19] As a result of the political consciousness that was burgeoning among *Indigéniste* writers of the second half of the 1920s, as well as the generations that followed, many became actively engaged in the social transformation that was taking place in Haiti during and after the American Occupation. Many of the *Indigéniste* writers had done studies in various disciplines; their broad knowledge enabled them to assess and evaluate the multidimensional social and political problems in Haiti. Some were physicians, ethnographers, professors, and diplomats; others were ethnologists, sociologists, philosophers, and political theorists. Hence, more than a literary movement, the *Indigéniste* movement became a sociopolitical movement, whose purpose was to disclose the political and sociocultural predicament of Haiti; a situation which they viewed as an embarrassment to their ideal of autonomy. The sociopolitical state of the country was viewed as an utter humiliation brought by outside forces. Haiti had lost its *de facto* independence and, resultantly, the psychological and cultural esteem of Haitians continued to weaken. In 1928 Price-Mars published *Ainsi parla l'Oncle* (*So spoke the uncle*) to probe and shed light on the importance of folk and popular culture in Haiti's history and heritage. In *Histoire de la Littérature Haïtienne*, Raphaël Berrou and Pradel Pompilus point out that

> *Ainsi parla l'Oncle*, en invitant les intellectuels haïtiens à prendre conscience des valeurs de civilisation du monde noir qui font leur patrimoine culturel, ajoutait à l'indigénisme une dimension proprement africaine: écrivains, musiciens, peintres, architectes, artisans, gens du monde comprirent la leçon et ce fut un renouveau de tout notre mode de penser, de sentir et de vivre...*Ainsi parla l'Oncle* est l'ouvrage capital et, à juste titre, le plus célèbre du docteur Price-Mars. Il a exercé l'influence la plus décisive et la plus durable sur l'évolution culturelle, politique et sociale de notre pays après 1915.[20]

> *Ainsi parla l'Oncle*, by inviting Haitian intellectuals to become aware of the values of black civilization, which is their cultural inheritance, added a dimension specifically African: writers, musicians, painters, architects, artisans and lay people understood the lesson, and that was a renascence of our entire way of thinking, feeling and living. . . . *Ainsi parla l'Oncle* is the major and, rightly so, the most renowned of doctor Price-Mars' works. It has had the most decisive and lasting influence on the cultural, political and social evolution of our country, since 1915.

His later work, *Formation Ethnique Folk-Lore et Culture du Peuple Haïtien* (*Ethnic Formation, Folk-Lore and Culture of the Haitian People*), published in 1939, expounded on the role of folklore in Haiti to emphasize that Haiti's cultural salvation lies in its lore. Price-Mars theorized that if by definition folklore includes the total of beliefs, superstitions, myths, fables, songs, and riddles on which are founded the primitive life of a nation and constitute the base of its culture, then Haiti must preserve its traditions.

> Si par définition, le folk-lore est la somme des croyances, superstitions, légendes, contes, chansons, devinettes, coutumes sur lesquelles repose la vie primitive d'un peuple et constitue les fondements de sa "culture", il n'est pas un pays qui possède un plus riche fond de traditions orales que la nôtre. Et ces traditions sont d'autant plus profondes et merveilleuses qu'elles remontent aux origines mêmes de la race.[21]

> If by definition folk-lore is the sum of beliefs, superstitions, myths, tales, songs, riddles, customs on which is based the primitive life of a people and constitutes the foundation of its "culture," then no country possesses a richer oral tradition than ours. And these traditions are as profound and marvelous as they date back to the very origin of the race.

Aware that the non-written knowledge of a people includes everything from its past and present culture, everything that is omitted in the written history of civilization and the doctrines of what are considered official religions, Price-Mars stressed that in order to avoid cultural erasure literature should reflect the nation's lore. Thus, *Formation Ethnique* and *Ainsi parla l'Oncle* sought to galvanize a national intersubjectivity among Haitian elites and intellectuals in order to impel them to analyze the complexity of Haitian society. Furthermore, Price-Mars asserted that without the valorization of Haitian mores—whether derived from Africa, Europe, or formed in the New World—the elite class will continue to live through illusory beliefs constructed on what it imagines to be French traditions and customs. Moreover, it will continue to view itself as superior to the masses, whose phenotype and traditions reveal an obvious kinship to Africa. Within the social and political contexts it is worth noting that the elite's superiority was simultaneously *illusory* and *realistic*. The rationale for viewing itself as superior was an illusion; however, the economic and political power the class acquired from its illusion of superiority remains very real. The manipulation of race and color dynamics for economic gain became the major cause of class division in Haiti. The implication of such chasm, which created two nations within one nation, is twofold: on a cultural and social level, it impeded the creation of a unified community, and on an economic and political level, it maintained the continuous exploitation of the masses.

Education and Religion

Throughout the 1900s, Price-Mars worked to ameliorate the sociopolitical situation the Occupation exacerbated. For him, the acute political anarchy that existed in Haiti during the Occupation was preceded by a moral anarchy of which the elite class was the accomplice, for its members erroneously calculated they would politically benefit from the intervention. Thus, the masses were doomed from the inception of the intervention, since they had to contend with a joint force of exploiters; that is, the covetousness of the Haitian elite and the despoliation of American officials.[22] However, as time progressed, a considerable number of Haitian elites also became dispossessed of their posts and privileges as American officials occupied and controlled the administration of the country.[23] And so, if the American Occupation aggravated the sociopolitical dynamic in Haiti it also, paradoxically, impelled the elite toward self-reflection—if only temporarily.

La Vocation de l'élite (published during the American Occupation) was an appeal to impress the elite class to build Haiti's cultural pride and reclaim its political independence. To assume such responsibility Price-Mars judged it critical that the elite class, which constituted the country's intellectual base, is composed of individuals of character and integrity. Hence, he proposed the implementation of an educational program that would intellectually and morally prepare Haitians in general and the elite class in particular. He advised that the government unhesitatingly implement another curriculum that would replace or modify the existing one, a program "qui consacrera enfin la refonte totale de [l'] enseignement public de telle façon que la préparation morale de l'élite à venir égale en intensité sa préparation intellectuelle" ("that will finally focus on the complete restructuring of public education to the point that the moral preparation of the elite becomes equal, in intensity, to its intellectual preparation").[24] Similar to numerous black leaders, Price-Mars called for a program that would contextualize the subjects taught to Haitian youths and adults. A specific education, along with the universal education in philosophy and the human condition, would teach individuals moral responsibility and national pride, and by extension, meet the contry's needs. He reasoned:

> Si l'éducation est une tentative de modeler l'homme selon un idéal déterminé, il me semble que tout système de pédagogie doit d'abord connaître le tempérament du peuple auquel on se propose de l'appliquer. C'est la première considération, je suis tenté d'affirmer que c'est la considération essentielle qui doit dominer une entreprise d'éducation collective.[25]

Early in the twentieth century Price-Mars advocated the creation of vocational institutions similar to Booker T. Washington's Tuskegee Institute. Price-Mars met Booker T. Washington in Paris in 1903 while pursuing his studies in France. In 1904, when President Nord Alexis sent Price-Mars and Dr. Audain to the United States, as Haitian representatives to the Louisiana Purchase Centennial Exposition in St. Louis, Price-Mars wrote to Washington and asked for his consent to visit Tuskegee Institute.[26] After two weeks in the South, where he observed Booker T. Washington's Tuskegee program, he concluded that Haiti was in need of a similar institute, which would set the country's industrial and agricultural progress in motion. In a series of articles published in 1912, Price-Mars suggested vocational institutions for urban areas and agricultural institutions for rural *provinces*, where a center would be created in each of the Departments of the country. These centers would have the capacity to accommodate 500 to 600 students and Anglo-Saxon teachers "to create—concurrently with scholarly centers elementary and agricultural systematic education disseminated throughout our rural sections."[27] The elite class opposed the idea of Anglo-Saxon teachers because they were wary such undertaking would eventually dismantle the French educational model that was ingrained in Haiti's educational system. Because Price-Mars understood the concerns of Haitian scholars, he emphasized—similar to Du Bois who stressed the importance of intellectualism to balance Booker T. Washington's Tuskegee Institute—that technical institutions would not replace intellectual institutions but would work in tandem. He argued that with technical training "not only would the level of living of the mass of Haitian peasants rise, but more importantly, collective labor communes could be formed and out of these could come a more equitable social and political system."[28]

Equally important, while Price-Mars was calling for a general pedagogical reform, he was also advocating intellectual opportunity for Haitian women. Like figures such as Maria Stewart, Edward Blyden, Anna Julia Cooper, and Amy Jacques-Garvey, he believed the advancement of a society depends on the education of its women.[29] He argued that the position a society assigns to its women demonstrates the order of preoccupations within that society. Furthermore, the position assigned is a logical consequence of the society's concept of life itself. Haitian women of the elite class, he noted, were reared to only be objects of luxury and desire, to the point that their idea of life and happiness "se résume tout simplement *à paraître, rien qu'à paraître*" ("simply sums up to *appearance, nothing but appearance*"), while the mass of Haitian women were reared to serve as working machines, "le plus excellent outil de travail . . . la bête de ferme" ("the most execellent work tool . . . the farm animal").[30] In both cases, however, neither class of women was prepared for intellectual work and the activism that could serve the country and their community.

Along with education reform was the religious appeal. One of the main cultural aspects under attack during the Occupation was Vodouism. To analyze the religious dimension of Haitian culture Price-Mars explored the origins of such religions as Catholicism, Buddhism, and Hinduism, in order to assert Vodou's place amidst world religions. Similar to other religious believers and practitioners, he contended, Vodou adepts believe in the existence of the Supreme Being and of the spirits, who watch over the living. Price-Mars emphasized in 1916, and reiterated in 1928, the conviction that Vodou is one of Haiti's main inheritances from Africa, particularly Dahomey, from where it has been noted a great number of slaves in Saint-Domingue arrived. Furthermore, in *Vôdou et Magie: Psychologie Haïtienne* (1937) J.C. Dorsainvil probed the origins of the religion to assert that the word *Vodou* is from the *Fongbé* dialect—one of the languages in Dahomey—which was part of *Ewe*.[31] In *Formation Ethnique Folk-Lore et Culture du Peuple Haïtien*, Price-Mars explained:

Quoiqu'il en soit, la religion des esprits ou des dieux, autrement dit la religion du vodou avec son ritualisme enchevêtré et sa formidable puissance traditionnelle qui est l'ossature même de l'organisation sociale et politique du Dahomey et particulièrement du royaume de Ouida d'où sont venus tant d'esclaves à Saint-Domingue—cette religion là a également fourni le cadre des croyances des masses populaires haïtiennes. Il va de soi, que l'organisation religieuse tout entière du Dahomey ne se retrouva pas intégrale à Saint-Domingue dans les conditions où la traite s'est opérée et selon les modalités de la vie de l'esclave dans la colonie.[32]

At any rate, the religion of the spirit or the gods, stated differently, the vodou religion, with its perplexed rituals and its formidable traditional power, which is the social and political structure of Dahomey, particularly the kingdom of Ouida, from where so many slaves in Saint-Domingue arrived—this religion also established the framework for the beliefs of the Haitian masses. It stands to reason that the entire religious structure of Dahomey is not found in its integrality in Saint-Domingue, considering the conditions of the slave trade and the mode of life of the slave in the colony.

Though the religion the slaves created in Saint-Domingue took a different form from traditional African religions, because of the mixture of various ethnicities and the influence of Catholicism, the connection remains evident. Moreover, the enslaved Africans who were brought to Saint-Domingue arrived with religious beliefs and mores that were ingrained in their social and political lives.[33] Thus, their way of conceiving and experiencing life in the New World was also based on religious beliefs. By tracing the history and analyzing the inherited social structure in Haiti, the publications of *Formation Ethnique Folk-Lore et Culture du Peuple Haïtien* and *Ainsi parla l'Oncle* helped legitimize Haiti's religious, moral, and cultural resistance during the American Occupation. Faced with another threat of cultural erasure, in addition to the existing French cultural preponderance, proponents of the *indigéniste* movement responded by speaking against the ostracism of Vodou. They acknowledged the religion as a non-extractable element within Haiti's social system.

If *Ainsi parla l'Oncle* was a defense of Haitian culture, it was equally a defense of black identity as well as the valorization of black Africa and its heritage. In fact, in 1919 Price-Mars proudly informed Haitians of the accomplishments of their congeners in the United States. He noted that they have remarkable musicians such as Dunbar, Coles, and the Johnson brothers. He also complimented "eminent" mathematicians, historians, and sociologists of impressive intellectualism such as Dr. Du Bois and Dr. Blyden, and persuasive orators such as Washington.[34] In 1956, during a homage ceremony dedicated to Jean Price-Mars, Léopold Sédar Senghor described *Ainsi parla l'Oncle* as a pioneer and exemplary text. Senghor lauded Dr. Price-Mars as one of the most notable figures of sociopolitical history. He declared,

Il est des noms qui sonnent comme un manifeste. Tel me fut révélé le nom du Dr. Price-Mars. . . . Je lus *Ainsi Parla L'Oncle* d'un trait, comme l'eau de la citerne, au soir, après une longue étape dans le désert. . . . Me montrant les trésors de la négritude qu'il avait découverts sur et dans la terre haïtienne, il m'apprenait à découvrir les mêmes valeurs, mais vierges et plus fortes sur et dans la terre d'Afrique. . . . Par quoi le 15 octobre 1956 sera le quatre-vingtième anniversaire de la négritude.[35]

There are names that ring like a revelation. As such I was revealed the name of Dr. Price-Mars. . . . I read *Ainsi parla l'oncle* uninterruptedly, like water from the fountain, at night, after a long journey in the desert . . . unveiling to me the treasures of négritude he had discovered on and within Haitian soil, he was teaching me to discover the same values, but purer and stronger, on and within the soil of Africa. . . . This is the reason October 15, 1956 will be the eightieth anniversary of négritude.

Senghor's metaphor of the fountain is significant. If he received *Ainsi parla l'Oncle* as "water from a fountain, after a long trip in the desert," it was because Price-Mars' concept of self-reclamation came at a time when blacks were in need of self-valorization, in the hope of destroying the constant pressure of the politics of assimilation that was taking place around the globe, but more particularly in France. For Senghor, the "treasures" Price-Mars discovered on Haitian soil and discussed in his book, gave readers the possibility to acknowledge African inheritances in Haiti and the black Diaspora. Because the homage ceremony was in honor of Price-Mars' eightieth birthday, Senghor declared 1956 the eightieth birthday of *Négritude*.

The Junction: Indigénisme and Négritude

In the 1930s the *Indigéniste* movement went beyond national barriers to dialogue with writers of literary and sociopolitical movements of the black world, such as the *New Negro Renaissance*, *Négritude*, and the *Afrocriollo* movements. *Indigéniste* writers were familiar with the works of intellectuals such as Langston Hughes, Claude McKay, and Nicolás Guillén. According to Raphaël Berrou and Pradel Pompilus, the literary works of Maurice Casséus (*Viejo*, 1935), Roussan Camille (*Assaut à la nuit*, 1940), and Jacques Roumain (*Bois-d'ébène*, 1945), all reflected an *Indigénisme* that reached out to the world and addressed the problems of peasantry and proletariat in Haiti and throughout the globe.[36] Through the presentation of cultural exchanges and dialogues with writers of the Diaspora, the manifestation of Black Internationalism became apparent in the texts of *Indigéniste* writers.

In 1945, one year after his death, Jacques Roumain's *Bois-d'ébène* was posthumously published by his wife. *Bois-d'ébène* is a collection of four poems:
"Bois-d'ébène" ("Ebony-Tree"), "l'Amour la Mort" ("Love Death"), "Sales
nègres" ("Dirty Negroes"), and "Nouveau sermon nègre" ("New Negro
Sermon"). "L'Amour la Mort" is a love poem that illustrates the despair of
the protagonist at the death of his lover. "Bois-d'ébène," "Sales nègres," and
"Nouveau sermon nègre," are poems that depict and vociferate the black condition around the world. In "Bois-d'ébène," Roumain writes,

> Nègre colporteur de révolte
> tu connais tous les chemins du monde
> depuis que tu fus vendu en Guinée
>   * * *
>
> Mais je sais aussi un silence
> de vingt-cinq mille traverses de Bois-d'Ebène
> sur les rails du Congo-Océan
> mais je sais
> des suaires de silence aux branches de cyprès
> des pétals de noirs caillots aux ronces
> de ce bois où fut lynché mon frère de Georgie
> et berger d'Abyssinie
>   * * *
>
> Afrique j'ai gardé ta mémoire Afrique
> tu es en moi
> Comme l'écharde dans la blessure
> Comme fétiche tutélaire au centre du village
> fais de moi la Pierre au centre du village
> de ma bouche les lèvres de ta plaie
> de mes genoux les colonnes brisées de ton abaissement . . .[37]
>
>
> Negro peddler of rebellion
> you know all the routes of the world
> since you were sold in Guinea
>   * * *
>
> But I also know a silence
> a silence of twenty-five thousand negro corpses
> twenty-five thousand railroad ties of Ebony Wood
> Under the iron rails of the Congo-Océan
> but I know
> the shrouds of silence in the cypress branches
> the petals of black bloodclots on the brambles
> in that woods where they lynched my brother of Georgia
> and, shepherd of Abyssinia,
>   * * *

> Africa I kept your memory Africa
> you are in me
> Like the splinter in the wound
> Like a guardian fetish in the village center
> make me a catapult stone
> of my mouth the lips of your wound
> of my knees the broken columns of your abasement . . .[38]

Bois-d'ébène, similar to "Sales nègres," resonates revolt. In "Sales nègres" the poet declares that Negroes no longer acquiesce to serving whites; no longer bow with such submissive words as "oui missié, oui mon pè, yes Sir, oui Blanc, si señor." Roumain noted the refusal of the Negro twice in Creole, once in English, in French, and in Spanish. The emphasis on the multilingual "no" to the injustices of white masters, underscores the common past of blacks— the Atlantic Slave Trade, the Middle Passage, and the slavery system—their present situation of plantation life, and their unanimous call to revolt. In *Bois-d'ébène* Roumain points out that the Negro who now propagates the call to revolt, had known different slave ports and had traveled through different countries of the world since the day he/she was sold from Africa. The mention of different "paths" or "*chemins*" symbolizes the various countries to which the slaves were brought. Underlining the common experiences of slaves, "Bois-d'Ebène on the Congo Ocean" is a metonymy for the slaves in the pits during the Middle Passage. The poet discloses that he keeps the memories of Africa deep within; symbolically, "as a splinter in a wound, as a guardian of fetish in the center of the village"; he finally requests, "make me your catapult stone." The last metaphoric imploration holds two references: biblically, it alludes to David and Goliath; historically, it is the practice (during the nineteenth and twentieth centuries) of diffusing the common history of the black race, and of heralding a call to revolt. By addressing common black issues, Roumain's poems simultaneously express the national and international dimensions of the *Indigéniste* movement.

Similarly, toward the end of *Cahier d'un retour au pays natal* (*Notebook of a return to the native land*) Césaire depicts the *négrier* as a space of rebellion. In *Cahier*, it was on the slaveship or the *négrier* the slaves suddenly stood up against the slavers. It was on the *négrier* they rebelled against their maltreatment as cattle and chattel.[39] In the poem, Césaire offers his definition of the *nouvelle négritude*. Similar to Alain Locke's "New Negro," the *nouvelle négritude* is one of liberation and self-reclamation. Césaire writes:

> Je dis hurrah! La vieille négritude
> progressivement se cadavérise
> l'horizon se défait, recule et s'élargit
> et voici parmi des déchirements de nuages la

fulgurance d'un signe
le négrier craque de toute part . . . Son ventre se
convulse et résonne . . . L'affreux ténia de sa cargaison
ronge les boyaux fétides de l'étrange nourrisson des
mers!
Et ni l'allégresse des voiles gonflées comme une
poche de doublons rebondie, ni les tours joués à la
sottise dangereuse des frégates policières ne l'empê-
chent d'entendre la menace de ses grondements
intestins

En vain pour s'en distraire le capitaine pend à sa
grand' vergue le nègre le plus braillard ou le jette à la
mer, ou le livre à l'appétit de ses molosses

La négraille aux senteurs d'oignon frit retrouve dans
son sang répandu le goût amer de la liberté

Et elle est debout la négraille

la négraille assise
inattendument debout
debout dans la cale
debout dans les cabines
debout sur le pont
debout dans le vent
debout sous le soleil
debout dans le sang
  debout
  et
  libre[40]

I say right on! The old negritude
progressively cadavers itself
the horizon breaks, recoils and expands
and through the shredding of clouds the flashing of a sign
the slave ship cracks everywhere . . . Its belly convulses and
resounds . . . The ghastly tapeworm of its cargo gnaws the
fetid guts of the strange suckling of the sea!
And neither the joy of sails filled like a pocket stuffed with
doubloons, nor the tricks played on the dangerous stupidity of
the frigates of order prevent it from hearing the threat of its in-
testinal rumblings

In vain to ignore them the captain hangs the biggest loud-
mouth nigger from the main yard or throws him into the sea,
or feeds him to his mastiffs

Reeking of fried onions the nigger scum rediscovers the bitter
taste of freedom in its spilled blood
And the nigger scum is on its feet

the seated nigger scum
unexpectedly standing
standing in the hold
standing in the cabins
standing in the deck
standing in the wind
standing under the sun
standing in the blood
    standing
    and
    free[41]

Césaire celebrates the death of the *vieille négritude*, where blacks were kept chained in the pit of the slaveship, where "voracious hounds" threw off board the slaves they believed were rebellious or would be useless to the slave system in the New World. The "hounds" or "*molosses*" are references to the slavers on the ship who inflicted various forms of punishment on the slaves, and carried out their assassination. For Césaire, with the death of the *vieille négritude* began the dismantlement of the limitations slavers had set for the slaves. And, through the metaphoric dissipation of the clouds that covered the négrier, was sudden hope. In his line "Le négrier craque de toute part. . . . Son ventre se convulse et résonne," Césaire depicts the beginning of the collapse of the slave trade system, where the convulsion in belly of the ship signifies the disturbance and revolt of the slaves taking place in the very pit of the ship. The numerous repetitions of "debout" reinforce the emphatic call to freedom and the urgency to take a stand for justice, for "la négraille aux senteurs d'oignon frit retrouve dans son sang répandu le goût amer de la liberté."[42]

Césaire's depiction of the revolt in the belly of the slaveship holds another significance; in 1939 Césaire's poem appealed to blacks of the Diaspora—particularly his compatriots in Martinique—to take a stand for justice and freedom during a period when social and financial misery remained prevalent. He wrote:

Et je me dis Bordeaux et Nantes et Liverpool et
New York et San Francisco

pas un bout de ce monde qui ne porte mon empreinte digitale
et mon calcanéum sur le dos des gratte-ciel et ma
crasse
dans le scintillement des gemmes !
Qui peut se vanter d'avoir mieux que moi?
Virginie. Tennessee. Géorgie. Alabama
Putréfactions monstrueuses de révoltes
inopérantes,
marais de sang putrides
trompettes absurdement bouchées
Terres rouges, terres sanguines, terres consanguines.[43]

And I say to myself Bordeaux and Nantes and Liverpool and
New York and San Francisco
not an inch of this world devoid of my fingerprint
and my calcaneus on the spines of skyscrapers and my filth in
the gilitter of gems!
Who can boast of being better off than I?
Virginia. Tennessee. Georgia. Alabama
Monstruous putrefaction of revolts
stymied
marshes of putrid blood
trumpets absurdly muted
Land red, sanguineous, consanguineous land.[44]

    Bordeaux, Nantes, Liverpool, New York and San Francisco were some of the major ports where slaves were disembarked; where the Western world molded and assigned an identity to the slaves brought from Africa. The enslaved Africans have also marked the Western world in many ways, for even in 1939 the blood of people of African descent continued to tint American, European, and African soils. The *nouvelle négritude* Césaire called for in *Cahier* was a négritude where the revolts in Virginia, Tennessee, Georgia, and Alabama would be successful, and blacks would have social and political justice. In 1969 Césaire explained that his concept of négritude was not anti-white but anti-injustice. Furthermore, the négritude he conceived was one of self-liberation and valorization. In an interview published in *Nouvelles littéraires*, he emphasized that while the concept of négritude was not racist, the race dimension was inevitable and indispensable. "S'il n'y avait pas eu le racisme blanc, on n'aurait jamais parlé de négritude. . . . C'était une base de départ; à aucun moment, ni Senghor ni moi n'avons voulu nous enfermer dans un monde clos. La négritude restait un humanisme, car elle a une vocation pour l'universel" ("If white racism did not exist, we would never have to speak of négritude. . . . That was the starting point; at no point did Senghor nor myself wanted to alienate ourself from the world. Négritude remains humanism because it has a universal vocation").[45]

Notes

1. Jean Price-Mars, *La Vocation de l'élite* (Port-au-Prince: Imprimerie de Compiègne, 1928) 68.

2. Berrou, Pompilus, *Histoire de la Littérature Haïtienne*, 7–8.

3. Frantz Fanon, *Black Skin, White Masks* (New York: Grove Press, 1967).

4. Ibid., 8.

5. Jean Price-Mars, *Ainsi parla l'Oncle* (Port-au-Prince: Imprimerie de Compiègne, 1928) ii.

6. Michel-Rolph Trouillot, *Haiti: State Against Nation* (Port-au-Prince: Editions Fardin, 1986) 80–84.

7. Price-Mars, *Ainsi parla l'Oncle*, ii.

8. Price-Mars, *La vocation*, 185.

9. In *Quelques vues politiques* published in 1934, Dr. J. C. Dorsainvil reflects on the educational, economic, social, and political issues in Haiti. Similar to leaders such as Edward Blyden and Marcus Garvey, Dorsainvil advances that each race has its particular idiosyncracies. With the same logic, he argues that one of the major problems in Haiti is that of an education where the study of the contribution of Africa in Haiti's customs is neglected. He explains: "l'erreur foncière de notre pédagogie sociale a été de ne point tenir compte de cette autorité de la race, d'avoir voulu faire d'un groupement violemment arraché de la terre d'Afrique, un peuple de pure culture française." Berrou, Pompilus, *Histoire le la Littérature Haïtienne*, 758.

10. Price-Mars, *Ainsi parla l'Oncle*, ii.

11. Berrou, Pompilus, *Histoire de la Littérature Haïtienne*, 9.

12. Ibid., 7.

13. Les Frères de l'Instruction Chrétienne, *Histoire D'Haïti*, 214.

14. Magdaline Shannon, *Jean Price-Mars, the Haitian Elite and the American Occupation, 1915–1935* (St. Martin's Press, Inc., 1996) 7.

15. Ibid., 7. Also see: Les Frères de l'Instruction Chrétienne, *Histoire D'Haïti*, 215.

16. Shannon, *Jean Price-Mars and the American Occupation*, 7.

17. Les Frères de l'Instruction Chrétienne, *Histoire D'Haïti*, 223.

18. Berrou, Pompilus, *Histoire de la Littérature Haïtienne*, 12.

19. Trouillot, *Haiti: State Against Nation*, 131.

20. Ibid., 11, 721.

21. Jean Price-Mars, *Formation Ethnique Folk-Lore et Culture du Peuple Haïtien* (Port-au-Prince: V. Valcin Imprimeur, 1916) 42–43.

22. Price-Mars, *La vocation*, 76.

23. Ibid., 107.

24. Price-Mars, *La vocation*, 79.

25. Ibid., 68 (see translation in the chapter's opening quotation).

26. Shannon, *Jean Price-Mars, the Haitian Elite and the American Occupation*, 19.

27. Ibid., 23.

28. Ibid., 20.

29. Ibid., 95.

30. Ibid., 97, 103.

31. J.C. Dorsainvil, *Vôdou et Magie: Psychologie Haïtienne* (Port-au-Prince: N. Telhomme, 1937) 174.

In the Fon dialect Vodou means god or the spirit of god; it also means the representation or symbol of a spirit. The word Vodou, which originally referred to spirit, came to signify a religion in Saint-Domingue.

32. Price-Mars, *Formation Ethnique*, 47.

33. For other texts on the origin of Vodou in Haiti, see Alfred Métraux, *Voodoo in Haiti* (1958); Albert Raboteau, *Slave Religion* (1980); Joan Dayan, *Haiti, History, and the Gods* (1995); Michael A. Gomez, *Exchanging Our Country Marks* (1998).

34. Price-Mars, *La Vocation*, 177–78.

35. Berrou, Pompilus, *Histoire de la Littérature Haïtienne*, 734. See translation in the opening quotation of this present text's introduction.

36. Berrou, Pompilus, *Histoire de la Littérature Haïtienne*, 12.

37. Jacques Roumain, *When the Tom-Tom Beats* (Washington, DC: Azul Editions, 1995) 72–78.

38. Ibid., 73–79.

39. Aimé Césaire, *Cahier d'un retour au pays natal.* 1939. (Paris: Présence Africaine, 1983) 60–65.

40. Ibid., 60–61.

41. Aimé Césaire, *Notebook of a Return to the Native Land.* (Connecticut: Wesleyan University Press, 2001) 47–48.

42. Césaire, *Cahier*, 61.

43. Ibid., 24–25.

44. Césaire, *Notebook*, 15–16.

45. Owusu-Sarpong, *Le Temps Historique*, 204.

7

Aimé Césaire: *Négritude* and the Lessons of Decolonization

En particulier avec l'accès à l'indépendance des pays africains, nous sommes entrés dans le moment de la responsabilité. Les noirs désormais doivent faire leur histoire [. . .] on s'interroge soi-même, on essaye de comprendre; or, dans le siècle où nous sommes, la poésie est un langage qui nous paraît plus ou moins ésotérique. Il faut parler clair, parler net, pour passer le message. Et il me semble que le théâtre peut s'y prêter—et il s'y prête bien.

Particularly with the African countries' attainment of independence, we entered the period of responsibility. Henceforth, blacks must make their history [. . .] we reflect and try to understand; now in this present century, poetry is a language that seems more or less esoteric. One must speak clearly and concisely to convey the message. It seems that theatre can accomplish the task—and it accomplishes it well.

—Aimé Césaire[1]

THE *NÉGRITUDE* MOVEMENT GREW in the mid-1930s during the height of *Indigénisme* and the *New Negro Renaissance*. In France, the *Négritude* movement was preceded by three literary currents: *Revue du monde noir*, *Légitime Défense*, and *L'Etudiant Noir*. The *Revue du monde noir* (1931–1932) was created by the Haitian, Dr. Léo Sajous and, the Martinican, Paulette Nardal; Dr. Sajous assumed the role of director and Paulette Nardal that of secretary. The motto of the *Revue du monde noir* was "Pour la paix, le travail et la justice par la liberté, l'égalité et la fraternité," ("For peace, work and justice, through liberty, equality and fraternity").[2] *Légitime Défense* (1932) was published by René Ménil, Jules Marcel Monnerot, Etienne and Thélus Léro. *L'Etudiant Noir* (1934) was launched by Aimé Césaire, Léopold Sédar Senghor, and Léon Gontran Damas. These journals, similar to the *Crisis* and the *Negro World*, made possible the publications of many black artists living in France and abroad. The *Revue du monde noir* and *Légitime Défense* were French/English bilingual journals which sought to publish articles from both Anglophone and Francophone intellectuals. In an interview, Paulette Nardal explained that the publication of a bilingual journal which would be of service to the race was originally Dr. Léo Sajous' idea. A journal that would facilitate dialogues among blacks of different nationalities and languages, he thought, was urgently needed. Dr. Sajous "felt if he could found a common journal of some kind, to include all sorts of articles, scientific, literary, geographical, etc., and a corresponding page on which all kinds of questions from Negroes everywhere could be answered, it would help draw Negroes all over the world together."[3] In *Aimé Césaire: Un Homme à la Recherche d'une Patrie*, Georges Ngal explains that the *Revue du monde noir* was a space of encounter for all black writers living in France, as well as a space for the propagation of Pan-African ideology. The *Revue du monde noir* and *Légitime Défense* made possible textual dialogues between writers of the Harlem New Negro, Afro-Cubanism, the Indigéniste and Griot movements in Haiti, and Afro-Antillanismo in Puerto Rico.[4]

From the nineteenth century onward, the *Revue du monde noir*, *Légitime Défense*, and *L'Etudiant Noir*, along with other social and literary movements of the Diaspora, were groundworks for the *Négritude* movement. The term "*Négritude*" was coined in 1939, when it appeared in Césaire's *Cahier d'un retour au pays natal*. The *Négritude* movement promulgated four crucial points. First, it advocated the reclamation and valorization of African heritage and culture. Second, it contended that the alienation from, and the negation of, African culture tend to lead—consciously or subconsciously—to feelings of inferiority and, by extension, tend to damage black nations or communities. Third, it stressed the point that to liberate themselves from centuries of constructed and imposed identity, Africans and persons of African descent ought to seek to affirm and define their own identity. Lastly, it encouraged *Négritude* writers to question Western education and neo-colonialism, insofar as their impact on black intellectuals. The literary works of Aimé Césaire, from the second half of the 1930s onward, reiterated the value of an African past for the liberation and advancement of the black Diaspora.

The publications of Césaire's *La Tragédie du Roi Christophe* (*The Tragedy of King Christophe*) 1963 and, *Une Saison au Congo* (*A Season in Congo*) 1966, present the sociopolitical conditions of blacks in Africa and the Diaspora. King Henry Christophe and Patrice Lumumba are depicted as symbolic figures who illustrate the dilemma of revolutionary black leaders. During the late 1950s and early 1960s many African countries procured nominal independence but remained under direct or indirect European ruling. Concurrently, in the 1950s and 1960s, blacks of the United States were also undertaking difficult battles to attain true freedom—beyond *de jure* emancipation. In the Caribbean, blacks continued their fight for freedom and recognition, as they struggled to combat divisions based on colorism and unequal social privileges.

In the plays, King Christophe and Lumumba transcend their individualism to represent the mental disposition of black nations emerging out of slavery and colonization. In a 1969 interview published in *Magazine Littéraire* Césaire explained that at the historic point of black liberation movements he prefers theater, because it is generally the easiest literary genre to grasp; as such, it enables blacks—whether literate or illiterate—to understand the situation at play. The language of theater is less opaque and esoteric to human understanding, and the visual dimension helps the spectators identify with the characters.

> Effectivement je donne ma préférence à la forme théâtrale; je crois que les événements extérieurs y sont pour quelque chose. Le monde noir traverse une phase difficile. En particulier avec l'accès à l'indépendance des pays africains, nous sommes entrés dans le moment de la responsabilité. Les Noirs désormais doivent faire leur histoire [. . .] On s'interroge soi-même, on essaye de comprendre; or, dans le siècle où nous sommes, la poésie est un langage qui nous paraît plus ou moins ésotérique. Il faut parler clair, parler net, pour faire passer le message. Et il me semble que le théâtre peut s'y prêter—et il s'en prête bien.[5]

> Indeed, I prefer the theatrical genre; I think the external events play a part. The black world is going through a difficult phase. Particularly with the African countries' attainment of independence, we entered the period of responsibility. Henceforth, blacks must make their history [. . .] we reflect and try to understand; now in this present century, poetry is a language that seems more or less esoteric. One must speak clearly and concisely to convey the message. It seems that theatre can accomplish the task—and it accomplishes it well.

Throughout the 1960s Césaire expressed the need for a Negro theater in Africa. In 1969 he published *Une Tempête*. Significantly, the subtitle of *Une Tempête*, is "Théâtre d'après 'La Tempête' de Shakespeare, adaptation pour un théâtre nègre." "A play based on Shakespeare's 'Tempest': Adaptation for a Negro theater." *Une Tempête* is fundamentally the questioning of world order, where Caliban (the slave) revolts against the oppression of Prospero (the colonialist). And so, the purpose of a Negro theater, for Césaire, is to create a space for observation, self-questioning and examination, in order to incite a sense of responsibility within each individual and the community. To further explain his choice of theater Césaire affirms that

> Si depuis quelque temps j'ai surtout écrit pour la scène, c'est parce que je sens que l'Afrique a besoin, a soif de théâtre. Le théâtre est un art éminemment social qui est directement appréhendable. Je veux un théâtre actuel en prise directe sur nos problèmes. Le drame doit être une prise de conscience, il est un "donner-à-voir," un "donner-à penser."[6]

> If for a while I have specifically written for the stage, it is because I feel that Africa needs and is thirsty for theater. Theater is an art that is eminently social and directly comprehensible. I want a current theater, directly tuned to our problems. The drama must be a conscious awakening; it is a "donner-à-voir," a "donner-à-penser."

The era of independence and human rights struggles of the 1950s and 1960s exposed the need for self-examination, questioning, and understanding among blacks. Within that context, Césaire captures the past and present problems of the race in order to raise a level of social and political consciousness that would induce a *revolution of mentalities* among the black audience— spectators and/or readers. The play, for Césaire, serves as a mirror from which black folk can see themselves through the representation of their ancestors and contemporaries. It is the "*donner-à-voir.*" In plays, the characters in question are *alive*; spectators hear their voices as they observe their actions. Thus, the problems posed are seen in actuality and, as a result, the sensibility of each spectator becomes more acute. It is the "*donner-à-penser.*"

La Tragédie du Roi Christophe

In *La Tragédie du Roi Christophe,* Césaire uses historical facts on the reign of King Christophe in order to present a play that could have a didactic effect on black readers and spectators. In factual Haiti, after the assassination of Dessalines in 1806, Christophe governed the North of the Republic of Haiti, while Pétion, and later Boyer, governed the South. After Pétion's reelection in 1811, Christophe proclaimed himself the King of Haiti, *Roi Henry 1er,* and reigned in the North.[7] In the North he established an empire and sought to teach the people dignity in being black. King Christophe allotted plantations to the nobles of his kingdom and requested that each nobleman maintains the productivity of his respective lands. Because the dukes, counts, and barons had no other source of income, they brought their lands to the "peak of productiveness."[8] The King's orders, stated in *Code Henry*, required every adult male and female to work a set amount of hours per day. They worked from dawn to eight o'clock in the morning, and were then allowed an hour off for breakfast on location; they worked from nine to noon with a two-hour break until two in the afternoon, and then worked from two until dusk.[9] King Christophe led by example. The King followed a strict work ethic and was, as John W. Vandercook reported in 1928, "the greatest builder and the greatest planter in his kingdom. . . . In one year his plantations had produced 10,000,000 pounds of coffee, two-thirds of the kingdom's total export of that commodity."[10] The *Sans Souci* palace, where Christophe resided, was surrounded by vast and fertile lands that were continuously planted and reaped. Christophe built seven royal palaces and fifteen châteaux, all of which were surrounded by cultivated lands.[11]

Henry 1er was a stringent king; he unyieldingly used his power to build schools and churches, and to rebuild cities and edifices that were burned down during the war of independence and the various revolts that followed.[12] During his presidency and, later, his reign, Christophe regularly and attentively oversaw the economy of the republic and of the kingdom. Every morning each intendant, namely the ministers of treasury and customs, brought his report to the King.[13] Though Christophe accumulated personal wealth, he used a considerable amount of the monetary riches that were generated to "bring teachers from England and set up schools, to reclaim the devastated plantations that had three-quarters reverted to jungle; to enforce law and morality and the code of civilised nations."[14] During the reign of Henry Christophe Haiti became rich. In *Black Majesty* Vandercook reports that "under the stimulus of the work laws the port of Cap Henry alone had, in one year, besides sugar, exported 20,000,000 pounds of coffee, 5,000,000 pounds of cacao, 4,000,000 of cotton, and a quantity of logwood, fruit, and other minor country products."[15]

In *La Tragédie du Roi Christophe*, Césaire exposes the challenges of building a nation out of a community that had experienced the dehumanizing effects of the slave trade, who had toiled daily on the plantations (from dusk to dawn), and who had been mercilessly whipped, debased, and tortured to death in the New World. Césaire's play depicts Christophe's effort to form an independent and responsible nation. In the play, Christophe's baron and secretary, Vastey, addresses an assembly of people on the social and political program of the King. He explains:

Le monde entier nous regarde, citoyens, et les peuples pensent que les hommes noirs manquent de dignité! Un roi, un cour, un royaume, voilà, si nous voulons être respectés, ce que nous devrions leur montrer. Un chef à la tête de notre nation. Une couronne sur la tête de notre chef! Cela, croyez-m'en, calme-rait bien des têtes dont les venteuses idées peuvent à n'importe quel moment, ici, sur nos têtes, déchaîner la tempête![16]

The whole world is watching us, citizens, and the nations think that black men have no dignity. A king, a court, a kingdom, that's what we've got to show them if we want to be respected. A leader at the head of our nation. A crown on the head of our leader. Believe me, that will quiet the military philanthropists who think we need their kind of order.[17]

At the outset one would note a remarkable parallelism between the empha-sis King Christophe—the factual man and the character Césaire portrays in his play—placed on external trappings and accoutrements of nationhood and Marcus Garvey's symbols of nationhood. In chapter 2, we examined Garvey's effort to establish a black nation as well as his reasons for creating and pub-licly parading the symbols that validate nationhood, i.e., the flag, the anthem, the soldiers, and officers. The motivation for national and royal trappings, as King Christophe and Garvey viewed it, was to show the world the dignity of black folk. For Christophe, the formation of a kingdom that is governed by a black king gives the race the respect it had been denied since the slave trade. Vastey's exclamation, "Une couronne sur la tête de notre chef! Cela, croyez-m'en, calmerait bien des têtes dont les venteuses idées peuvent à n'importe quel moment, ici, sur nos têtes, déchaîner la tempête!" underlines that the governance of a black king would deter France from trying to re-establish slavery in Haiti. In 1807, however, the king observed that the other enemy of Haiti's independence was, unconsciously, the Haitian people, who, after the horrific labors of slavery, equated independence with complacency, with complete erasure of discipline and hard work. In his speech to the people, King Christophe vehemently points out,

Assez! Qu'est-ce que ce peuple qui, pour une conscience nationale, n'a qu'un conglomérat de ragots! Peuple haïtien, Haïti a moins à craindre des Français que d'elle-même! L'ennemi de ce peuple, c'est son indolence, son effronterie, sa haine de la discipline, l'esprit de jouissance et de torpeur. Messieurs, pour l'honneur et la survie de ce pays, *je ne veux pas qu'il puisse jamais être dit, jamais être soupçonné dans le monde que dix ans de liberté nègre, dix ans de laisser-aller et de démission nègre suffiront pour que soit dilapidé le trésor que le martyr de notre peuple a amassé en cent ans de labeur et de coups de fouet.* Aussi bien, qu'on se le dise dès à présent, avec moi vous n'aurez pas le droit d'être fatigués. Allez, Mes-sieurs! Allez, dispersez-vous! (Emphasis added)[18]

That'll do! What kind of a nation is this whose national occupation is gossip-ing! Haitian People! Haiti has less to fear from the French than from itself.

This people's enemy is its indolence, its effrontery, its hatred of discipline, its self-indulgence, its lethargy. Gentlemen, for the honor and survival of this nation, I don't want it ever to be said, I won't have the world so much as suspect, that ten years of black freedom, ten years of black slovenliness and indifference, have sufficed to squander the patrimony that our martyred people has amassed in a hundred years of labor under the whip. You may as well get through your heads this minute that with me you won't have the right to be tired. Very well, gentlemen. Disperse.[19]

King Christophe struggled to create a new national consciousness and a body of hard-working citizens, in lieu of what he calls "a conglomeration of gossips" who spend their time in idle conversations. In his view, the spirit of indolence, indiscipline, and somnolence that the newly freed slaves developed, were hindrances to the progression of the young nation. He earnestly urged the people to distinguish between slavery and hard work—as Toussaint Louverture previously did—for the development of one's nation.[20] He predicted that approximately less than ten years of *laissez-aller* or *laissez-faire* would deplete the resources that the slaves had worked inhumanly hard for and had assembled with blood and sweat. Furthermore, he believed that the new black nation had to prove itself to the rest of the world and establish its self-respect among other nations. Césaire's utterances through the respective discourses of King Christophe and Vastey reflect his familiarity with the political history of the New World's first black King. In a chain of cross-generational and cross-geographic teachings, the speeches in Césaire's play also reiterate the philosophies of Marcus Garvey. Like Césaire, Garvey had come to construct and formulate his philosophies from his knowledge of the political history of such men as "Edward Blyden, Barclay, and Johnson of Liberia, Frederick Douglass of the United States, Toussaint Louverture, Jean-Jacques Dessalines and Henri Christophe of Haiti, and Lewis of Sierra Leone."[21]

In act 1, scene 7 of *La Tragédie*, during an anniversary dinner to celebrate his crowning, King Christophe's wife asks him not to demand so much of the people and of himself. The King's reply to his wife and his close entourage outlines his belief in strict governance. He was convinced that blacks should work harder than other races in order to advance; for only *they* inherited residual effects of the slave trade. In a metaphoric analogy between the world and the pit of the slaveship, King Christophe explains that it is from there blacks are attempting to climb out; it is from the pit that they are screaming, and aspiring to air, light, and sun.

Tous les hommes ont mêmes droits. J'y souscris. Mais du commun lot, il en est qui ont plus de devoirs que d'autres. Là est l'inégalité. Une inégalité de sommations, comprenez-vous? A qui fera-t-on croire que tous les hommes, je dis tous, sans privilège, sans particulière exonération, ont connu la déportation, la traite, l'esclavage, le collectif ravalement à la bête, le total outrage, la vaste insulte que tous, ils ont reçu, plaqué sur le corps, au visage, l'omni-niant crachat! Nous seuls, Madame, vous m'entendez, nous seuls, les nègres! Alors au fond de la fosse! C'est bien ainsi que je l'entends. Au plus bas de la fosse. C'est là que nous crions; de là que nous aspirons à l'air, à la lumière, au soleil. Et si nous voulons remonter, voyez comme s'imposent à nous, le pied qui s'arcboute, le muscle qui se tend, les dents qui se serrent, la tête, oh! la tête, large et froide! Et voilà pourquoi il faut en demander aux nègres plus qu'aux autres: plus de travail, plus de foi, plus d'enthousiasme, un pas, un autre pas, encore un autre pas et tenir gagné chaque pas! C'est d'une remontée jamais vue que je parle, Messieurs, et malheur à celui dont le pied flanche![22]

All men have the same rights. Agreed. But some men have more duties than others. That's where the inequality comes in. In the challenge. Does anyone believe that all men, all I say, without privilege, without special exemption, have known capture, deportation, slavery, collective reduction to the level of animals, the monstrous insult, the total outrage that we have suffered, the all-denying spittle plastered on our bodies, spat in our faces. We alone, Madame, do you hear me, we blacks. From the bottom of the pit we cry out for air, light, the sun. And if we're going to climb out, don't you see that we need tense muscles, clenched teeth, and cool clear heads—ah yes, heads! And that's why I have to ask more of blacks than of other people, more faith, more enthusiasm, a step, another step, and still another, and never a step backward.[23]

In principle everyone should have the same rights, however reality reveals differently. In his speech, King Christophe argues that though black folk are equal to members of other races and ought to be treated as such, their past and fate are different; therein lies their imposed inequality. Because the history of black folk is remarkably different from that of other races, it is important that blacks have greater faith and work harder in order to shape their destiny. Step by step they should strive to climb out of the pit into which they were thrown. "Malheur à celui dont le pied flanche," wretched will the one whose strength gives out and misses a step, for he/she will fall back to the bottom of the pit. King Christophe's severity, as he explains it, was an effort to show newly freed slaves the possibility of realizing seemingly impossible goals. For the seemingly impossible actions will undo the fate that was laid out for them, will help them surpass their history of slavery and menialism, and will defy what they have been led to accept as the law of Nature. "Ce peuple doit se procurer, vouloir, réussir quelque chose d'impossible! Contre le Sort, contre l'Histoire, contre la Nature."[24] For King Christophe, the ultimate symbol representing the free nation was the standing of the solidly towering *Citadelle La Ferrière*. In *Black Majesty*

Vandercook describes the Citadelle as "a fortress larger and more massive than the Tower of London, yet it straddles a mountain peak three thousand feet above the sea. It is the most impressive structure ever conceived by a negro's brain or executed by black hands in all the world in all the tens of thousands of years of the race's history."[25] King Christophe observed that every nation has its monument of self-proclamation; Haiti must erect a monument that represents its national freedom and dignity.

> Porté par nos mains blessées, le défi insensé! Sur cette montagne, la rare pierre d'angle, le fondement ferme, le bloc éprouvé! Assaut du ciel ou reposoir du soleil, je ne sais, la première charge au matin de la relève! Regardez, Besse. Imaginez, sur cette peu commune plate-forme, tournée vers le nord magnétique, cent trente pieds de haut, vingt d'épaisseur les murs, chaux et cendre de bagasse, chaux et sang de taureau, une citadelle! Pas un palais. Pas un château fort pour protéger mon bien-tenant. Je dis la Citadelle, la liberté de tout un peuple. Bâtie par le peuple tout entier, hommes et femmes, enfants et vieillards, bâtie pour le peuple tout entier! Voyez, sa tête est dans les nuages, ses pieds creusent l'abîme, ses bouches crachent la mitraille jusqu'au large des mers, jusqu'au fond des vallées, c'est une ville, une forteresse, un lourd cuirassé de pierre . . . Inexpugnable, Besse, inexpugnable! Mais oui, ingénieur, à chaque peuple ses monuments! A ce peuple qu'on voulut à genoux, il fallait un monument qui le mît debout. Le voici! Surgie! Vigie.[26]

> Extravagant venture of our bare hands! Insane challenge of our wounded hands! On this mountain a solid cornerstone, a firm foundation. Assault of heaven or sun's resting place, I do not know—fresh troops charging in the morning. Look, Besse. Imagine on this very unusual platform, turned toward the north magnetic pole, walls one hundred and thirty feet high and thirty feet thick, lime and bagasse, lime and bull's blood, a citadel. No, not a palace. Not a fortress to guard my property. No, the citadel, the freedom, of a whole people. Built by the whole people, men and women, young and old, and for the whole people. Look, its head is in the clouds, its feet dig into the valleys. It's a city, a fortress, a battleship of stone. Impregnable, Besse, impregnable. Yes, Mr. Engineer, to every people its monuments. This people, forced to its knees, needed a monument to make it stand up. There it is. Risen! A watchover! (Spellbound).[27]

The *language* Césaire chooses here is very poetic. The specific choice of words and the rhythm of each line, illustrate the impassioned disposition of the King. In a stanza it would read as follow:

> Porté par nos mains blessées,
> le défi insensé!
> Sur cette montagne, la rare pierre d'angle,
> Le fondement ferme,

le bloc éprouvé ! Assaut du ciel
ou reposoir du soleil,
Je ne sais, la première
Charge au matin de la relève![28]

(Transposition mine)

The principal image in the King's speech is of solidity. The solidity he aspires to simultaneously represents the state of the Citadelle and the nation. He associates the construction of the Citadelle with the creation of nationhood. The image of the bleeding hands carrying stones to accomplish a difficult task, that of a fortress aiming for the sky and the sun, stresses Christophe's belief that blacks—Haitians in particular—should aim beyond what they were taught to be their limitations or horizons; for social and political possibilities are arbitrary constructs of Man. In his earnest command, Christophe exclaims, "Porté par nos mains bléssées, le défi insensé!" in order to build a nation that European powers were convinced to be a chimera. Through the symbolism of the Citadelle, the King presents the image of a nation that has changed from a kneeling to an upright position. His statement, "à ce peuple qu'on voulut à genoux, il fallait un monument qui le mît debout,"[29] is uttered to remind the citizens of their freedom from slavery. In *Cahier* (1939), when Césaire exclaims "la négraille assise, inattendument debout, debout dans la cale,"[30] he also portrayed the image of a "standing" people to describe revolt and liberation from slavery. However, King Christophe's austere determination—both the factual leader and Césaire's character—to create a nation that would eventually become equal to other free nations, started to ignite resentment among some Haitian officials who viewed him as a despot. Though many believed the King imposed excessive demands on a group of people who were physically and psychologically exhausted from the labors of slavery, they did not have the power to contest his authority.

In 1811, however, at the time when King Christophe became physically paralyzed, the people began to revolt and a number of his soldiers started an alliance with Boyer, who was governing the South of Haiti. In *Black Majesty* Vandercook explains that the *Code Henry*, which required intense labor for all Haitians, had an explosive in it, "specially since just over the border in Pétion's republic universal idleness was both permitted and practiced. Christophe knew this. But he had resolved to build, no matter how many bricks were cracked."[31] Sir Home Riggs Popham, who was then the commander-in-chief of the West Indian fleet from England, had an admiration for Christophe's achievements in Haiti.[32] In 1818 Popham cautioned King Christophe of his work laws as unwise. He informed and advised the King: "In the South they say your subjects are no better than slaves and that you are a second Dessalines. You are going too fast. Pétion has an army and if you ever stumble he will be over the border and at you, and every man and woman in Haiti who confuses idleness and independence will join him. . . . Sorry."[33] As Popham cautioned, in 1820 the mutiny began. The rebels plundered the treasury in Le Cap, looted the King's châteaux, and set fire to his plantations.[34]

In *La Tragédie*, King Christophe deplores the ingratitude of the people. Metaphorically linking the people to the land, he lamented planting ambitious seeds into a barren soil. "Semences ambitieuses, ai-je dit, pour vos terres fastidieuses. . . . J'ai tâché de mettre quelque chose dans une terre ingrate,"[35] ("I tried to put something into an inhospitable land").[36] The seeds of hard work and responsibility he planted on Haitian soil did not germinate; at the end the people showed resentment toward his efforts, and finally betrayed him. Incapable of psychologically coping with his physical paralysis, and disobedience from the people and the army, King Christophe—as did the factual King—shoots a bullet into his head. Before his suicide, the King implores mother Africa to help him come back to the ancestral land and to take him in her arm like a child who has returned home.

> Afrique! Aide-moi à rentrer, porte-moi comme un vieil enfant dans tes bras et puis tu me dévêtiras, me laveras. Défais-moi de tous ces vêtements, défais-m'en comme, l'aube venue, on se défait des rêves de la nuit. . . . De mes nobles, de ma noblesse, de mon sceptre de ma couronne. Et lave-moi! Oh, lave-moi de leur fard, de leurs baisers, de mon royaume! Le reste, j'y pourvoirai seul.[37]

> Africa, help me to go home, carry me like an aged child in your arms. Undress me and wash me. Strip me of all these garments, strip me as a man strips off dreams when the dawn comes. . . . Strip me of my nobles, my nobility, my scepter, my crown. And wash me, oh, wash me clean of their grease paint, their kisses, wash me clean of my kingdom. I'll attend to the rest alone.[38]

In the King's last words, Césaire shows the tragedy of a man who genuinely wanted to create a dignified black nation. However, the vestiges of slavery on Haiti's soil, the world's social, political, and economic politics with the new Republic, along with the King's rigid approach, rendered his endeavors unattainable. The King's insurmountable leadership dilemma was to maintain agricultural and economic prosperity within a non-industralized and ostracized country. It translated into excessive and forced manual labor for the people. In order for the new Republic to provide for its citizens and assert its position on the international market, the King believed austere governance was essential. Thus, the practice of his concept of "discipline" and "responsibility" was instrumental, if the newly freed black nation were to advance. "Damnation!" he exclaimed frustratingly. "Other peoples had time to build step by short step, over the centuries. Our only hope is to take long steps, year by groaning year."[39] ("Bougre! Les autres ont fait à petits coups de siècles. Où est pour nous le salut, si ce n'est que nous ferons nous—à grands coups d'années, à grands ahans d'années?"[40] It was with the understanding the newly freed black nation needed strict ruling that Christophe rigidly governed Haitians. The King had the reputation for magical omnipresence because he used a brass telescope to watch workers from a distance.[41] In 1818, in response to Sir Popham's advice regarding his work laws, Christophe replied,

> You do not understand. . . . My race is as old as yours. In Africa, they tell me, there are as many blacks as there are white men in Europe. In Saint-Domingue, before we drove the French out, there were a hundred negroes to every master. But we were your slaves. Except in Haiti, nowhere in the world have we resisted you. We have suffered, we have grown dull, and, like cattle under a whip, we have obeyed. Why? Because, m'sieu, we have no pride! And *we have no pride because we have nothing to remember.* Listen! It is a drum, Sir Home. Somewhere my people are dancing. It is almost all we have. The drum, laughter, love for one another, and our share of courage. . . . Perhaps if we had something we could show you, if we had something we could show ourselves, you would respect us and we might respect ourselves. . . . I am thinking of the future m'sieu, not of now. I will teach pride if my teaching breaks every back in my kingdom! (Emphasis added)[42]

However, more than the indolence of Haitians, the division and the tension between King Christophe in the North and Pétion—later Boyer—in the South, also served as another hindrance to the prosperity of the republic. The geographic cleavage also represented the separation and underlying resentment between mulattoes and full-blooded blacks; a situation that is also part of the vestige of slavery, and which hindered unity within the newly-freed nation. Finally, one could argue that the formation of an independent black nation is a challenging undertaking, which thus far has been faced with various obstacles—both internal and external oppositional forces. Césaire's 1966 play, *Une Saison au Congo*, presents another example of the tragic black leader, and the contradictions of independence.

In *Le temps historique dans L'œuvre théâtrale d'Aimé Césaire*, Albert Owusu-Sarpong argues that like Kwame Nkrumah, Jomo Kenyatta, Sekou Touré, and Patrice Lumumba, King Henry Christophe was the misunderstood leader. He represents the intellectual leader who dedicates his life to the decolonization of his nation but who then becomes the most alienated individual from society. *La Tragédie* and *Une Saison* depict the leader who is alienated, because a significant portion of the population do not fully understand the arduous work and psychological strength that are required to survive external sabotage, gain economic independence and advance a newly liberated country to prosperity.

Upon nominal independence, too many tend to suddenly abandon the liberation struggle, usually because of an illusory belief of sociopolitical attainment. Therefore, they immediately become disappointed in, and resentful toward, the leader who requires the surpassing of oneself for the benefit of the nation and its continuous prosperity.

Une Saison au Congo

In *Une Saison au Congo* Césaire presents the tragedy of Lumumba, an activist who by 1961 became isolated from the people on behalf of whom he unrelentingly fought. Lumumba was at once betrayed by his ministers, who were the "collaborators" of the Belgian government; the government against which the Congo needed to free itself. Lumumba's goal was that of a unified Congo, which had been divided into ethnic factions, provincialism, and other artificial genres of separatism placed by the Belgian government in order to maintain its authority. In 1958 the Belgian Congo, which hitherto was politically isolated from the rest of Africa, began to participate in the independence struggles in the continent. During the Brussels Exhibition of 1958 several hundred Africans from all parts of the Congo and Ruanda-Urundi met in Belgium. There, the Africans became conscious of the race dynamics in their home country as well as the importance of Congolese unity.[43] During the same year France offered to its territories in West and Equatorial Africa the choice of immediate independence or autonomy under French leadership. It was also in 1958 that France proffered independence to French Congo, Brazzaville, which was subsequently known as the Congo Republic.[44] The independence of the Congo Republic heightened the urgency for liberation amidst Belgian-colonized Congolese. The first All-African People's Conference—which met in Accra on December 5, 1958, to discuss and plan the independence movements and the unity of African countries—also raised Belgian-colonized Congolese's desire for independence and unity with the rest of the continent.[45] During the Accra conference Lumumba declared:

> This historic conference which brings us together, politicians of all the countries of Africa, shows us that in spite of frontiers and ethnic differences, we are of one mind and have the same desire to make our continent a happy one, free from anxiety, and from the fear of colonial domination. Down with colonialism! Long live the Congolese nation! Long live an independent Africa![46]

In addition to the Accra conference, in 1958 Joseph Kasavubu—the Abako leader—delivered an inaugural speech as *bourgmestre* (burgomaster) of the

Dendale commune during which he took a sharp political turn and criticized the Belgian policy in the Congo.[47] Inevitably, the growing liberation consciousness of the people exacerbated the crisis of the Belgian Congo. The crisis in the Congo, in Léopoldville in particular, grew out of the social and political dissatisfaction of the people. The overpopulation and poverty in Léopoldville were dire. In *The Belgian Congo* Ruth Slade compares the social situation in three of the Congo's important cities—Bazzaville, Katanga, and Léopoldville—to underline the particularity of Léopoldville's plight, which caused the riots of January 1959. She explains:

> The influx of Africans to Leopoldville had been insufficiently controlled, and there had been no time to extend the excellent housing schemes carried out in some parts of the city to cover the whole area inhabited by Africans. Faced with this mass of population, paternalism was impotent; in the Katanga, where the problem had not to be faced on so large a scale, it was more adequate. In Elisabethville there is nothing to be seen comparable to the worst parts of the African city of Leopoldville. Certainly the misery in Leopoldville was less than in Brazzaville; it was not this, however, which struck the Africans, but rather the racial discrimination in such things as salaries and housing conditions in Leopoldville itself.[48]

On January 4, 1959, the Abako supporters who had gathered to hear Arthur Pinzi's—*bourgmestre* of the Kalumu commune, and Minister of Foreign Affairs—report on his recent trip to Belgium, ardently spoke of justice and independence.[49] When the police invaded the crowd with the use of firearms, "anger spread throughout the native city, and the cry of independence was taken up; the pent-up fury of many months was unloosed; Europeans were attacked and churches, schools, hospitals, and social centers destroyed. The Europeans gave way to panic, the Army was called in, and the repression was violent."[50] Consequently, Joseph Kasavubu, Gaston Diomi and Arthur Pinzi were arrested without evidence of their involvement in instigating the riots. On January 13, 1959, King Baudouin of Belgium announced the future independence of the Congo. He declared that "it is [the Belgians] firm intention, without undesirable procrastination but also without undue haste, to lead the Congolese populations forward towards independence in prosperity and peace."[51] Following these events, by mid-March 1959 Arthur Pinzi, Gaston Diomi, Joseph Kasabubu, Daniel Kanza, and Simon Nzeza were released from prison and flown to Belgium.[52] During the period of preparation for Congolese independence a number of political groups were organized in Léopoldville; namely, the *Mouvement de Regroupement de Populations du Congo*, which aimed at regrouping the Bakongo; the *Inter-fédérale*, which united the non-Bakongo ethnic groups of Léopoldville; the *Union Progressiste*

Congolaise, the *Parti Démocrate Congolais*, and the *Mouvement pour le progrès national congolais*, which focused on independence and unity.

In September of 1959 the *Parti Solidaire Africain* was formed. The P.S.A., which was a party of extremists led by Antoine Gizenga, wanted to establish a federal republic in the Congo. The P.S.A. allied with the Abako—headed by Kasavubu—to oppose the *Mouvement National Congolais* led by Patrice Lumumba. Lumumba wanted a unitary state with a strong central government.[53] In November of 1959 the branch of the M.N.C. which opposed Lumumba, was headed by Albert Kalonji. Kalonji's branch formed a cartel with the Abako and the P.S.A., and published a joint memorandum demanding a united but federal Congo. In January 1960, the Round Table Conference, which lasted a month, was convened in Brussels to discuss the future of the Congo on the eve of independence. However, upon their return to the Congo new alliances and divisions were formed among the various political parties. For a brief period of time—less than a month—Lumumba's branch of the M.N.C. joined up with Kalonji's branch. Antagonism grew between the extremists of the Abako who wanted to establish a republic of the Lower Congo, which would stretch into Angola and the French Congo and the moderates. Kasavubu had then consented to a federal Congo. The P.S.A. led by Antoine Gizenga left the Abako cartel and shifted to Lumumba's party. Hence, Gizenza and members of the P.S.A. started to support Lumumba's view of a strong central government.[54] Gizenga would remain Lumumba's right hand man and would continue the fight against the secession of Katanga after Lumumba's death.

With the establishment of a strong central government, Lumumba wanted to aim at diminishing and eventually erasing ethnic divisions. Combating provincialism and ethnic factions, however, proved to be a difficult if not a nearly impossible task, considering those issues still exist in twenty-first century Africa. In *The Belgian Congo*, Slade argues that the conflict in Kasai between the Baluba and the Lulua significantly contributed to the crisis of 1959.[55] The Baluba were among the groups in the Eastern Congo who fled from the Arab slave traders and settled in South Kasai and North Katanga. The Lulua, which was then the largest tribe in Kasai, allowed the Baluba to occupy land near Luluabourg. In time, the Baluba socially and economically prospered and outnumbered the Lulua. In 1959, with the prospect of elections with universal suffrage, the Lulua became apprehensive about the Baluba's accretion of power. Their fear led to tension and violence. In July 1959 the Lulua attacked the Baluba villages, and constant outbreaks between the two groups continued until independence in June 1960.[56] Unlike the demography in Kasai, the Baluba were the minority in Katanga. As the majority, the Katangese reserved the best positions for themselves. The oppression of the

Baluba in Katanga—who subsequently chose Lumumba as their leader—also added to the chaos of 1959.[57]

In *Une Saison au Congo* Césaire depicts the effects of colonialism in order to produce a cathartic and didactic impact on his spectators. Act 1 of scene 5 presents a dialogue between individuals each representing a different ethnic group. The dialogue Césaire depicts in his play interprets the conflict that arose between the Baluba, the Lulua and the Kantagese in 1959-factual Congo. The conversation outlines the atmosphere of division in Congo at the dawn of independence (*Dependa*). Here, the three characters include *le joueur de Sanza, le tribaliste Mukongo,* and *un Mungala.*

Le joueur de Sanza: Dipenda! On ne nous l'apporte pas, c'est nous qui la prenons, citoyens!

Le tribaliste Mukongo: Peu importe! Donnée ou arrachée, ce que je sais, c'est que maintenant que nous avons Dipenda, il faudra que tous les Bengalas rentrent dans leurs villages. Le pays est gâté avec tous ces Bengalas-là!

Un Mungala: Attention, monsieur, ne vous provoquez pas. C'est nous qui sommes bien bons de tolérer qu'un Mukongo soit président de la République, qu'un Mukongo nous gouverne; cette place revient à un homme du fleuve! Vive Jean Bolikango! Jean Bolikango au pouvoir!

Le joueur de Sanza: Allons! Messieurs, calmez-vous! plus de querelles ethniques. Ne laissons pas le colonialisme diviser pour régner! Dominons ces querelles tribales! Qu'il n'y ait plus parmi nous de Bengalas, de Bakongos, de Batételes, mais seulement des Congolais! libres, unis, organisés! Allons, célébrons notre unité autour d'une bonne bière, je vous paie à boire, messieurs![58]

Sanza Player: Listen to me, citizens. Nobody's bringing us Dependa. We're taking her.

The Bakongo Tribesman: It's all the same. Maybe they're giving us Dependa and maybe we're taking her, but one thing is for sure: Now that we've got her, we're going to send all those Bengalas back to their villages. The Bengalas are wrecking the country.

First Man: Watch your step, sir. Don't try to provoke us. If you ask me, it's pretty nice of us to put up with a Bakongo president, to let a Bakongo rule us. By rights a river man should have the job. Jean Bolikango! That's the man! Hurrah for Jean Bolikango!

Mpolo: That's enough, gentlemen. Calm down. Let's not have tribal quarrels. That's just what the colonialists want. Divide and rule, that's their motto. We've got to stop being Bengalas, Bakongos, and Batetelas. From now on we're all jus plain Congolese, free, united, and organized. Let's all drink a good glass of beer to our unity. Be my guests, gentlemen.[59]

The *joueur de Sanza* reiterates Lumumba's philosophy; he is also the didactic voice of Aimé Césaire. *Le joueur de Sanza* implores the *Mukongo* and the *Mungala* to cease ethnic confrontation by urging them to eschew the divisive plot the colonialists orchestrated, in order to rule more effectively. He further supplicates his listeners to transcend ethnic quarrels, so they no longer speak in terms of Bengalas, Bakongos, Batételes, but to speak as a free, organized, and united Congolese nation. It is with an analogous logic to that of the *joueur de Sanza* that in scene 7 of act 1, *la Speakerine* (announcer) calls for an African "moral rearmament," or a "revolution of mentalities" on the radio.

Ici le réarmement moral africain. Au travail citoyens! au travail! Je dis au travail, comme je dirais "aux armes"! C'est qu'une guerre est commencée, Congolais, la Guerre pour l'avenir du pays. Aussi bien la mobilisation des classes laborieuses doit-elle être totale, inconditionnelle, consciente, volontaire! Les jours que le Congo a vécus sont semblables à une époque préhistorique. Mais avec l'indépendance nous avons accédé à l'âge historique, et l'âge de l'Histoire, citoyens c'est l'âge du Travail. Au travail! Au travail, citoyens![60]

This is the voice of African Moral Rearmament. Get to work, citizens. To work! And when I say "to work," it's the same as if I were saying "to arms." We are at war, citizens, at war for the future of the Congo. The mobilization of the working classes must be total, unconditional, deliberate, voluntary. The Congo has been living in prehistoric times. With independence we have acceded to the historical age, and that means the age of hard work. To work, citizens! To work![61]

The *speakerine* sees the period of Congo's reconstruction as a period of war. Indeed, rebuilding requires a period of combat against the colonial mentality that usually threatens the future of a nation. To win the war on colonialism and, equally important, to prevent neo-colonialism, the Congolese must work in harmony with one another, and they must work hard. According to the *speakerine*, their work must be unconditional, conscientious, and voluntary. Taking place simultaneously in scene 8, which is situated in Kalina, is a protest march of Congolese soldiers against Lumumba as the Prime Minister of Congo. One of the important conversations in scene 8 occurs between Lumumba and one of his ministers who during the political unrest, begins to show his hesitation and nervousness regarding the independence of Congo. In his speech, Lumumba outlines the price of independence and the indispensable commitment it demands from each leader for its viability.

Nous aurons tout, et en même temps? Et tout de suite: la révolte, le sabotage, la menace, la calomnie, le chantage, la trahison. Vous avez l'air étonnés! C'est ça, le pouvoir: la trahison, la mort peut-être. La mort sans doute. Et c'est ça le Congo! Comprenez: Le Congo est un pays où tout va vite. Une graine en terre

aujourd'hui, et demain un buisson, que dis-je, une forêt! en tout cas, les choses
qui vont vite iront leur train.[62]

There's going to be trouble, every kind of trouble before you can say Jack Sprat:
mutiny, sabotage, threats, slander, blackmail, and treason. You look surprised.
That's what power means: betrayal, maybe death. Yes, death and no maybe.
That's the Congo. The Congo, you see, is a country where things go gast. A seed
in the ground today, tomorrow a bush, no, tomorrow a forest. In any case, the
things that move quickly will keep on moving quickly.[63]

He continues his reflection in the presence of the delegation of soldiers who
entered the room.

Pendant cinquante ans, on a gardé la bouche close et tremblé devant le Belge, à
ne pas accorder à un gouvernement congolais, à un gouvernement de Congolais, à un gouvernement de frères qui vient seulement de s'installer, le délai de
quelques mois qu'il réclame pour étudier les dossiers et faire le tour des problè-
mes![64]

For fifty years they've kept their mouths shut and trembled at the sight of a
Belgian. And now they refuse to give a Congolese government, a government of
their brothers, the few months' time it needs to get its bearings.[65]

For Lumumba, the consequences of independence for black leaders are
revolt, sabotage, threats, slander, blackmail, or betrayal. Lumumba's theory
has been proven by history; for, revolt, sabotage, slander, blackmail, betrayal,
or death were the lot of political leaders such as Toussaint Louverture, Marcus
Garvey, W. E. B. Du Bois, Martin Luther King, and Malcolm X—to name a
few. Lumumba also observed the Congolese's intolerance for the governance
of native officials. He points out that for fifty years Congolese soldiers and
civilians have silently endured and trembled in acquiescence when facing the
dominance of the Belgian government. However, they quickly grow impatient
with the newly born Congolese government made of indigenous officials,
and refuse to accord it time to settle down and tackle the problems that have
plagued the Congo since the inception of Belgian colonization. In his introduction to Lumumba's speeches, Jean-Paul Sartre argues that the reason for
such intolerance was not only because of ethnic and provincial separatism,
which created an inherent division, but it was also because of class division.
The class division that Europeans created in the Congo was a tactic to better
serve their colonial purposes.

In the introduction to *Lumumba Speaks: The Speeches and Writings of Patrice
Lumumba, 1958–1961*, Jean-Paul Sartre comments on the problems of direct
and indirect control the Belgian government exerts on the Congo. Furthermore,

he underscores the steadfast commitment and leadership that was needed from the Congolese people in order to restructure their country. Sartre explains:

> Patrice dreams of a unifying power that will rally all the people, acting everywhere, bringing harmony, a community of action, throughout the country, receiving information from the most remote hamlet, collating this information and using it as the basis of a political policy, sending information and orders to the representatives of this power back by the same route to the tiniest hamlet. The government splits the colonized into individual atoms and unifies them from *the outside*, as subjects of the same king. Independence will be merely an empty word unless the cohesion *imposed* from *the outside* is replaced by unification from *the inside*.[66]

In his analysis Sartre points to the politic of European direct and indirect control in Africa, and the unprincipled strategy that divided the continent. The complicity between European imperialists and unscrupulous African "leaders" depleted Africa of its resources and destroyed the basic structure of the society—both its secular and religious institutions. Sartre further contends that one of the factors of Lumumba's failure was his unawareness of the fact that the Belgians *reared* collaborators, who because of the brainwash process they underwent, were against the political independence of Congo.[67] Sartre explains: Lumumba "does not know that the mother countries that have been in control want to give nominal power to the 'natives,' who will govern more or less consciously, in such a way as to further colonial interests."[68] He further explains that these men "have been handpicked in Europe, that they all belong to the class that has been recruited and trained by the colonial administration."[69]

Contrary to Sartre's opinion, Lumumba became aware of the Belgian plot early enough. However, his awareness and actions could not cope with such a staunchly established system, a system that had mentally *made* and corrupted the majority of Congo's schooled class. Paradoxically, it was precisely the schooling they received that programmed them to work in the interests of the Belgian government and their own materialistic goals, but to the detriment of the Congolese people and the country. In scene 11 of act 1, situated in the Congolese parliament, Césaire outlines a speech delivered by Lumumba. For Césaire, the speech demonstrates Lumumba's level of awareness of the Belgian conspiracy.

> Et moi, je vous assure, messieurs, que nous ne voyageons pas assez. Ah! Que pour ma part, j'aurais voulu pouvoir me multiplier, me diviser, être moi-même innombrable pour être partout à la fois présent. Matadi, Boma, Elisabethville, Luluabourg, pour pouvoir déjouer partout l'inombrable complot de l'ennemi!

Car il éclate partout le complot de l'ennemi! Ce complot, le complot belge, je le vois ourdi dès le premier jour de notre indépendance, ourdi par des hommes travaillés de dépit et époinçonnés de haine. Je le vois, sous les traits du général Massens. . . . Le complot belge? je le vois en la personne de l'ambassadeur de Belgique à Léo. . . . Le complot belge? je le vois en tenue de général, préparant méthodiquement, et ce, dès le premier jour, son lâcher de parachutes et ses raids de soulards. Le complot belge? C'est le traité d'amitié que les Belges avaient signé avec nous, déchiré comme un chiffon de papier.[70]

I for my part, gentlemen, assure you that we don't travel enough. Ah, I wish I could multiply and divide myself, so as to be everywhere at once. In Matadi, in Boma, in Elisabethville, in Luluabourg, to crush the enemy's many-headed plot. For the plot is everywhere. Ever since the very first day of our independence, I've seen the Belgians, men ravaged by hatred and eaten by resentment, hatching their plot. General Massens stirring up the militia against the government, representing us as a gang of politicians and unscrupulous profiteers. . . . From the very first day General Massens has been setting the scene for his raids, working up a pretext for his mercenaries to step in. That's the Belgian plot, gentlemen. Their treaty of friendship with us? As far as they are concerned it's a scrap of paper.[71]

Metonymically, Lumumba enumerates the tactics of the Belgian plot. These schemes are the ambassador to Belgium in Léopoldville, Belgium methodical operation in Congo, and the treaty of friendship the Belgian government signed with the Congo. They all represent the Belgian scheme to maintain control in Congo. In scene 7, act 2 of Césaire's play, Lumumba's wife, Pauline, warns him of his trusting nature in comparison to the cunning politicians who have been trained to sabotage any attempt to native political power in Congo. Pauline frantically describes animals associated with subtle trap and gradual infestation: termites, toads, spiders, and the crawling vermin of envy.[72] In the play Césaire further uses a number of predatory and bloodsucking animals to describe the Belgian and their Congolese "collaborators." With similar animal-like metaphoric enumeration, in scene 8 of act 1 Lumumba refers to the Belgians as carnivorous animals: vultures, falcons and hawks, whose practices are killing the Congolese people through the ethnic wars they fuel, and whose predatory habits are devouring the Congo's economy and manpower.[73]

Lumumba was, thus, aware of the conspiracy; he worked relentlessly to mobilize the Congolese people and prevent the realization of the Belgian plot. In the same speech, Lumumba does not only urge the Congolese but all Africans to take action. He asks:

Congolais, allez-vous laisser assassiner notre indépendance si chèrement conquise? Et vous, Africains, mes frères, Mali, Guinée, Ghana, vers vous aussi, par-delà les frontières du Congo, nous crions. Afrique! Je te hurle! Croient-ils donc à l'Afrique une lourdeur à l'oreille? Ou lui croient-ils une faiblesse autour du cœur? Ou croient-ils la main de l'Afrique trop courte pour délivrer? Je sais bien que le colonialisme est puissant. Mais je le jure par l'Afrique: tous unis, tous ensemble, nous percerons le monstre par les narines! D'ores et déjà, mes frères, le Congo a remporté une grande victoire.[74]

People of the Congo, we have paid dearly for our independence. Are we going to let them throttle it now? And you, my brother Africans, Mali, Guinea, Ghana, we cry out to you across our borders. Africa! Do they think Africa is deaf? Or faint-hearted? Or do they think Africa is too feeble to deliver us? I know the colonialists are powerful. But I swear to you by Africa: All of us united, together, will subdue the monster. Brothers, already the Congo has won a great victory.[75]

Again, Lumumba acknowledged the power of colonialism, but he also believed in Africa's power to attain unity. A united Africa, as he viewed it, cannot be fainthearted. It was with that understanding that he wrote to Kwame Nkrumah, who was then the president of Ghana. In response, Nkrumah dispatched Ghanaian troops for the use of the United Nations in order to protect Lumumba and establish order in Congo. In the play, Césaire depicts the situation where in September 1960 the United Nations used Ghanaian troops against Lumumba to prevent his use of the national radio, while Radio Brazzaville, which was controlled by the French, continued to transmit "the most violent sort of propaganda" against him.[76] On September 12, 1960, Nkrumah sent a response letter to Lumumba, expressing his disappointment in the action of the United Nations. He wrote,

My dear Patrice,
    I appreciate your point of view perfectly, and I can see and understand the difficult situation you find yourself with regard to the Ghanaian troops in Leopoldville. I too find myself in an embarrassing and vexing situation used in the Congo, even though I am fighting tooth and nail, day and night, in your favor. . . . If Ghanaian troops are to be put entirely at your disposal, then you and your government must find some way of declaring that Ghana and the Congo are as one in this fight. This is the only way that will allow my Ghanaian troops to operate legitimately with Congolese forces.[77]

The suggestion that Ghana join forces with the Congo and operate as one in the struggle for liberation from Belgian imperialism, reinforces the emphatic call for Pan-Africanism that both Lumumba and Nkrumah had been advocating. Though the colonial foundation in the Congo was too deeply and strongly entrenched for both Lumumba and Nkrumah to eradicate, they nonetheless maintained the lessons of courage, integrity, and unity.

It is precisely the lessons of safeguarding one's independence and national prosperity that Césaire sought to teach younger generations of Africans and those of African descent. To de-colonize and establish independence, a nation must find its dignity, it must rid itself of every complex of inferiority and convince itself that it can and must do without the colonizer. And so, the youth of Africa and the black Diaspora must receive a relevant education, so they no longer serve as collaborators or intermediaries for the colonial system. It has been established that the rebuilding of a country means, primarily, the psychological revolution and the re-education of its people. In both cases, in Congo and Haiti, the people held a false notion of independence. Furthermore, it is also through relevant education that black nations will reduce the social gap between the masses and the elite or the national bourgeoisie. As Césaire demonstrates, Lumumba was betrayed by his national bourgeoisie, whose covetousness and quest for dominance led to its cooperation with colonial powers, and the hindrance of true independence.

The sacrifices and death of black leaders remain significant for the continuation of liberation and advancement movements. In *Aimé Césaire: Un homme à la recherche d'une patrie* Georges Ngal argues that the individual death of these leaders matters little in the sense that their death helps create a psychological sensibility among the people. Hence, "s'il meurt, c'est pour revivre, pour continuer à défier la mort grâce à la conscience créée par lui dans le peuple. En réalité sa révolution est permanente, continue" ("if he dies, it is to live again, to continue to defy death through the consciousness he awakened in the people. In fact his revolution is permanent, continuous").[78] The physical death of the leader paradoxically heightens national and race consciousness as well as a sense of responsibility among future generations. Moreover, the physical death motivates successive leaders to re-launch the struggle that was started but was hindered midway. Though he is dead, Lumumba represents Africa's continuous struggle for politicoeconomic independence and unity.

Sartre declares that Lumumba was not, and could not have been, the hero of Pan-Africanism. He was its martyr, because "his story brings into the light of day, for all to see, the intimate relationship between independence, unity, and the fight against the trusts. His death is a cry of alarm; in and through him, the whole continent dies in order to be born again."[79] Contrarily, Lumumba is simultaneously a hero and a martyr of Pan-Africanism. It is precisely because Lumumba heroically suffered the calumnies of the Belgian government and its collaborators, and it is because he fearlessly sacrificed his life for the Black Nationalist struggle and continental Pan-Africanism, that he became a martyr. As a leader and hero, Lumumba aimed at defending the Congo against psychological as well as sociopolitical assaults coming from within and without the country.

Notes

1. Albert Owusu-Sarpong, *Le Temps Historique dans L'Œuvre Théâtrale d'Aimé Césaire* (Paris: Editions L'Harmattan, 2002) 19.

2. Ngal, *Aimé Césaire: Un Homme à la Recherche d'une Patrie*, 49.

3. Edwards, *The Practice*, 119. Quoted from Eslanda Goode Robeson's "Black Paris," part II *Challenge* 1, no. 5 (June 1936): 11–12.

4. Ngal, *Aimé Césaire: Un Homme à la Recherche d'une Patrie*, 49.

5. Ibid., 19.

6. Ibid., 20.

7. Les Frères de l'Instruction Chrétienne, *Histoire D'Haïti*, 133.

8. John Womack Vandercook, *Black Majesty* (New York: The Literary Guild of America, 1928) 134.

9. Ibid., 134. Also see Hubert Cole, *Christophe King of Haiti*, 209.

10. Vandercook, *Black Majesty*, 136.

11. Ibid., 136.

12. Hubert Cole, *Christophe King of Haiti* (New York: The Viking Press, 1967) 238–44.

13. Les Frères de l'Instruction Chrétienne, *Histoire D'Haïti*, 132.

14. Cole, *Christophe King of Haiti*, 21.

15. Vandercook, *Black Majesty*, 136.

16. Aimé Césaire, *La Tragédie du Roi Christophe* (Paris: Présence Africaine, 1963) 28.

17. Aimé Césaire, *The Tragedy of King Christophe*, trans. Ralph Manheim (New York: Grove Press, Inc., 1970) 18.

18. Césaire, *La Tragédie*, 29.

19. Césaire, *The Tragedy*, 18.

20. Césaire, *La Tragédie*, 26–29. For the philosophies of the factual King, see John Womack Vandercook, *Black Majesty*, 1928; C. L. R. James, *The Black Jacobins*, 1963; Hubert Cole, *Christophe King of Haiti*, 1967.

21. Levine, "Marcus Garvey and the Politics of Revitalization," 111.

22. Césaire, *La Tragédie*, 59.

23. Césaire, *The Tragedy*, 41–42.

24. Ibid., 62.

25. Vandercook, *Black Majesty*, 4.

26. Césaire, *La Tragédie*, 62–63.

27. Césaire, *The Tragedy*, 44–45.

28. Ibid., 63.
One could transpose into poetic form King Christophe's entire speech to his entourage and note the close link between Césaire's rhythmic language of theater and that of poetry. Though from the standpoint of delivery Césaire believes that the majority of black spectators are more apt to apprehend the message from a play, his rhythmic presentation of the two genres remains akin.

29. Ibid., 63.

30. Césaire, *Cahier*, 61.

31. Vandercook, *Black Majesty*, 134.

32. Cole, *Christophe King of Haiti*, 259.

33. Vandercook, *Black Majesty*, 144.

34. Cole, *Christophe King of Haiti*, 17.

35. Césaire, *La Tragédie*, 138.

36. Césaire, *The Tragedy*, 86.

37. Césaire, *La Tragédie*, 147.

38. Césaire, *The Tragedy*, 90.

39. Ibid., 87.

40. Césaire, *La Tragédie*, 139.

41. Cole, *Christophe King of Haiti*, 195; Vandercook, *Black Majesty*, 157.

42. Vandercook, *Black Majesty*, 144–45.

43. Ruth Slade, *The Belgian Congo* (London: Oxford University Press, 1960) 45. Colin Legum, *Congo Disaster* (Baltimore: Penguin Books, 1961) 55.

44. Ibid., 45–46.

45. Ibid., 46. The three Congolese who attended the All-African People's Con-fererence as representatives of the Mouvement National Congolaise were Patrice Lumumba, president of the M.N.C.; Gaston Diomi, *bourgmestre* of the Ngiri-Ngiri commune of Léopoldville; and Joseph Ngalula, editor of *Présence Congolaise*. Legum, *Congo Disaster*, 56.

46. Ibid., 47.

47. Ibid., 48.

48. Ibid., 49.

49. Ibid., 49.

50. Ibid., 49.

51. Ibid., 50.

52. Ibid., 51.

53. Ibid., 59.

54. Ibid., 71.

55. Ibid., 61.

56. Ibid., 61–62.

57. Ibid., 65.

58. Aimé Césaire, *Une Saison au Congo* (Paris: Editions Seuil, 1973) 24.

59. Aimé Césaire, *A Season in Congo*, trans. Ralph Manheim (Washington, D.C.: Ubu Repertory Theater Publications, 1990) 82.

60. Césaire, *Une Saison*, 33.

61. Césaire, *A Season*, 92.

62. Césaire, *Une Saison*, 35.

63. Césaire, *A Season*, 94.

64. Césaire, *Une Saison*, 35–36.

65. Césaire, *A Season*, 94.

66. Patrice Lumumba, *Lumumba Speaks: The Speeches and Writings of Patrice Lu-mumba, 1958–1961.* 1963. (Boston: Little, Brown and Company, Inc., 1972) 19.

67. The term *Collaborator* holds different meanings and refers to three types of African groups. *Collaborator* refers to Africans who worked within the European system, with the belief that they can make a difference and change the system for the better. The term also refers to Africans who worked for the colonial system for personal gain; as a result, they served as intermediaries between Europeans and the masses of Africans, to the detriment of the latter. Thirdly, the term also refers to a group of Africans who were conscious of the oppression of the European system but believed they did not have a choice but to work in that system in order to earn a living. In French-speaking Africa the equivalent term is *évolué(s)*. The évolués were schooled to become allies of European rulers in overseeing and establishing the stability of colonial institutions in Africa. *Intermediaries* is the term used in the United States, particularly during the 1960s and 1970s, in reference to blacks who were chosen to work and serve as cushion between the governmental system and the black community. The position of members of all three groups, i.e., collaborators, évolués, and intermediaries was ambiguous; for, while some were only motivated by self-interest, others were interested—on different levels—in the advancement of black folk.

68. Lumumba, *Lumumba Speaks*, 23–24.

69. Ibid., 24.

70. Césaire, *Une Saison*, 43.

71. Césaire, *A Season*, 102.

72. Césaire, *Une Saison*, 71–72; Césaire, *A Season*, 128.

73. Césaire, *Une Saison*, 37–38.

74. Césaire, *Une Saison*, 44.

75. Césaire, *A Season*, 102.

76. Lumumba, *Lumumba Speaks*, 409.

77. Ibid., 408.

78. Ngal, *Aimé Césaire: Un Homme à la Recherche d'une Patrie*, 195.

79. Ibid., 51.

8

Nicolás Guillén and the *Afrocriollo* Movement: The Valorization of African Heritage in Hispanic Culture

Like a wisp of smoke around the fire—
    And the tom-toms beat,
    And the tom-toms beat,
And the low beating of the tom-toms
    Stirs your blood.

             —Langston Hughes[1]

Entends-tu ces voix: elles chantent l'amoureuse douleur
Et dans le morne, écoute ce tam-tam haleter telle la gorge
      d'une noire jeune fille.
Ton âme, c'est le reflet dans l'eau murmurante où
      tes pères ont penché leurs obscurs visages
Et le blanc qui te fit mulâtre, c'est ce peu
      d'écume rejeté, comme un crachat, sur le rivage.

Do you hear those voices: they're singing love's heartache
And in the mournful darkness, hear that tom-tom panting
      like a young black girl's breasts.
Your soul is the reflection in the murmuring water where
      your ancestors bent their dark faces
And the white man who made you a mulatto is this bit of
      sea spume cast out, like spit, upon the shore.

             —Jacques Roumain[2]

IN RESPONSE TO THE RACE AND CLASS politics of the nineteenth and twentieth centuries—inherited from the slavery era—the world witnessed the rise of intellectual and activist men and women who would forever change the mentality of the global community. Within the Hispanic Caribbean, the Afro-Cuban poet Nicolás Guillén became the voice of sociopolitical consciousness. By the late 1920s he emerged as the activist who did much to incite the articulation process of liberation thought in Cuba and, subsequently, helped to instill black esteem at home and abroad. Prior to the late 1920s, two trends of thoughts and emotions came from white Hispanic writers of South America, Central America, and the Caribbean. The first tier was occupied by writers who viewed blacks as savages and black art as uncontrollable and maniac. Such view was mainly, if not solely, based on the confidence and self-valorization black artists displayed, and racist white Hispanic writers found unacceptable. White Hispanic writers responded with envy and vexation to the level of self-assertion and the degree of self-pride coming from a people they judged inferior. Among such writers one would find José Carlos Mariátegui (the Peruvian journalist and political philosopher), Rubén Darío (the Nicaraguan poet, journalist, and diplomat), and César Vallejo Mendoza (the Peruvian poet). While the intellectual significance of those writers within the greater Hispanic literary canon is conceded, one must take into account their response to the emerging black voice of the time; a reaction which was overtly condescending and vilifying. The second tier was composed of white Hispanic writers who were part of the Negrista poets' school of thought. Unlike Mariátegui's, Darío's, and Vallejo's blatant disdain for blackness, Negrista writers demonstrated a certain level of recognition for black culture. However, though their works were seemingly less caricatural than their predecessors, they nonetheless perpetuated stereotypical representations of black life. Such distorted portrayal was accepted through the guise of the *exotic*, which essentially translated into *lasciviousness*. The well-known writers of Negrista include Luis Palés Matos (the Puerto Rican poet, known for the introduction of "Afro-Antillano" in Hispanic America), Fernando Ortiz (the Cuban essayist), and Alejo Carpentier (the Cuban novelist and essayist).

Keeping with and capitalizing on the Negro vogue that was prevalent in Europe and the United States, the Negrista genre and its Negrismo content depicted black images based on European and Euro-American primitivism. As Richard Jackson explains in *Black Literature and Humanism in Latin America*, each writer was "more interested in atavism, ritual and entertainment than the black per se."[3] Ortiz utilized his anthropological research on African culture as contrivance to perpetuate and further persuade Cubans of the *presupposed* connection between blackness and crime in Cuba. With prejudiced examinations of black life, Ortiz propagated his belief that the race was composed of "people with primitive mentalities and strong proclivities to lust and violence."[4] These canonical theories came to influence acclaimed Negrista writers such as Matos and Carpentier. Carpentier's first novel, *Ecué Yambá O*, which is a complicated amalgamation of racist theory and an appreciation of black culture, remains one of the most popular and contradictory Negrista writings. While the writer set out to reveal his notion of inherent facets of black culture, he in fact presented, by and large, a novelistic version of Ortiz's theories. The culture Carpentier depicted in *Ecué* is based on biased interpretations of the *other*, his *subjects*, imbued with a myriad of stereotypes attributed to blacks, are nothing short than his intellectual environment's creation of blackness. It is thus not surprising that the superficiality in content renders the novel obsolete among scholars interested in the history and culture of African descendants. As Jackson succinctly expresses, "Carpentier seemingly only caught hold of the outer garment of the black Cuban in *Ecué Yambá O*, as he himself has often acknowledged his inability to 'get inside' the black culture he tried to depict in his first novel"; hence, "the characters are not 'universal' or 'human;' the novel is simply a false, nativistic, documentary exercise written at the height of primitivism; and the novel simply and perhaps innocently propagates a racist, negative, and stereotyped image of blacks, both Haitian and Cuban."[5]

By the 1940s, surely due to the global effects of the sociopolitical philosophies of such movements as Pan-Africanism, New Negro Renaissance, Indigénisme, Garveyism, Afrocriollo, and Négritude, white Hispanic writers such as Matos and Carpentier began to rethink their presentation of Afro-Cuban culture. More significantly, the Afro-Cuban poet Nicolás Guillén emerged as *the* engaged voice of black culture within Hispanic America of the 1930s and 1940s. As an ideological proponent of the broader *Afrocriollo* movement in Cuba, Guillén expressed the particularities of a foundational African heritage, to balance the cult of Europeanism; he further emphasized the reality of *Mulatez*, the essence of a great number of Cubans and Hispanic Americans.

Nicolás Guillén and the Emergence of an Afro-Cuban Expression

Though Nicolás Guillén started his vocation as a poet with the publication of his first poems in the journal *Camagüey Gráfico* (between the years 1919–1920), and later with *Cerebro y Corazón* in 1922 (which was published about half a century later, in 1977), his article "Camino de Harlem" published in 1929, marked his first race conscious writing. With "Camino de Harlem" began Guillén's social criticism on the unjust, prejudiced, and racist treatment blacks endured in Cuba. To counterbalance the daily practice of insult, maltreatment, and violence against blacks on his native land, Guillén's article introduced Harlem as the locus of cultural consciousness, political engagement, and self-pride, where blacks were unrelentingly pushing for social justice and recognition. His conviction was that Cuba ought to accept the essence of its mixed heritage as a nation—i.e., both its African and European components—and the Cuban sociopolitical structure must value the foundational African contribution to society; moreover, African descendants must be treated as respectable citizens. Following Guillén's first prosaic race-based writing ("Camino de Harlem"), his *Motivos de son* became the poetic voice of black aesthetics and social consciousness. *Motivos de son* (published in April of 1930) appeared after and in the midst of three influential international factors: the global sociopolitical momentum of the Garvey movement, the actualization of the twentieth century New Negro philosophy (most remarkably in Haiti and the United States) and, lastly, Guillén's personal encounter and poetic connection with the renowned Harlem Renaissance poet Langston Hughes.

As examined in chapters 1 and 5, Garveyism was a consequential movement with both direct and indirect influence on black thought and politics throughout the African Diaspora. Blacks in Cuba, composed of native Afro-Cubans as well as Haitians and Jamaicans who had migrated to the island to work on sugar cane fields, played an important role in sustaining the vision of the Universal Negro Improvement Association. By 1926 Cuba had the second highest number of U.N.I.A. branches in the world; the United States maintained first place. Between the years of 1902–1932 the majority of immigrants to arrive in Cuba were Spaniards (778,481 citizens), Haitians (190,989 citizens), and Jamaicans (120,989 citizens).[6] The growing black population in Cuba and its need for social justice and protection under the law also meant adherence to Garvey's philosophy of race uplift. Accordingly, "the U.N.I.A. became firmly entrenched among the black workers in Cuba and in time became mutual aid society, race uplift organization, and quasigovernment for the black population. It was practically the only effective attempt to look after their interests."[7] Throughout the 1920s the U.N.I.A.'s Black Star Line traveled with different cargos to Cuba, Haiti, Jamaica, Panama, and Costa Rica; each ship was received with pride and enthusiasm, as the inhabitants considered the voyages an initial stage to equitable trades and cultural exchanges between blacks. In 1930 Garvey was denied entry in Cuba for the same reasons he was banned from Europe and European colonies in Africa; his philosophies inspired blacks to take a stand against social violence and political oppression, as a result he was viewed as disturbing the nations' *peaceful* status quo.

The 1912 massacre of thousands of blacks (which occurred after a non-violent protest against oppression) laid bare the deeply rooted racism that existed, and marked the apogee of genocide against blacks within Cuba.[8] Keeping with its mission to psychologically and physically safeguard members of the race and defend their political and social interests, the U.N.I.A. assumed the responsibility to protect blacks in Cuba. Notwithstanding the subsequent dismantlement of numerous U.N.I.A. branches and the prohibition of Garvey's entrance in Cuba, the seed of race consciousness and the call to justice had been planted. Concurrent with Garvey's international movement and its impact, cultural movements in Haiti and the United States also contributed to the psychological strength of Afro-Cubans in general, as well as the preoccupation of Guillén's poetry and essays during the 1930s. As discussed in chapters 4 and 5, the turn of the twentieth century marked the birth of a New Negro spirit and intellectualism within the United States, with Harlem as the *Mecca*. With the emergence of the New Negro spirit and thought was the burgeoning of the cultural movement expressed in the works of New Negro Renaissance artists. Chapter 6 examined the development of a cultural renaissance in Haiti, particularly during the American occupation. The cultural ideology of the Indigéniste movement fomented the political and social philosophy adopted by the *Noiriste* adherents and writers.[9] Through the different currents coming out of Harlem and Port-au-Prince, pride in blackness and the esteem of African heritage started to germinate among the Cuban masses. Hughes' sojourn in Cuba and his first encounter with Nicolás Guillén (in March 1930) brought a new philosophical dimension to the island; he motivated the poetic race conscious utterance of the Afro-Cuban poet. Guillén's "Negro Bembón" ("Thick-lipped Negro")—from his seminal work *Motivos de son*—is the assertion of the race dignity that emerged in the nineteenth century and was prevalent by the 1920s.

> ¿Por qué te pone tan bravo,
> cuando te dicen negro bembón,
> si tiene la boca santa,
> negro bembón?
>
> Bembón así como ere
> tiene de tó;
> Caridad te mantiene,
> te lo dá tó.
>
> Te queja todavía,
> negro bembón;
> sin pega y con harina,
> negro bembón;
> majagua de drí blanco,

negro bembón;
sapato de dó tono,
negro bembón . . .

Bembón así como ere,
tiene de tó;
¡Caridad de mantiene,
te lo dá tó![10]

How come you jumps salty
when they calls you thick-lipped boy,
if yo' mouf's so sweet,
thick-lipped cullud boy?

Thick-lipped as you is
you got everything.
Charity's payin' yo' keep.
She's givin' you all you need.

Still you go around beefin',
thick-lipped cullud boy.
No work an' plenty money,
thick-lipped cullud boy.
White suit jes' spotless,
thick-lipped cullud boy.
Shoes two shades o' honey,
thick-lipped cullud boy.

Thick-lipped as you is
you got everything.
Charity's payin' yo' keep,
She's givin' all you want.[11]

The rhythmic short verses and the repetition of "negro bembón" within each stanza is the reproduction of the son in its poetic and written form. Moreover, the repetition of "negro bembón" is the exclamation of the Negro self-affirmation, consistent throughout the black Diaspora. "Negro bembón" is, thus, the reiteration of the growing expression of self-esteem and the acceptance of the total Negro essence and culture also present in the poems of Langston Hughes, Jacques Roumain, and Aimé Césaire. It is also the affirmation of the "black is beautiful" later asserted and manifested in the Black Power movement: "¿Porque qué te pone tan bravo, cuando te dicen negro bembón, si tiene la boca santa, negro bembón? . . . Bembón así como ere . . . negro bembón . . . negro bembón . . . negro bembón . . . negro bembón . . .

Bembón así como ere." In its entirety *Motivos de son* presents the daily life concerns of the Afro-Cuban: embarrassment and pride; it depicts the emotional turmoil of an unjust life, and records the inescapable toil along with the cultural dances of endurance and joy. As Roberto Márquez notes in *Man-Making Words*, it "gave a new, less picturesque texture, an element of a more penetrating realism and increased social density, to the Afro-Hispanic poetry movement of that time and previewed the seminal, constitutive importance of that indigenous popular form."[12] The poem "Canto Negro" is the unaltered voice of the Afro-Cuban.

> ¡Yambambó, yambambé!
> Repica el congo solongo,
> repica el negro bien negro;
> congo solongo del Songo
> baila yambó sobre un pie.
>
> Mamatomba,
> serembe cuserembá
>
> El negro canta y se ajuma,
> el negro se ajuma y canta,
> el negro canta y se va.
> Acumeme serembó
> aé
> yambó,
> aé.
>
> Tamba, tamba, tamba, tamba
> tamba del negro que tumba
> tumba del negro, caramba,
> caramba, que el negro tumba:
> ¡yamba, yambó, yambambé![13]

Motivos de son is the expression of African song and rhythm. With the stress on the sound of the drum ("tamba, tamba, tamba, tamba), it reveals a broader scope of Cuba's cultural substructure. Equally important, through such verses as "el negro bien negro" and "congo solongo del Songo" the *son* brought about a level of recognition and pride to blackness, until then not respected even among Afro-Cubans who had come to internalize the Negrophobic sentiments of their environment. As Jackson keenly notes in *Black Writers in Latin America*, Guillén tried to dismantle the blacks' own phobia, "his own fear of being black and of identifying with his *son*, his *rumba*, and his *bongo*."[14]

In his collection *Tengo* (published in 1964) the poem "Vine en un barco Negrero" ("I Came on a Slaveship") explores the journey from the slaveship to the new land. Guillén's historical trajectory is important to the affirmation of the New Afro-Cuban identity, as it underlines their roots in Africa as well as their transition to the American continent.

> Vine en un barco negrero.
> Me trajeron.
> Caña y látigo el ingenio.
> Sol de hierro.
> Sudor como caramelo.
> Pie en el sepo.
>
>   * * *
>
> O'Donnell, Su puño seco.
> Cuero y cuero.
> Los alguaciles y el miedo.
> cuero y cuero.
> De sangre y tinta mi cuerpo.
> Cuero y cuero.
>
>   * * *
>
> ¡Oh Cuba! Mi voz entrego.
> En tí creo.
> Mía la tierra que beso.
> Mío el cielo.
> Libre estoy, vine de lejos.
> Soy un negro.
>   La Yagruma
>   de nieve y esmeralda
>   bajo la luna.[15]
>
> I came on a slaveship.
> They brought me.
> Cane, lash, and plantation.
> A sun of steel.
> Sweat like a caramel.
> Foot in the stocks.
>
>   * * *
>
> O'Donnell. His dry fist.
> Lash and more lash.
> The constables and the fear.
> Lash and more lash.
> My body blood and ink.
> Lash and more lash.
>
>   * * *

> Oh Cuba! I give you my voice.
> I believe in you.
> The land I kiss is mine.
> Mine the sky.
> I am free, I came from far off.
> I am a Black man.
> > The Yagruma
> > of snow and emerald
> > beneath the moon.[16]

In "I Came on a Slaveship" the poet recollects the physical and psychologi-cal brutality of the plantation, but comes to view Cuba as his land; the land that was fertilized with the sweat and blood of the African ancestors. "¡Oh Cuba! Mi voz entrego. En tí creo." "I Came on a Slaveship" is the celebration of life: the poet's life, the lives of those who survived the savagery of slavery, the celebration of the prosperity of the land that all the slaves nourished. His proclamation of liberty in the verse "libre estoy, vine de lejos" is timely, if we are to remember the liberation movements of the 1950s and 1960s in Africa and the Diaspora.

In 1934 Guillén published "West Indies, Ltd." Though "I Came on a Slave-ship" was published in 1964, its subject matter precedes "West Indies, Ltd." in terms of historical and ideological contents. "West Indies" is the transition from Africanness to creoleness. In its development, the poem addresses the multicultural and multiracial aspects of the Caribbean.

> Aquí hay blancos y negros y chinos y mulatos.
> Desde luego, se trata de colores baratos,
> pues a través de tratos y contratos
> se han corrido los tintes y no hay un tono estable.
> (El que piense otra cosa que avance un paso y hable.)[17]

The mixture of the races and cultures creates continuous changes in the Caribbean. Furthermore, the Caribbean ports receive the world as they are the ports of vacation or correspondence for many. Yet, the paradox is: not-withstanding the temporary intermingling of people, the Caribbean remains a point of race prejudice and sharp class separation. ". . . me río de ti, porque hablas de aristocracias puras, de ingenios florecientes y arcas llenas. ¡Me río de ti negro imitamicos, que abres los ojos ante el auto de los ricos, y que te avergüenzas de mirarte el pellojo oscuro, cuando tienes el puño tan duro!"[18]

The poem unmasks the *abstract* multiculturalism to reveal the absurdity of the West Indies, where the working and peasant classes can only find subsistence if they work with no rest. "Me matan, si no trabajo, y si trabajo, me matan: siempre me matan, me matan, siempre me matan!"[19] As Jacques

Roumain would later write in *Gouverneurs de la rosée* (*Masters of the dew*), "the poor work in the sun, the rich play in the shade. Some plant, others reap. Certainly we ordinary folks are like a pot. It's the pot that cooks the food, that suffers the pain of sitting on the fire. But when the food is ready, the pot is told, 'You can't come to the table, you'd dirty up the cloth.'"[20] Discerningly, Guillén exclaims his reality and perception of the Caribbean.

> West Indies! West Indies! West Indies!
> Este es el pueblo hirsuto,
> de cobre, multicéfalo, donde la vida repta
> con el lodo seco cuarteado en la piel.
> Este es el presidio
> donde cada hombre tiene atados los pies.
> Esta es la grotesca sede de *companies y trusts*.
> Aquí están el lago de asfalto, la minas de hierro,
> las plantaciones de café,
> los *ports docks*, los *ferry boats*, los *ten cents* . . .
> Este es el pueblo del *all right*,
> donde todo se encuentra muy mal;
> éste es el pueblo del *very well*,
> donde nadie está bien.[21]

If Guillén pays particular attention to colorism and race politics in the Caribbean, the dynamic of class structure is also an essential dimension of his poetry; as we have come to comprehend, colorism and class are indissolubly linked within the region. Moreover, it is not an innovative observation to state that in the Caribbean a darker hue usually equals relegation to the lower rungs of the social scale, while a lighter hue means membership to the higher echelon of the social ladder. What is noteworthy is that as early as 1934 Guillén forthrightly describes the West Indies as the location where everything seems *all right* (from a touristic and elitist perspective) but where nothing goes well for the unfortunate and underprivileged inhabitants. "West Indies, Ltd." is an overt social, political, and economic criticism of Cuba and the Caribbean, insofar as the interrelation of race, color, and class. Three years after the publication of "West Indies, Ltd.," in 1937, Guillén joined the Communist Party where he continued the struggle for social justice, until his death in 1989.

The Poetry Engagé of Guillén, Hughes, and Roumain

The ideological union of Jacques Roumain, Langston Hughes, and Nicolás Guillén strengthened their individual and collective commitment to race and class justice. Guillén's encounter with Roumain in 1937 occurred during the latter's exile from Haiti. In 1934 Roumain founded the Haitian Communist Party; he was later arrested and imprisoned until 1936. Upon his release he was promptly exiled. So, when Guillén and Roumain met in Paris, their role in their respective country, the Caribbean and the greater world was well defined. It was to change the plight of the urban proletariat and the rural peasant class. Roumain's most renowned work (*Gouverneurs de la rosée*)—which was translated into Spanish by Nicolás Guillén and into English by Langston Hughes, with the assistance of René Piquion and Mercer Cook—depicts the oppression and the daily economic struggle of the masses. In *Gouverneurs* the protagonist Manuel returns to Haiti (after spending fifteen years in Cuba where he worked in sugar cane fields) to find his village destitute: drought, abject poverty, oppression, and exploitation of the masses by the powerful few, as well as discord among family members, caused by enmity over land (for survival). Aware that these problems are not limited to Haiti, in his long poem, "Bois-d'ébène," Roumain emphasizes the belief that the socioeconomic movement of the proletariat should be international; furthermore, it should simultaneously include and transcend race.

> Ouvrier blanc de Détroit péon noir d'Alabama
> peuple innombrable des galères capitalistes
> le destin nous dresse épaule contre épaule
> et reniant l'antique maléfique des tabous de sang
> nous foulons les décombres de nos solitudes[22]

> White worker of Detroit black sharecropper of Alabama
> countless multitudes of capitalist galleys
> destiny unites us shoulder to shoulder
> and repudiating the ancient malefice of blood taboos
> we trample down the ruins of our solitude[23]

Roumain died in 1944, at the age of 37. Unlike many black intellectuals who later withdrew from the party because of its shortcomings in regard to race matters, Roumain did not live long enough to see and evaluate the party's lack of commitment to the peculiar black condition. Nonetheless, Roumain's and Guillén's adherence to the Communist party, and their cross-ideologies, strengthened their activism in the cause of the masses. In his "Eligía a Jacques Roumain," Guillén praises Roumain's character and humanitarian deeds. Expounding on Roumain's metaphor of Haiti as a "blood-soaked sponge," Guillén utilizes the analogy to reflect on the possibility of social stability on the island, after many decades of bloodshed.

Él, Monsieur Jacques Roumain,
que hablaba en nombre
del negro Emperador, del negro Rey,
del negro Presidente
y de todos los negros que nunca fueron más que . . .

                    * * *

Negros descalzos frente al Champs-de-Mars
o en el tibio mulato camino de Petionville,
o más arriba,
en el ya frío blanco camino de Kenskoff:
negros no fundados aún,
sombras, zombíes,
lentos fantasmas de la caña y el café,
carne febril, desgarradora,
primaria, pantanosa, vegetal.

                    * * *

El va a exprimir la esponja,
él va a exprimirla.

Verá entonces el sol duro antillano,
cual si estallara telúrica vena,
enrojecer el pávido océano.

Y flotar sin dogal y sin cadena
cuellos puros en suelta muchedumbre,
almas no, pero sí cuerpos en pena.

Móvil encendio de afilada lumbre,
lamerá con su lengua prometida
del fijo llano a la nublada cumbre.

¡Oh aurora de los tiempos, encendida!
¡Oh, mar, oh mar de sangre desbordado!
El pasado pasado no ha pasado.
Le nueva vida espera nueva vida.[24]

He, Monsieur Jacques Roumain
who spoke for the black
Emperor, the black King,
the black President,
and for all the Blacks who never came to more than . . .

                    * * *

barefoot Blacks on the Champs-de-Mars,
and on the brown and lukewarm way to Petionville;

or further up, on the cold, white road to Kenskoff.
Blacks not even born:
shadows and Zombies,
languid ghosts of cane and coffee;
anxious, tearing, primary,
swampy, vegetable flesh.

He will come to squeeze the sponge,
he'll come to squeeze that sponge . . .

And then a hard, Antillian sun
will see the bursting of telluric veins,
will watch a timid ocean turning red.

And watch pure necks without a collar or a chain
float high in daring masses,
not yet souls but flesh in pain.

A soaring flame of piercing heat
will flash in trenchant tongues
from plain to cloudy peak.

Oh, dawn of time in flames!
Oh, sea, oh sea of overflowing blood!
The past of yesterday has not gone by;
new life hopes for life renewed![25]

Guillén's attention to the value of Roumain's writing in relation to his activism underscores the significance of art work in the sociopolitical movements of the twentieth century. In his lamentation of Roumain's death Guillén hopes to see a new life for the masses, on behalf of whom both he and Roumain rallied.

From the 1920s onward the politics of race, colorism, and class shaped black thought both in the Caribbean and the United States. In the United States, however, the dynamics of race obscured class politics for a long time, while such politics was prevalent and apparent in the Caribbean. One would note that from the triumvirate's writings the socialist preoccupation of Guillén and Roumain far surpassed Hughes' class concerns. On the other hand, Hughes' race focus inspired Guillén's and Roumain's writings on the relational complexity of race and colorism. Guillén's 1958 poem, "Ríos," is reminiscent of Hughes "The Negro Speaks of Rivers" (1922). "Ríos," similar to "The Negro Speaks of Rivers," holds the symbolism of the spirit, of the soul. While "The Negro Speaks . . ." refers to the human soul, that of the poet's and his African ancestors' ("I've known rivers ancient as the world and older than the flow of human blood in human veins. My soul has grown deep like the rivers."), "Ríos" focuses on the soul of the "land"; by extension, the collective behavior and spirit of those who occupy the land.

> Tengo el Rin, del Ródano, del Ebro,
> tengo los ojos llenos;
> tengo del Tíber y del Támesis,
> tengo del Volga, del Danubio,
> tengo los ojos llenos.
>
> pero yo sé que el Plata,
> pero yo sé que el Amazonas baña;
> pero yo sé que el Missipi,
> pero yo sé que el Magdalena baña;
> yo sé que el Almendares,
> pero yo sé que el San Lorenzo baña;
> yo sé que el Orinoco,
> pero yo sé que bañan
> tierras de amargo limo donde mi voz florece
> y lentos bosques presos en sangrientas raíces.
> ¡Bebo en tu copa, América,
> en tu copa de estaño,
> anchos ríos de lágrimas!
>
> Dejad, dejadme,
> Dejadme ahora junto al agua.[26]
>
> With the Rhine, the Rhone, the Ebro,
> my eyes are filled.
> With the Tiber, the Thames,
> the Volga, the Danube,
> my eyes are filled.
>
> But I know the Plata,
> and I know the Amazon bathes.
> But I know the Mississippi,
> and I know the Magdalena bathes.
> I know the Almendares,
> and I know the San Lorenzo bathes.
> I know the Orinoco,
> I know they bathe
> lands of bitter slime where my voice blooms,
> and languid jungles chained by bloody roots.

America, I drink from your cup,
from the tin cup,
great rivers of tears!

Oh, leave me, leave me,
leave me now
. . . close to the water.[27]

The rivers in Guillén's "Ríos" are the people and their diverse political and social cultures that settled in the Americas. Guillén enumerates rivers from East and West Europe, as he speaks of rivers flowing through the Caribbean, South America, and the United States. There is a double reference to America (the Continent) and America (the United States) in Guillén's " . . . America . . . great rivers of tears . . . lands of bitter slime . . . languid jungles chained by bloody roots. America, I drink from your cup . . . "[28] Throughout his activist and writing career, Guillén remained critical of race injustice in the Americas (including the United States) and Europe; as he also weighed the relationship between the United States and Cuba. It is evident that his friendship with Langston Hughes was based not only on their common love for verses but also on their stand against racism and the exploitation embedded within the capitalist system. Though Hughes did not adhere to the Communist party he wrote about the various sociopolitical revolutions and class struggles of the countries he visited throughout the years: Mexico, Cuba, Haiti, and Spain.

With cross influences, Hughes, Roumain, and Guillén bolstered each other's commitment to awaken a significant level of race consciousness at home and abroad, in order to advocate the rights of the underprivileged. Their poetry and novels presented facets of black life that were treated by very few writers of their time. As Cobb points out, the three poets portrayed the total black experience; such approach "released them from the need of *proving* anything, for they perceived the strengths, the defeats, the patient endurance as well as the rebellion of the poor, what refined and corrupted, and they made no apologies for what they presented in their works."[29] Their knowledge of foreign languages made possible the exchange of their sociopolitical ideas as well as the appreciation of one another's literary work. Hughes' fluency in French and Spanish afforded him the opportunity to translate Guillén's and Roumain's work into English. Translation made their works accessible to a broader audience; by extension, the *prise de conscience* their poems, novels, essays, and manifestoes awakened, inspired succeeding generation of writers to continue to investigate the politics of race, colorism, and class.

Notes

1. Langston Hughes, "Dance Africaine," *The Collected Poems of Langston Hughes*, ed. Arnold Rampersad (New York: Alfred A. Knopf, 2002) 28.

2. Roumain, *When the Tom-Tom Beats*, 24, 25.

3. Edward J. Mullen, *Langston Hughes in the Hispanic World and Haiti* (Connecticut: Archon Book, 1977) 25.

4. Ibid., 24.

5. Ibid., 25.

6. Dominga González Suárez, "Análisis de las causas de la immigración en Cuba (1902–1932)," *Revista de la Universidad de Oriente*, Publicación trimestral, 55 (1984): 159–71.

7. Martin, *Race First*, 49.

8. It certainly goes without saying, but nonetheless worth underlying, that black denigration was not particular to Cuba, but rampant throughout Hispanic America.

9. See chapter 6. *Noiriste* members insisted that dark complexioned Haitians be given the same opportunities as their lighter complexioned compatriots.

10. Nicolás Guillén, *Elégies et Chansons Cubaines*, trans. Claude Couffon (Paris: Editions Pierre Seghers, 1959) 10.

11. Edward J. Mullen, *Afro-Cuban Literature: Critical Junctures* (Westport: Greenwood Press, 1998) 207.

12. Nicolás Guillén, *Man-Making Words*, trans. Roberto Márquez and David Arthur McMurray (Amherst: University of Massachusetts Press) x.

13. Nicolás Guillén, *Nueva Antología Mayor* (La Habana: Editorial Letras Cubanas, 1979).

14. Richard L. Jackson, *Black Writers in Latin America* (Alburquerque: University of New Mexico Press, 1979) 82.

15. Guillén, *Man-Making Words*, 184, 186.

16. Ibid., 185, 187.

17. Guillén, *Elégies*, 22.

18. Ibid., 26.

19. Ibid., 40.

20. Jacques Roumain, *Masters of the Dew* (Portsmouth: Heinemann Educational Publishers, 1978) 51.

21. Guillén, *Elégies*, 34, 36.

22. Roumain, *When the Tom-Tom Beats*, 80.

23. Ibid., 81.

24. Guillén, *Man-Making Words*, 96, 98.

25. Ibid., 97, 99.

26. Guillén, *Man-Making Words*, 2, 4.

27. Ibid., 3, 5.

28. Ibid., 5.

29. Martha Cobb, *Harlem, Haiti and Havana* (Washington D.C.: Three Continents Press, Inc., 1979) 143.

9

The Principles of Self-Governance and Black Power in the Writings of Kwame Nkrumah and Malcolm X

<hr>

History shows, then, that as a result of these unusual forces in the education of the Negro he easily learns to follow the line of least resistance rather than battle against odds for what real history has shown to be the right course. . . . The education of the Negro, then, becomes a perfect device for control from without. Those who purposely promote it have every reason to rejoice, and Negroes themselves exultingly champion the cause of the oppressor.

—Carter G. Woodson[1]

Kwame Nkrumah: The Principles of African Unity and Governance

IN *CONSCIENCISM*, KWAME NKRUMAH argues the following:

A colonial student does not by origin belong to the intellectual history in which the university philosophers are such impressive landmarks. *The colonial student can be so seduced by these attempts to give a philosophical account of the universe, that he surrenders his whole personality to them.* When he does this, he loses sight of the fundamental social fact that he is a colonial subject. In this way, he omits to draw from his education and from the concern displayed by the great philosophers for human problems, anything which he might relate to the very real problem of colonial domination, which, as it happens, conditions the immediate life of every colonized African. . . . This defective approach was suffered by different categories of colonial student. Many of them had been handpicked and, so to say, carried certificates of worthiness with them. These were considered fit to become enlightened servants of the colonial administration. (Emphasis added)[2]

At the outset Nkrumah underscores the distinction between Universal Humanism, which views the actions and accomplishments of all human beings as interrelated, and an abstract universalism, which aims at erasing diversity and varying philosophies to the dominating benefits of one group. It was with similar reservations that in 1943 Césaire responded to the French Communist Party's politic of subjugating the issues of black folk to the interests of the party. He clarified:

> Je ne m'enterre pas dans un particularisme étroit. Mais je ne veux pas non plus me perdre dans un universalisme décharné. Il y a deux manières de se perdre: par ségrégation murée dans le particulier ou par dilution dans 'l'universel'. Ma conception de l'universel est celle d'un universel riche de tout particulier, de tous les particuliers, approfondissement et coexistence de tous les particuliers.[3]

> I do not burry myself within a strict particularism. But I do not want to lose myself in a lifeless universalism either. There are two ways of losing oneself: by segregating the self within the particular or by dilution in the 'universal.' My concept of the universal is that of a universal rich with all particulars, the deepening and coexistence of all particulars.

A mis-education based on the theory of an empty universalism destroys the black student's ability of critical thought and deforms his/her personality. According to Nkrumah—as we analyzed in chapter 7 with the betrayal of Patrice Lumumba—these students were chosen by the colonialists and were formed as future "collaborators" or "intermediaries" of the colonial administration. The abstract education they received negated the need of the country. Such education was in discord with the social milieu; thus, did not contribute to Africa's struggle toward independence. Nkrumah argued that even in the case where the individual did acquire a certain level of social consciousness, it was usually not as profound as to understand the historical development of the country, and the fundamental nature of the struggle. In *Consciencism* Nkrumah explains that

> from his wobbly pedestal, he [the student] indulged in the history and sociology of his country, and thereby managed to preserve some measure of positive involvement with the national processes. It must however be obvious that the degree of national consciousness attained by him was not of such an order as to permit his full grasp of the laws of historical development or of the thoroughgoing nature of the struggle to be waged, if national independence was to be won.[4]

To increase the number of students who would become involved in the national process, in 1948 Nkrumah founded Ghana National College. The formation of the college evolved as a measure to educate ten students who were expelled from their educational establishments for having protested the detention of Nkrumah and five of his colleagues. Upon his release, Nkrumah rented the Oddfellows Hall on M'Carthy Hill in Cape Coast to house the students, and arranged for three teachers—who were also fired for having protested his arrest—to teach those students. Because of lack of funding, he could not afford to pay the teachers, who agreed to work without pay until the finances were in order. Given the story behind the establishment of the college, Nkrumah viewed it as an opportunity to nurture the minds of courageous and determined young Africans. In a speech given on July 20, 1948, he explained to teachers, parents, and students that the inauguration of the college would be the "launching of an educational enterprise which may prove a significant landmark when the history of our hectic times comes to be written." Furthermore, he believed Ghana National College's challenging task was "to liberate the minds of our youth so that they should be ready to tackle the many problems of our time."[5] The objective of the college was to teach its pupils the best of African culture combined with Western culture.

> The times are changing and we must change with them. In doing so we must combine the best in Western culture with the best in African culture. The magic story of human achievement gives irrefutable proof that as soon as an awakened intelligentsia emerges among so-called subject people, it becomes the vanguard of the struggle against alien rule. It provides the nucleus of the dominant wish and aspiration, the desire to be free to breathe the air of freedom which is theirs to breathe. If we cannot find breadth of outlook and lofty patriotism in our schools and colleges, where else, in the name of humanity, can we find them?[6]

Through the program of Ghana National College, Nkrumah aimed at preparing a group of hard working, responsible, and conscientious intellectuals who would work to ameliorate Ghana's social and political predicament. The education the college offered was structured in relation to the students' background and Ghana's national needs. Nkrumah urged students to develop their analytical ability and study the lessons of history. He advised them to work arduously and with sustained effort, for "as never before" he explained, "we want thinkers—thinkers of great thoughts. We want doers—doers of great deeds. Of what use is your education if you cannot help your country in her hour of need?"[7] The program of the college proved to be such a success that in the following years Nkrumah founded over a dozen Ghana national secondary schools and colleges, which later led to the founding of the University of Ghana. The creation of the secondary schools and colleges was crucial in preparation for self-governance. In *Africa Must Unite*, Nkrumah argues that when an "awakened intelligentsia" rises from within its nation, the body of revolutionary intellectuals that has been formed becomes the leadership force in the fight against foreign governance.[8] Furthermore, he points out that in the need to stifle the intellectual growth of young Africans, imperial powers opt not to provide proper educational facilities and proper education for Africans. "I saw this connection quite soon in my career," he explains, "and it was one of the main reasons why I became a teacher for the first time. . . . The fact that most of my colleagues had, like me, been trained as teachers reflected their faith, too, in education as the key to our liberation and advance."[9]

With a similar vision, in 1951, the Bureau of Ghana Languages (which was originally known as the Vernacular Literature Bureau) was established. The purpose of the Bureau was to teach and valorize Ghanaian languages and culture. The establishment of the Bureau, in 1951, is the materialization of the thoughts the Kenyan writer Ngũgĩ Wa Thiong'o would later theorize in *Decolonising the Mind: The Politics of Language in African Literature*, in 1986. Thiong'o expounds on the critical role—written and spoken—African languages play in the cultural esteem of Africans and the preservation of their history and traditions. Thiongo explains that

> the choice of language and the use to which language is put is central to a people's definition of themselves in relation to their natural and social environment, indeed in relation to the entire universe. Hence language has always been at the heart of two contending social forces in the Africa of the twentieth century.[10]

Because the African struggle was equally continental as it was national, in 1961 the Ghana Institute of Languages was founded. The languages included: English, French, Spanish, Portuguese (the Western languages), as well as different African languages. Nkrumah envisaged that the institute would educate individuals who would eventually make possible and facilitate communication among black nations, particularly within Africa. In other words, the dissemination of Pan-Africanist philosophy and movement was the principal objective for the founding of the Ghana Institute of Languages.

In 1949 Nkrumah also articulated the program of the Convention People's Party (C.P.P.). The launching of the Convention People's Party, which sprung from the United Gold Coast Convention (U.G.C.C.), was a major vehicle in the struggle for independence. On June 12 of 1949, Nkrumah voiced the goals of the Party, which were:

(1) To fight relentlessly by all constitutional means for the achievement of full "Self-Government NOW" for the chiefs and people of the Gold Coast.

(2) To serve as the vigorous conscious political vanguard for removing all forms of oppression for the establishment of a democratic government.

(3) To secure and maintain the complete unity of the chiefs and people of the Colony, Ashanti, Northern Territories and Trans-Volta.

(4) To work in the interest of the trade union movement in the country for better conditions of employment.

(5) To work for a proper reconstruction of a better Gold Coast in which the people shall have the right to live and govern themselves as free people.

(6) To assist and facilitate in any way possible the realization of a united and self-governing West Africa.[11]

The party's main tasks were, one, to reconstruct the Gold Coast by establishing a democratic government and by ensuring the people better living conditions; and two, to create a unified and self-governing West Africa. In regard to the unity of the Gold Coast, and West Africa in general, the objective of the C.P.P. was to extirpate ethnic divisions, which hindered the nationalist movement. Nkrumah noted in countries where colonialists triumphed in dividing the nationalist movement into ethnic confrontations, the struggle against the colonial system usually—if not always—loses its impetus and, by extension, the possibility for unity is generally halted. As Nkrumah viewed it, the C.P.P. was the people. Similar to Garvey, Nkrumah believed that a successful national movement should include and work with the masses.

In *Africa Must Unite*, as in *Ghana: The Autobiography of Kwame Nkrumah*, Nkrumah discusses his reason for leaving the U.G.C.C. In 1948 he left the U.G.C.C. to form the C.P.P. because members of the former wanted him to withdraw from the masses. "Unwilling to come down to the masses," he explains, "whom they scorned as 'flotsam and jetsam,' it was not surprising that those leaders failed to make headway with the ordinary people, and were constantly rejected by them."[12] The aim of the C.P.P. was to reach and assemble Ghanaians of all classes under a strong and organized political party. Nkrumah's paper, the *Accra Evening News*, which first appeared on September 3, 1948, was the C.P.P.'s main vehicle of propagation. The paper's motto, "We prefer self-government with danger to servitude in tranquility," was coined to emphasize the need for independence and self-government; moreover, it served to remind Africans that freedom and political governance were only possible through self-organization. On January 14, 1949, Nkrumah wrote in the *Accra Evening News* that "the strength of the organized masses is invincible. . . . We must organize as ever before, for organization decides everything."[13]

Garvey's philosophies and movement had a great influence on Nkrumah's sociopolitical thought. There are three main comparisons to be drawn between the two leaders in their approach to freedom and advancement for Africans and people of African descent. The first comparison lies in the creation of Ghana National College and Garvey's School of African Philosophy, which provided crash courses for organizers of the Universal Negro Improvement Association. Though the schools served two different groups, i.e., Ghana National College was created to educate African youths, while the School of African Philosophy was established to educate adults, both institutions were established to educate and prepare future leaders. Secondly, there is also a notable comparison between Garvey's U.N.I.A. and Nkrumah's C.P.P., to the extent that both organizations emphasized political and social independence as well as the role of the mass of people in the struggle for advancement. Thirdly, comparing the U.N.I.A.'s motto (written in the *Negro World*) to the motto of the *Accra Evening News'* (which published the philosophy of the C.P.P.), it is clear that in both cases the message was self-governance through unity and organization. The *Negro World's* motto "One Aim, One God, One Destiny," "A newspaper devoted solely to the interests of the Negro Race," and the *Accra Evening News'* "We prefer self-government with danger to servitude in tranquility," can be viewed as both analogous and complementary to each other. In *Ghana: The Autobiography of Kwame Nkrumah*, Nkrumah affirms that Garvey's philosophy and movement taught him invaluable lessons of leadership. Recounting his political preparation years in England, which he entitles "Hard Times," Nkrumah reveals:

> My aim was to learn the technique of organization. I knew that when I eventually returned to the Gold Coast I was going to be faced with this problem. I knew that whatever the programme for the solution of the colonial question might be, success would depend upon the organization adopted. I concentrated on finding a formula by which the whole colonial question and the problem of imperialism could be solved. I read Hegel, Karl Marx, Engels, Lenin and Mazzini. The writings of these men did much to influence me in my revolutionary ideas and activities, and Karl Marx and Lenin particularly impressed me as I felt sure that their philosophy was capable of solving these problems. But I think of all the literature that I studied, the book that did more than any other to fire my enthusiasm was *Philosophy and Opinions of Marcus Garvey* published in 1923. Garvey, with his philosophy of "Africa for Africans" and his "Back to Africa" movement, did much to inspire the Negroes of America in the 1920s.[14]

While Nkrumah admired Garvey and esteemed his philosophies, he also discerned a distinction between his own geopolitical agenda and that of his ideological predecessor. In his autobiography, Nkrumah underscores *Black* nationalism as the focal point of Garvey's philosophy, while he directed his foremost attention to *African* nationalism.[15] The distinction Nkrumah drew between Black Nationalism and African Nationalism clarifies his primary focus on a continental Pan-Africanism which would be part of the greater Black Nationalist program. Nkrumah wanted to address issues pertaining to the African continent in order to raise African sociopolitical consciousness and create African unity. We have examined—in chapter 1—that Garvey also advocated African nationalism within the greater Black Nationalist program, albeit with a different organizational perspective than Nkrumah put into practice during the 1950s and 1960s. Garvey's aborted plan was to create a politically and economically self-reliant and unified Africa, with Africans and African descendants of the Diaspora. The principle on which Garvey persisted during his time and later Nkrumah earnestly urged Africans was that the revolution program should seek freedom first. Correspondingly, the slogan of the C.P.P. became "Seek ye first the political kingdom"; for, the attainment of national and continental independence cannot be realized without the political structure that must serve as the base for economic growth and social betterment.

From 1958 until the end of his presidency, Nkrumah organized and/or participated in a number of conferences which brought together African leaders who were working for the unification of Africa. In 1958 the first conference of Independent African States was held. On November 23rd of the same year Ghana and the Republic of Guinea united to form the core components of the Union of African States. In December 1958 the first All-African People's Conference—which met in Accra—hosted sixty-two delegates from African nationalist organizations. In July 1959 Nkrumah and the presidents of Liberia and Guinea met to discuss the questions of African emancipation and unity.[16] At their 1959 meeting, they drafted the Declaration of Principles and named the organization for African political union, the "Community of Independent African States." The principles of the Community were that

> members of the Community would maintain their own national identity and constitutional structure; and each member of the Community would agree not to interfere in the internal affairs of any other member. The general policy of the Community would be to build up a free and prosperous African Community for the benefit of its peoples, and the peoples of the world. The policy would be founded on the maintenance of diplomatic, economic and cultural relations, on a basis of equality and reciprocity, with all the states of the world which adopted positions compatible with African interests. One of its main objectives would be to help African territories not yet free to gain their independence.[17]

The motto of the Community, which was "Independence and Unity," underlined the idea that African territories must first become free nation-states in order to be successfully unified. Within the community of free states, each nation maintained its identity and remained in control of its internal affairs while strengthening political, economic, and cultural relations with one another. One of the Community's main objectives, in addition to the strengthening of free nation-states, was to help African territories that were not yet free gain their independence. Following the 1959 meeting of the Declarations of Principles, which was held in Sanniquellie (Northern Liberia) on December 24, 1960, Nkrumah met Guinea's president Sekou Touré, and Mali's president Modibo Keita, at Conakry; during that meeting they formed a special committee which met in Accra. During the Accra meeting, which lasted from the 13th to the 18th of January, they formulated proposals for a Ghana-Guinea-Mali Union. From the 27th to the 29th of April, Nkrumah, Touré and Keita met again in Accra and agreed on the creation of a Charter. The union of the three countries became known as the Union of African States (U.A.S).[18]

The Union of African States' main objective was to form a United States of Africa. Its members knew that even though African countries have been divided by territorial boundaries and, due to years of colonization, Africans have converted to different religions, have experienced Western cultural influences, their "sense of one-ness" surpassed all the differences that have been created. Nkrumah explained that their *one-ness* does not derive simply from their colonial past, nor does it derive from the fact that they have common aims; "it is something which goes far deeper," he explained, "[he] can best describe it as a sense of one-ness in that [they] are *Africans*. In practical terms, this deep-rooted unity has shown itself in the development of Pan-Africanism, and, more recently, in the projection of what has been called the African Personality in world affairs."[19] With this sense of one-ness, the aim of the Union—as was the objective of the Community—was to help facilitate national struggles for independence and form a strong body of United States of Africa.

Nkrumah attributed the defeat and death of Lumumba to the impotence of a divided Africa. He argued that the crisis in the Belgian Congo was a display of realistic dangers of colonialism, neo-colonialism, and balkanization. He further explained that foreign business interests and the policies of the cold war dominated the Congo's political scene and prevented early intervention by the United Nations. However, even when the United Nations became involved in the Congo, it operated in the interests of the Belgian government and against the sovereignty of Lumumba's government. As we discussed in chapter 7, in Césaire's play *Une Saison au Congo*, the United Nations used

Ghanaians forces—which Nkrumah voluntarily dispatched in order to help Lumumba—against Lumumba and denied him the use of the national radio to defend himself and rally what remained of his national allies. In *Africa Must Unite*, Nkrumah maintains that "if at that time, July 1960, the independent states of Africa had been united, or had at least a joint military high command and a common foreign policy, an African solution might have been found for the Congo; and the Congo might have been able to work out its own destiny, unhindered by any non-African interference."[20]

Nkrumah viewed Lumumba's death and the situation in the Congo as a "valuable object lesson" which proved to Africans and their leaders the absolute need for unity. It is noteworthy that in the late 1930s Garvey made a similar observation in reference to the 1935 Italian invasion in Ethiopia. His warning and criticism was that the lack of organization and unity among black folk subjected them to impotency when facing racial aggression. During the nineteenth century, Blyden—as discussed in chapter 3—also maintained that Africa, which for centuries has been largely instrumental in the development of the Western Hemisphere, remained powerless and incapable of responding to the continual threats European powers were exercising against the sovereignty of Haiti and Liberia.[21] It was in light of such situations that Blyden called for "African power."

> Some great centre of the race where our physical, pecuniary and intellectual strength may be collected. We need some spot whence such an influence may go forth in behalf of the race as shall be felt by the nations. We are so scattered and divided that we can do nothing. The imposition began last year (1861) by a foreign power upon Haiti, and which is still persisted in, fills every black man who has heard of it with indignation, but we are not strong enough to speak out effectually for that land. When the same power attempted an outrage upon the Liberians, there was no African power strong enough to interpose. So long as we remain thus divided, we may expect impositions.[22]

Throughout his years of preparation and activism, Nkrumah remained conscious of the urgency for African unity and power. The various conferences that took place and the different unity organizations that were created from the late 1950s to the early 1960s, showed the awareness of a number of African leaders of the need for alliance in order to attain political and social freedom. Before the Second World War, only Liberia, Ethiopia, and Egypt were independent. By 1959, Ghana, Sudan, Morocco, Tunisia, Libya, and Guinea, had also gained their independence. In 1960, Nigeria, the Congo, French Togoland, French Cameroons, and Somalia became free. By 1961, Sierra Leone, Tanganyika, Uganda, and Nyasaland gained their independence; and since then many other African countries also gained their independence.[23]

In 1957, at the occasion of Ghana's independence, Nkrumah proclaimed the purpose of African nationalism.

> African nationalism was not confined to the Gold Coast—the new Ghana. From now on it must be Pan-African nationalism, and the ideology of African political consciousness and African political emancipation must spread throughout the whole continent, into every nook and corner of it. I have never regarded the struggle for the Independence of the Gold Coast as an isolated objective but always as a part of a general world historical pattern. The African in every territory of this vast continent has been awakened and the struggle for freedom will go on. It is our duty as the vanguard force to offer what assistance we can to those now engaged in the battles that we ourselves have fought and won. Our task is not done and our own safety is not assured until the last vestiges of colonialism have been swept from Africa.[24]

Before and since his statement, Nkrumah and many African leaders were actively engaged in numerous political and social organizations dedicated to the precepts of Pan-Africanism. Equally important, just as Nkrumah understood that the independence of the Gold Coast was not an isolated achievement, he also knew that Africa was not a secluded continent and should, therefore, work in relation with the greater world. For Nkrumah, the progress of Africa within the greater world community also signified its contribution to global advancement. Thus, continental Pan-Africanism extended toward two other objectives: (a) global Pan-Africanism—the aim for political, economic, and social development for all blacks, and (b) Universal Humanism. Just as preceding black literary, political, and social movements—such as Indigénisme, Négritude, New Negro Renaissance, Garveyism, and earlier forms of the Pan-African movement—have influenced the preparation of leaders of the 1950's *Pan-African* movement, the struggle for African nationalism and unity also had significant effects on black leaders of the Western Hemisphere, as well as on subsequent literary and social movements; namely, Martin Luther King, Malcolm X, Kwame Touré (Stokely Carmichael), and the Black Arts movement.[25]

Malcolm X and the Teachings of Black Power

In his speech, "On going back to Africa," delivered on December 12, 1964, Malcolm X offered his views on the need for lasting political independence and unity amidst African nations. Moreover, he pointed out the significant impact of a free black Africa on the freedom of black folk in general. He declared:

When the African continent in its independence is able to create the unity that's necessary to increase its strength and its position on this earth, so that Africa too becomes respected as other huge continents are respected, then, wherever people of African origin, African heritage or African blood go, they will be respected—but only when and because they have something much larger that looks like them behind them. . . . With Africa getting its independence, you and I will have more of a chance. I believe in that 100 per cent.[26]

Malcolm often drew the connection between the fate of Africa and that of people of African descent of the world. Linking the Modern Civil Rights Movement and the Liberation Movements of Africa, he asserted that black folk will only gain respect in the United States and elsewhere when black Africa is respected and able to serve as a support base and home for all blacks. Malcolm X's earlier solution to the race problem in America was similar to Blyden's and Garvey's; he proposed a physical return to Africa. Later—similar to Du Bois' Pan-Africanist ideology, Jean Price-Mars' Indigéniste philosophy, and Aimé Césaire's Négritude precepts—he came to propose a cultural, philosophical, and psychological "return" for those who choose to stay in their respective native country. The "return" meant collaborative work and mutual support, on all dimensions of society, between Africans and blacks of the Western Hemisphere. He explained that "the spiritual bond that would develop between us and Africa through this cultural, philosophical, and psychological migration, so-called migration, would enhance our position here, because we would have our contacts with them acting as roots or foundations behind us."[27] Even if black folk opt to physically stay in their country of birth, he added, they should simultaneously "return" to Africa and work within the framework of a global Pan-Africanism or Black Internationalism. By 1964—after his pilgrimage to Mecca—Malcolm began to internationalize the black freedom movement. During his speech entitled "The Black Revolution," he proposed that blacks start to conceptualize civil rights in terms of human rights because human rights transcend national laws. Moreover, human rights include global civil and political rights, irrespective of nationality and race. Once the civil rights struggle is extended beyond America's boundaries, "once it is expanded beyond the level of civil rights to the level of human rights, it opens the door for all our brothers and sisters in Africa and Asia, who have their independence, to come to our rescue."[28]

Comparable to his predecessors, the fundamental political principle in Malcolm X's philosophy remained Black Nationalism. After his break from Elijah Muhammad and the Nation of Islam in 1964, and during his announcement of the formation of the Muslim Mosque, Inc., Malcolm declared that the political, economic, social, and cultural philosophies of the Mosque was going to be black nationalism. "Our people aren't religiously inclined," he explained, and so,

> The Muslim Mosque, Inc., will be organized in such manner to provide for the active participation of all Negroes in our political, economic, and social programs, despite their religious or non-religious beliefs. The political philosophy of black nationalism means: we must control the politics and the politicians of our community. They must no longer take orders from outside forces. We will organize, and sweep out of office all Negro politicians who are puppets for the outside forces.[29]

Similar to his precursors, the Black Nationalist agenda Malcolm envisaged surpassed religious denominations just as it transcended geographic barriers and territorial nationalities. In his speeches he often stressed the historical weight of race and racism. He counseled his audience that when black folk come together they should not come together as Baptists or Methodists, for they are not being mistreated because they are Baptists or Methodists, but because they are black. With the same logic he explained, "You don't catch hell because you're a Democrat or a Republican, you don't catch hell because you're a Mason or an Elk, and you sure don't catch hell because you're an American; because if you were an American you wouldn't catch hell. You catch hell because you're a black man."[30] Malcolm expanded his Black Nationalist scope to underscore that one cannot confine the race problems within the United States for "what happens to a black man in America today happens to the black man in Africa. What happens to a black man in America and Africa happens to the black man in Asia and to the man down in Latin America. What happens to one of us today happens to all of us."[31]

Within Malcolm X's philosophy of Black Nationalism, education was central. His education ideology was in accordance with many predecessors; it can particularly be placed in parallel with David Walker's, who urged blacks to take the initiative to educate themselves. In 1828 Walker headed the Massachusetts General Colored Association (M.G.C.C.), which called upon free blacks to unite on the national level.[32] In 1829 he began to secretly circulate his *Appeal* within slave communities in Massachusetts, in which he insistently advocated the need for education and self-knowledge. Slaveholders of the South believed Walker's *Appeal* fueled the revolutionary spirit of such men as Nat Turner.[33] If Walker's *Appeal* fomented revolutionaries to take arms and rebel against the injustices of slavery, it also aided in the formation of African-American literature. In his *Appeal*, Walker grounded his argument on education in order to awaken an educational consciousness that would help slaves free themselves from slavery. He lamented,

I pray that the lord may undeceive my ignorant brethren, and permit them to throw away pretensions, and to seek after the substance of learning. . . . I would crawl on my hands and knees through mud and mire, to the feet of the learned man, where I would sit and humbly supplicate him to instill into me which neither devils nor tyrants could remove, only with my life.[34]

David Walker's plea expressed the black slave's and the newly freed ex-slave's need for learning. In his text and secret meetings, Walker encouraged them to satisfy their need for knowledge. Later, Du Bois also maintained that black slaves and blacks of the Reconstruction era longed for education. According to Du Bois, their thirst for education is what propelled them to edify "bogus college and anemic academies." They wanted better employment than simply working as "hewers of wood and drawers of water."[35] Many black leaders thought it was acceptable for some members of a race to work as "hewers of wood and drawers of water"—figuratively speaking. However, they also believed that there is something gravely wrong when the majority of a race is subjected to menial and manual work. Similar to Malcolm X's analysis and conclusion of the race problem, Walker also concluded that whites would hinder any move toward true self-knowledge; hence, it was the responsibility of black folk to search and disseminate knowledge within their communities.

In *Appeal*, Walker affirms that if colored people were to acquire knowledge in this country, it would "make tyrants quake and tremble on their sandy foundation."[36] He argues that even the few white philanthropists who supported a certain level of education for blacks, would also hinder the creation of any efficient schools that would eventually compromise their power. However, contrary to white philanthropists' belief that black education would compromise whites' social structure, Malcolm argued that the impediment on black education, which has been maintained for centuries, was not solely detrimental to blacks but also to whites and others races. He contended that ignorance and greed, and the "skillfully designed program of miseducation that goes right along with the American system of exploitation and oppression," were poisonous to American society and the world. He postulated:

If the entire American population were properly educated—by properly educated, I mean given a true picture of the history and contributions of the black man—I think many whites would be less racist in their feelings. They would have more respect for the black man as a human being. Knowing what the black man's contributions to science and civilization have been in the past, the white man's feelings of superiority would be at least partially negated. Also, the feeling of inferiority that the black man has would be replaced by a balanced knowledge of himself. He'd feel more like a human being. He'd function more like a human being, in a society of human beings.[37]

Malcolm was convinced that relevant education for all minds, particularly relevant education for blacks, was the most important remedy for American society and humanity as a whole. However, once he became certain that Europeans and Americans judged their interests at odds with the needs of blacks, and therefore would not support their educational progress, Malcolm advised members of the race to create and control their own institutions. By creating and developing their own businesses, newspapers, schools, and so on, blacks would be able to rear and choose their own leaders, whom would be endowed with ideologies consonant with black folk's beliefs, personality, and sociopolitical objectives. In other words, black communities would be able to nurture leaders who are committed to creating independent black communities that would work in interdependence with the rest of the world. In the 1960s, Carmichael and Hamilton re-articulated Du Bois', Garvey's and Malcolm X's philosophy of blacks "must do for themselves" in their concept of Black Power. They defined the concept of Black Power as:

A call for black people in this country to unite, to recognize their heritage, to build a sense of community. It is a call for black people to begin to define their own goals, to lead their own organizations and to support those organizations. It is a call to reject the racist institutions and values of this society. . . . The point is obvious: black people must lead and run their own organizations. Only black people can convey the revolutionary idea—and it is a revolutionary idea—that black people are able to do things themselves. Only they can help create in the community an aroused and continuing black consciousness that will provide the basis for political strength.[38]

The call for Black Power meant raising black consciousness on the levels of self-respect, self-knowledge, and responsibility. With self-knowledge, self-confidence and a strong sense of responsibility, blacks would begin to build and organize their own civil and political institutions to later attain self-sufficiency, both as individuals and as a race. Malcolm X, and later exponents of the Black Power philosophy, were fighting for autonomy on every level. They requested control of the schools in their communities and the power to revise their own curriculum; they demanded qualified teachers and the intellectual freedom of those teachers; finally, they pointed out the necessity for conscientious administration. For, similar to the observations of Césaire, Garvey, and Nkrumah, Malcolm evaluated that a number of black leaders served as "collaborators," "intermediaries," or "puppets" to the white power structure and were one of the hindrances to black advancement. He associated their behavior with the schooling they received, and argued that American institutions purposely prepared those individuals to become weapons of domination for the white power structure. Malcolm also addressed the issue of differing leadership methods, which has been dividing black leaders and, by extension, weakening black liberation movements in the United States and the black Diaspora. Paying particular attention to American leaders and their integrationist/separatist factions, he urged them to focus more on the objective of the race and less on the methods of their contemporaries. He admonished that

> all of our people have the same goals, the same objective. That objective is freedom, justice, equality. All of us want recognition and respect as human beings. We don't want to be integrationists. Nor do we want to be separationists. We want to be human beings. Integration is only a method that is used by some groups to obtain freedom, justice, equality and respect as human beings. Separation is only a method that is used by other groups to obtain freedom, justice, equality or human dignity. Our people have made the mistake of confusing the methods with the objectives. As long as we agree on objectives, we should never fall out with each other just because we believe in different methods or tactics or strategy to reach a common objective.[39]

After numerous history lessons of sabotage, deceit, and betrayal, Malcolm observed, assessed, and expressed what proved to be one of the greatest obstacles to the race's progress; that of various internal conflicts. The conflicts were often based on differing personalities, methods, and ideological positions. One can trace the integrationist-separatist factions of the United States back to Martin Delany and Frederick Douglass, who after working together co-editing the *North Star*, went their separate ways in 1849, when Delany's separatist position became increasingly pronounced. The next well-known clash of integrationist and separatist positions was that of Garvey and Du Bois. While Garvey was postulating his back-to-Africa movement, Du Bois was fighting for equality within the United States. In the first half of the 1960s, Malcolm X stepped into the political scene and assumed a different position and approach from his contemporary Martin Luther King, Jr. Contrary to their predecessors, however, Malcolm X and Dr. King neither attacked nor denounced each other's leadership methods.[40] Instead, they viewed their approaches as complementary. The perceptive integrationist leader, sooner or later, realized the necessity for a certain level of separatism to allow the black community the opportunity to grow as a body of independent and responsible adults—as Delany's and Du Bois' shifting integrationist/separatist positions proved. Similarly, given the global dynamic of the world, separatist leaders were generally aware that it would be unrealistic for blacks to live separately, alienated from the rest of the world—as Blyden and Garvey remained aware. The prevalent separatist philosophy of the nineteenth and twentieth centuries called for independent black nations that would stay in contact with the greater world and would engage in cultural and commercial exchange with other races and nations. After a long history of conflict, disappointment, betrayal, and death, Malcolm learned that the underlying principle of each leader's philosophy was black empowerment through Black Nationalism. The elements of the black empowerment they all envisaged were self-respect, autonomy, and race progress.

Notes

1. Carter G. Woodson, *The Mis-Education of the Negro* (Washington, D.C.: The ASALH Press, 2005) 54.

2. Nkrumah, *Consciencism*, 2–3.

3. Ngal, *Aimé Césaire: Un Homme à la Recherche d'une Patrie*, 237.

4. Nkrumah, *Consciencism*, 3.

5. Nkrumah, *Ghana*, 91.

6. Ibid., 91.

7. Ibid., 92.

8. Kwame Nkrumah, *Africa Must Unite* (New York: Frederick A. Praeger, Inc., 1963) 43.

9. Ibid., 43–44.

10. Ngũgĩ Wa Thiong'o, *Decolonising the Mind: The Politics of Language in African Literature* (Portsmouth: Heinemann, 1986) 4.

11. Nkrumah, *Ghana*, 101.

12. Kwame Nkrumah, *Africa Must Unite* (New York: Frederick A. Praeger Inc., 1963) 54.

13. Ibid., 55.

14. Nkrumah, *Ghana*, 45.

15. Ibid., 53–54.

16. Nkrumah, *Africa Must Unite*, 141.

17. Ibid., 141.

18. Ibid., 142.

19. Ibid., 136.

20. Ibid., 138.

21. Esedebe, *Pan-Africanism*, 39.

22. Ibid., 40.

23. Nkrumah, *Africa Must Unite*, 52.

24. Nkrumah, *Ghana*, 290.

25. Têtêvi Godwin Tété-Adjalogo, *Marcus Garvey: Père de l'unité Africaine des Peuples* (Paris: Editions L'Harmattan, 1995, Tomes I, II).

26. Malcolm X, *Malcolm X Speaks: Selected Speeches and Statements* (New York: Pathfinder, 1989), 211.

27. Ibid., 210.

28. Malcolm X, *Malcolm X Speaks*, 51.

29. Ibid., 21.

30. Ibid., 4.

31. Ibid., 48.

32. Peter Hinks, *To Awaken My Afflicted Brethren: David Walker and the Problem of Antebellum Slave Resistance* (University Park: Pennsylvania State University Press, 1997) 93.

33. Andrews, *Classic African American Women's Narratives*, vii.

34. Ibid., 91.

35. Lewis, *W. E. B. Du Bois—Biography*, 548.

36. Hinks, *To Awaken My Afflicted Brethen*, 22.

37. Malcolm X, *Malcolm X Speaks*, 196.

38. Stokely Carmichael, Charles V. Hamilton, *Black Power: The Politics of Liberation in America* (New York: Random House, 1967) 44–46.

39. Ibid., 51.

40. Malcolm X, *Malcolm Speaks*, 54.

Conclusion

It cannot be denied that the wisest plan of education for any people should take cognizance of past and present environment, should note the forces against which they must contend, or in unison with which they must labor in the civilization of which they form part.

—Anna Julia Cooper [1]

Once they become aware of their own past history, they will no longer despair of the future of their own race, part of which seems, at the present time, to be slow in developing. They will give to their slower brothers a helping hand and try to love them better.

—Paulette Nardal[2]

WITH EACH FIGURE THE LEVEL OF sociopolitical consciousness was modified and re-formulated. In the 1850s Blyden and Delany began to reiterate and reshape Paul Cuffee's and Bishop Turner's ideology of repatriation. The crucial difference between leaders of the 1810s and those of the 1850s is that during the latter period the question of education became prevalent. As time evolved, leaders began to realize that in addition to the philosophy of repatriation, the need to educate black folk in the United States and Africa was critical. In the 1900s Du Bois and Garvey continued the advocacy for education, and began to pay closer attention to the black Diaspora in relation to Africa. It was also during the early 1900s that the appreciation for Negro art emerged in the United States, particularly through the New Negro Renaissance in Harlem as well as through the literary dimension of Garveyism.

Concurrently, from 1915 through the 1950s, Price-Mars and members of the Indigéniste movement in Haiti began to focus on the socioliterary movement that started to valorize Haitian culture and its African heritage. From the 1930s onward, the Négritude movement, which fed upon the ideologies of Indigénisme and the New Negro Renaissance, also began to emphasize the artistic connection of the black Diaspora. Through its socioliterary framework, the Négritude movement placed artists from various countries in direct contact with one another by publishing works from writers of various national backgrounds. With the collaboration of numerous diasporic writers, members of the Négritude movement reiterated and continued to reinforce self-reclamation, self-revitalization, and the valorization of their African heritage. During the same period the Afrocriollo movement began to gain impetus in Hispanic America. In the 1950s and 1960s, with the independence of various black nations in Africa and the Americas, Césaire, Nkrumah, Jacques-Garvey, and Malcolm X continued to ponder the limitations of leadership within the Diaspora. In addition to external factors, the detrimental sociopolitical behaviors included the issue of division, due to differing approaches and personalities, the problem of complacency among newly freed blacks, and the ensuing problem of disorganization.

The implications of each leader's writing and sociopolitical engagement are multidimensional. Their centuries-long advocacy for the indispensable studies in black history and culture led to the creation of Black Studies in the 1960s and 1970s. Like earlier thinkers, black educators and students of the 1960s were convinced that education in black history would increase self-respect and esteem among black students and would decrease leadership shortcomings in future leaders. Through the study of political history, students can learn of such conflicts as those between Booker T. Washington and W. E. B. Du Bois, based on class and ideological differences; and that of Garvey and Du Bois, which exacerbated into a class, colorist, and nationalist struggle. In the 1950s and 1960s, Kwame Nkrumah, Malcolm X, and Martin Luther King Jr. averted certain conflicts because they had studied the strengths and weaknesses of leaders such as Toussaint Louverture, Marcus Garvey, and W. E. B. Du Bois. If Nkrumah grew increasingly conscious of the effect of complacency and division after independence, it was because of the lessons learned from previous independent black nations. Similarly, if Malcolm X made the effort to cooperate with Martin Luther King, in spite of their religious and ideological differences, it was because he, too, had learned important lessons from predecessors. In the 1960s, Amy Jacques-Garvey sought to build and strengthen cooperation among leaders of the Diaspora by encouraging them to focus on their objectives, precluding insignificant methodological disagreements. In the 1940s she reached out to Du Bois—Garvey's prime rival.

The implementation of Black Studies sought to fulfill one major purpose: to formally educate blacks and other races for the benefit of the world community; for, as Malcolm X discerningly noted in 1964, if individuals were properly educated, i.e., "given a true picture of the history and contributions of the black man, many whites would be less racist in their feelings. They would have more respect for the black man as a human being. Knowing what the black man's contributions to science and civilization have been in the past, the white man's feelings of superiority would be at least partially negated." More importantly—or at least equally important—"the feeling of inferiority that the black man has would be replaced by a balanced knowledge of himself. He'd feel more like a human being, in a society of human beings."[3] Malcolm was adamant in his conviction that education was essential in the liberation of black and white folks alike. With more respect between different races, the level of acceptance would increase and the degree of tension would decrease. Like many black activists, education for Malcolm X meant more than the traditional curricula of colleges and universities; instead, the caliber of education to which he often referred entails deliberate investigations and teaching of black political, economic, social, and cultural history.

The sociopolitical travail undertaken by scholars and leaders of the Diaspora, throughout the nineteenth and twentieth centuries, led (in the twenty-first century) to a partial response to Marcus Garvey's question. During a speech delivered at Liberty Hall, New York, on November 22, 1922, Garvey posed the following question: "If the black man is to reach the height of his ambition in this country—if the black man is to get all of his constitutional rights in America—then the black man should have the same chance in the nation as any other man to become president, of the nation, or a street cleaner in New York. . . . Are they prepared to give us such political equality?"[4] Though it is arguable whether or not the election of President Barack Obama translates into the political equality Garvey conceived, it certainly is indicative of sociopolitical progress within the United States. It remains, however, that in light of physical liberation, juridical freedom, and the election of black presidents, the general plight of black folk in today's society (across the globe) is one of economic ruin, social devastation, moral complacency, and resignation. At this juncture of world politics the focus ought to remain on the role of black folk—scholars and activists in particular—in the continuous rehabilitation of the race. If in the 1950s and 1960s W. E. B. Du Bois became disillusioned with the talented tenth, it was not because of its intellectualist position but rather for the non-conciliatory gap between its intellectualism and the interests of the black community.

Notes

1. Cooper, "On Education," *The Voice of Anna Julia Cooper*, 250.
2. Hymans, *Léopold Sédar Senghor*, 274.
3. Malcolm X, *Malcolm X Speaks*, 196.
4. Garvey, *Philosophy*, 97–98.

Appendix: Biographical Overview

Edward Wilmot Blyden, Martin Robison Delany, William Edward Burghardt Du Bois, Zora Neale Hurston, Marcus Aurelius Garvey, Amy Jacques-Garvey, Jean Price-Mars, Aimé Césaire, Jane Nardal, Paulette Nardal, Osagyefo Kwame Nkrumah, and Malcolm X

Edward Wilmot Blyden (1832–1912)

Edward Wilmot Blyden was born in the Caribbean, on the island of St. Thomas in 1832. Blyden, whose parents descended from the Ibos, was born free during a time when the majority of blacks brought to the Caribbean were still enslaved. Blyden attended primary school in Charlotte Amalie, St. Thomas. From 1842 to 1844, his family resided in Porto Bello, Venezuela, where Blyden learned to speak Spanish.[1] Upon the family's return to St. Thomas in 1844, Blyden was placed under the tutelage of Reverend John Pray Knox, a white American pastor of the Dutch Reformed Church. Under the pastor's influence, Blyden decided to become a clergyman. To assist Blyden in his pursuit of becoming a clergyman, in 1850 Reverend Knox attempted to enroll his pupil in a theological college in the United States. His attempt was hindered, for Blyden was immediately denied acceptance to the college due to his race. After his experiences and awareness of the dire living condition of blacks in the United States, Blyden decided to migrate to Liberia in 1851. According to Hollis R. Lynch, Blyden noted that "the status of blacks in the United States was lowly and precarious; they were discriminated against politically, socially, and economically. Moreover, they lived in dread of being unscrupulously taken into slavery as a result of the operation of the newly passed Fugitive Slave Bill."[2]

Given the condition of blacks in the United States, and given the established social and political structures which excluded blacks as full citizens, Blyden began to reiterate Paul Cuffee's conviction that emigration to Africa was the only salvation for blacks in the New World. Liberia was the country of choice because it had gained its political independence in 1847 and became the black republic in Africa. By extension, Liberia also stood as the symbol of a future independent Africa. In Liberia, Blyden started his vocational studies as a clergyman as well as a schoolteacher in a Presbyterian establishment in Monrovia. In 1858 he was ordained Presbyterian pastor and concurrently became the principal of Alexander High School from 1858 to 1861. From 1862 to 1871 he held the position of Professor of Classics at Liberia College and also served as Secretary of State from 1864 to 1866. Blyden dedicated his professional life working for the development of the black republic and pushing for social and political dialogue between African countries. From 1875 to 1877 he served a second term as the principal of Alexander High School and shortly after, in 1877, he became Liberia's first ambassador to Britain, a position he held until 1878. From 1880 to 1884 he presided over Liberia College.[3] Blyden's blueprint for the college was ahead of his time, for as early as the 1880s he proposed a curriculum that would be in accordance with Africa's needs—educationally, economically, socially, and politically. He viewed studies in African history, culture, languages, and literature, as well as improved methods of tropical agriculture, as crucial subjects in the educational program of the college. In 1884 Blyden was discharged from the college as a punitive response to his frequent absences due to the various projects in which he was simultaneously engaged. Worst yet, he could not gain the favor and support of the faculty for his proposed curriculum because, according to Hollis R. Lynch, "his difficult temperament and paranoid dislike for mulattoes stood in the way of his working harmoniously with the faculty and Liberian trustees of the college."[4]

In 1892 Blyden held the post of ambassador to Britain. In 1900 he began his second professorial term at Liberia College; however, he quickly faced new contentions for his conceptual blueprint of the college, which he viewed as "revolutionizing the thoughts not only of the citizens of the Republic about themselves, but of other Africans, and of foreigners with regard to Africans."[5] In short, he envisaged a global benefit from a multifarious and thorough educational system in Africa. In 1901 Blyden permanently severed his ties with the college, as a result of his continuous struggle with the faculty regarding the blueprint he envisioned for the college. From 1901 to 1906 he held the position of Director of Muslim Education in Sierra Leone; in 1905 he also served as an ambassador to both Britain and France. The post as Director of Muslim Education in Sierra Leone was the last position Blyden occupied until his death in 1912. More importantly, his position as Director of Muslim Education in Sierra Leone gave him the opportunity to play an important role in improving the relationship between Muslims and Christians in Sierra Leone and Liberia.

In the midst of his various academic and government appointments, Blyden published numerous writings: books, essays, lectures, and letters. From his arrival in Liberia in 1851 until the early 1860s, he published a number of articles in the *Liberia Herald* and in American journals. These writings promoted the valorization of African history and culture, as well as the advocacy of black American settlement in Liberia. In 1862 he published *Liberia's Offering*, his first collection of essays; and in 1869 he published "The Negro in Ancient History," his first significant scholarly article. In 1872 he founded and edited his own weekly paper, *The Negro*. *The Negro* lasted two years, from 1872 to 1874; however, in spite of the paper's demise, he continued to edit many West African papers, particularly the *Sierra Leone Weekly News* and the *Lagos Weekly Record*. Throughout the 1870s he also published articles in the American Colonization Society's paper, the *African Repository*. In 1873 he published his travel account *From West Africa to Palestine*, and in 1887 he published *Christianity, Islam and the Negro Race*, which, arguably, became his greatest work and one of the most informative texts written on the religious history of the black race. Simultaneously, with the success of *Christianity, Islam and the Negro Race*, in 1887 Blyden also gave a number of lectures in Africa: "Elements of Manhood," "Unity and Self-Respect," and "Race and Study." The dominant message was that Africans were not to imitate Europeans but should "cultivate a distinct 'African Personality.'"[6] From 1906 to 1907 Blyden wrote numerous articles in the *Sierra Leone News* on the subject of African tradition and daily life, which he published as a book entitled *African Life and Customs* in 1908. Blyden was a prolific writer and an outstanding political figure who dedicated his life to examining and searching for viable solutions to the condition of Africans in Africa as well as throughout the world.

Martin Robison Delany (1812–1885)

Martin Robison Delany was born of a slave father and a free mother on May 6, 1812, in Charlestown, Virginia. In 1822 his mother moved to Pennsylvania with her children in order to escape the menace of imprisonment for teaching the kids to read and write. Later his father joined the family. In 1831 Delany moved to Pittsburgh where he worked as a barber and resumed studies at an establishment directed by a black Methodist minister, Reverend Lewis Woodson. Delany lived in Pittsburgh for twenty-five years, from 1831 to 1856, during which time he worked as an editor of abolitionist and moral reform newspapers. He attended Harvard Medical School in 1850 but left in 1851. In 1856 he moved to Chatham, Canada, and sailed to Liberia in 1859, where he met the two most prominent Pan-Africanists of his era, Edward Blyden and

Alexander Crummell. In 1859 Delany signed a treaty with the king of Abbeo-kuta in which the king agreed to allocate some land for the African-American settlement in Africa. Upon his return to Canada in 1861, Delany "organized a proposed colony of Canadian blacks."[7] The plan for a colony of Canadian blacks was not realized because of the "increasingly complex web of British imperial designs upon West Africa—especially the rivalry between the British missionaries in Abbeokuta and the English traders centered at Lagos."[8]

By 1862, though Delany continued his call for emigration of U.S. blacks to Africa, his interest in the Civil War took precedence over the emigration call and, by 1863 he began to recruit black soldiers for the war. In 1865 he was appointed the first black major in the United States Army. His increasing involvement with the United States' military was of a territorial nationalistic disposition, for he viewed the Civil War as an opportunity for blacks to obtain their freedom within the states. By the end of the 1870s Delany became disenchanted with his patriotic endeavors, after he had been the subject of a few government controversies which led to the Cainhoy riot in 1876.[9] By that time, he realized that he had lost his power within the United States. As another sociopolitical measure, he returned to Africa in 1878.

Delany was a laborious activist and prolific writer. His writings played a significant role in the propagation of Pan-Africanist ideas, as well as the establishment of freedom for blacks within the United States. In 1843 he founded the *Mystery* and worked as editor of the paper until 1847. From 1847 to 1849 he co-edited the *North Star* with Frederick Douglass. As the first and only black-controlled newspaper of the era, the *North Star* was seen as an educational vehicle for its readers. In 1852 Delany published one of his major books, *The Condition, Elevation, Emigration, and Destiny of the Colored People of the United States*, whose major purpose was

> to place before the public in general, and the colored people of the United States in particular, great truths concerning this class of citizens, which appears to have been heretofore avoided, as well by friends as enemies to their elevation. By opponents, to conceal information, that they are well aware would stimulate and impel them on to bold and adventurous deeds of manly daring; and by friends who seem to have acted on principle of the zealous orthodox, who would prefer losing the object of his pursuit to changing his policy.[10]

His 1852 work, which advocated black emigration to Central and South America, was written before his first voyage to Liberia and before his espousal of the idea of black emigration to Africa. From 1853 to 1854 he defended his call for emigration to Central and South America, and led (in August 1854) a National Emigration Convention in Cleveland, during which he presented his "Political Destiny of the Colored Race on the American Continent."[11] In the 1850s he continuously attacked the American Colonization Society and "its offspring" Liberia.[12] He envisaged that the mission of the Society was to rid America of its free blacks while maintaining non-threatening blacks in bondage. Furthermore, the Colonization Society would simply establish a subtle colony in Liberia with free blacks from the United States. So, he came to view Liberia as the "offspring" of the United States because for him it was essentially a colonial extension. In 1855 Delany further expressed his anti-Liberian position in the introduction to William Nesbit's book *Four Months in Liberia; or African Colonization Exposed.*[13] However, at the height of his nationalistic and South/Central America emigrationist plans, Delany visited Liberia in 1859 for the first time. After meeting Blyden and Crummell in Liberia, Delany became one of the advocates of black emigration to Africa. In 1859 Delany's *Blake; or the Huts of America* appeared in series in the *Anglo-African Magazine* and in 1861 the book appeared in its entirety for the first time in the *Weekly Anglo African*. In 1879, upon his return from his second and last trip to Africa, he published an ethnological work in which he "reversed the arguments of racist theorists and also maintained the pure-blooded African to be racially superior to the mulatto."[14] Delany died in 1885 in Xenia, Ohio, where his family resided.

William Edward Burghardt Du Bois (1868–1963)

W. E. B. Du Bois was born on February 23, 1868, in Great Barrington, Massachusetts. His father Alfred Du Bois was born in Haiti, of a Franco-Haitian background; his mother Mary Silvina Burghardt was the descendant of a slave named Tom from West Africa, who belonged to Conrad Burghardt, a Dutchman.[15] Du Bois was reared by his mother and did not know much about his father, whom he described as "gay and carefree, refusing to settle long at any one place or job."[16] Du Bois attended elementary school in Great Barrington. At the age of seventeen he left Massachusetts to attend Fisk University, from where he graduated in 1888. Immediately after his years at Fisk, he enrolled at Harvard to pursue studies in history, philosophy, and psychology. He became the first African American to receive a Ph.D. from Harvard. David L. Lewis describes Du Bois' dissertation, *The Suppression of the African Slave Trade, 1638–1870*, as "an outstanding example of new historiography of interpretation fused to fact that Hart [Albert Hart, Du Bois' professor] demanded of his students."[17] Before obtaining his Ph.D. from Harvard in 1895, he was also enrolled in advanced studies at the University of Berlin from 1892 to 1894, under the influence of Professor Gustav Schmoller. At the University of Berlin

Du Bois studied history and sociology. From 1894 to 1896 he taught at Wilberforce University in Ohio, as a professor of classics: Latin and Greek.

From Wilberforce, he accepted an invitation to the University of Philadelphia to conduct studies on the condition of the urban Negro. Following his research, in 1899 he published his sociological work *The Philadelphia Negro*. David Levering Lewis views Du Bois' unprecedented project as "the book that begins urban sociology in America."[18] Du Bois held a professorial position at Atlanta University from 1897 to 1910. During his years at Atlanta University, he published his second major work, *The Souls of Black Folk*, in 1903. According to Saunders Redding, who wrote the preface to the 1961 edition, the text began to raise a collective consciousness amongst African Americans. "With its publication, Negroes of training and intelligence, who had hitherto pretended to regard the race problem as of strictly personal concern and who sought individual salvation in a creed of detachment and silence, found a bond in their common grievances and language through which to express them."[19]

The *Crisis*, which Du Bois founded in 1910 and served as the Director of Publicity and Research of the National Association for the Advancement of Colored People, also functioned as a vehicle to raise cultural and sociopolitical consciousness among black folk. The N.A.A.C.P. was founded in New York City in 1909 as a response to, and as a measure, against the reoccurrence of the Springfield riot of 1908.[20] The organization was initially called the National Negro Committee; in 1910 it became known and incorporated as the National Association for the Advancement of Colored People. In 1934, however, Du Bois resigned from the N.A.A.C.P., after years of unfailing service, and returned to his professorial position at Atlanta University. From 1900 to 1945 he organized and/or participated in five Pan-African Congresses. Early in the 1900s Du Bois also organized the Niagara Movement (from 1905 to 1908), and started to publish the Niagara Movement's unofficial paper, *Horizon*. The purpose of the movement was to issue declarations of protest against the injustices of white America toward blacks.[21]

Du Bois represented the American Government in international affairs in many capacities. In 1923 he made his first trip to Liberia as the Plenipotentiary of the American Government and in 1945 he served as the consultant to the foundational session of the United Nations. In 1951 Du Bois had a fall out with the N.A.A.C.P. after years of political and social leadership. At the same time, he was tried in federal court on charges of "being an unregistered agent of a foreign power."[22] Even though Du Bois was not convicted, he became increasingly disillusioned with the United States and joined the Communist Party as a result. In 1961 Du Bois migrated to Ghana where he died on August 27, 1963. The date of Du Bois' death was doubly significant for African

Americans. It was also the day of the "March on Washington for Jobs and Freedom." Du Bois' body of work include *Dusk of Dawn, The Quest of a Silver Fleece,* and his *Selected Poems.*

Jean Price-Mars (1876–1968)

Jean Price-Mars was born in 1876 in Grande Rivière du Nord, Haiti, and was reared by his maternal grandparents after the death of his mother in 1879. His father, Jean Eléomont Mars, was a coffee planter and exporter. Jean Eléomont Mars was a direct descendant of a slave from Sénégal named Jean-Baptiste Mars. Jean-Baptiste Mars, nicknamed Belley, "had become a freeman in Saint Domingue, had fought at Savannah with the American troops in 1779, and later was elected to represent the blacks of Saint Domingue at the French National Convention which unanimously abolished slavery on February 4, 1794."[23] Price-Mars' maternal grandmother, Elizabeth P. Godart, was "a direct descendant of the black freeman who followed Ogé Chavannes to the scaffold in their effort to establish social equality on the bloody soil of Saint Domingue."[24]

Jean Price-Mars' father, Eléomont, was Protestant and the grandmother, Elizabeth, was Catholic. While Jean Price-Mars was exposed to both denominations, he grew up Catholic until adolescence. At the lycée, Price-Mars began to practice Protestantism and attended Baptist services on weekends.[25] Price-Mars' first teacher was his father, he taught him to read the Bible; his father also recounted to the young Price-Mars the fables of La Fontaine in French and Creole, in order to develop his linguistic ability. Later, Eléomont set up a school in his home to give the young Price-Mars companionship and simultaneously teach boys of the area. He taught them geography and used the fables of La Fontaine "to explain human nature, substituting Haitian animals or folkloric characters, such as Bouqui and Ti-Malice, for the French, as as well as speaking in creole to give his pupils a true sense of their environment."[26] Later Price-Mars attended grammar school at collège Grégoire du Cap-Haïtien, and in 1892 he started high school at Lycée Pétion. Price-Mars graduated from high school in 1895 and registered for medical school in the same year. His academic achievements gave him the opportunity to receive a scholarship and continue his medical studies in France. In 1900, however, he interrupted his medical studies to return to Haiti.[27]

A few years after his return to Haiti, Price-Mars began his political and diplomatic career in 1903 as Secretary of the Haitian Embassy in Berlin. From March to November 1904 he served as the official representative for a mission to the United States and in 1909 he was employed as the Secretary of the Haitian Legation in Washington.[28] In 1915 he traveled to Paris, where he would start a career as a sociologist. He returned to Haiti in 1917, two years into the American Occupation, and in 1919 he published a pamphlet entitled *La Vocation de l'élite*. *La Vocation* addressed the faction that existed between the elite and the mass of the people. It also examined the colorism and racism that exacerbated in Haiti during the American Occupation. During the American Occupation, Price-Mars also held the post of chairman to the department of National History and Civil Instruction at Lycée Pétion. In 1922 he resumed his medical studies interrupted in 1900, and became Dr. Price-Mars in 1923. He published his major ethnographical and sociological work *Ainsi parla l'Oncle* in 1928, and in 1929 he published *Une étape de l'évolution haïtienne*, which focused on the intellectual evolution of blacks in Haiti.

During the second half of the 1930s Price-Mars became a member of the *Groupe des Griots* that Lorimer Denis, François Duvalier, Carl Brouard, and Clément Magloire presided together. The group published their journal *Les Griots* on a trimester schedule, from 1938 to 1948, and on a weekly basis from 1948 to 1950.[29] Because members of the journal were medical and philosophical doctors in different fields, it became an important organ in the circulation of various psychological, sociological, ethnographical, ethnological, pedagogical, and political articles. In 1941 Price-Mars became senator of Haiti; in 1946 he served as Secretary of State of External Relations and was later nominated ambassador to the Dominican Republic. In 1953 he published *La République D'Haiti et la République Dominicaine* to explore the longstanding social and political relations between the Haitian Republic and the Dominican Republic. From 1956 to 1957 he served as the ambassador to the United Nations, as the Secretary of State of External Relations. From 1957 to 1959 he worked as the ambassador of Haiti in Paris.[30] Dr. Price-Mars died in Pétion-ville, Haiti, in March 1968.

Marcus Mosiah Aurelius Garvey (1887–1940)

Marcus Garvey was born on August 17, 1887, in St. Ann's Bay, Jamaica. His parents were of direct African stock; his father, Marcus Garvey Sr., was born within the Maroon society in the mountains of Jamaica. According to Garvey, his father was "a man of brilliant intellect and dashing courage. He was unafraid of consequences. . . . He was severe, firm, determined, bold and strong, refusing to yield even to superior forces if he believed he was right."[31] His mother was "a sober and conscientious Christian, too soft and good for the time in which she lived. She was the direct opposite of [his father]."[32] His mother gave birth to eleven children, out of whom only two survived: Marcus Garvey and his sister Indiana.

During Garvey's childhood, the black mass in Jamaica was living under extreme misery and oppression. As a member of that social class, Garvey grew up in an atmosphere of hunger, emotional pain, discrimination, humiliation, and overt racism. He attended school at St. Ann's Bay until the age of fourteen, when it became necessary to abandon his academic studies and seek employment for financial subsistence. He started as an apprentice to his godfather, Alfred E. Burrowes, who was a printer. The opportunity to work with his godfather enabled him to learn the various aspects of the printing business. "My apprentice master," according to Garvey, "was a highly educated and alert man. In the affairs of business and the world he had no peer. He taught me many things before I reached twelve, and at fourteen I had enough intelligence and experience to manage men."[33] At the age of sixteen he moved from St. Ann's Bay to Kingston and began to work as a printer with his uncle. His apprenticeship in rural Jamaica, and his new position as a printer, raised his confidence in his own intelligence and abilities as a leader. Later in life he explained that "I was strong and manly, and I made them respect me. I developed a strong and forceful character."[34] It was also during that period in Kingston that Garvey began to develop his oratorical skills.

> Struck by the skill of the speakers he heard at barbershop forums and debates in local parks, Garvey set about learning the art with his characteristic energy. He went from church to church absorbing the oratorical and platform styles of a variety of preachers. He would spend long hours alone in his room reciting potent gestures. As his confidence grew, Garvey took an increasingly active role in the Saturday night discussion groups at Victoria Pier, where speakers debated and explored subjects of every sort.[35]

During those years of personal and professional growth, Garvey became a foreman of one of Jamaica's largest printing companies. In 1910, disenchanted by the government's treatment of the working class and due to the failure of his first paper, the *Watchman*, Garvey left Jamaica for Central and South America. After he traveled to Costa Rica, Panama, Ecuador, Nicaragua, Honduras, Columbia, and Venezuela, Garvey returned to Jamaica in 1911 with the conclusion that black exploitation went beyond particular national barriers and was indubitably a global phenomenon. In Costa Rica, Garvey worked as a time keeper for a United Fruit Company banana plantation, labored on the pier at Port Limon, and edited *La Nación*. In Panama and Ecuador, he "observed the universal degradation of the black race, worked intermittently to finance his travels, started another small paper in Colón, Panama, and agitated among black workers."[36] In 1912 he traveled to England to plead the cause of Jamaicans who were being maltreated in Jamaica and abroad. After a two-year stay in England, he returned to Jamaica in 1914 and founded the Universal Negro Improvement and Conservation Association and African Communities' League, which would later become the Universal Negro Improvement Association (U.N.I.A.).

In Jamaica Garvey lacked support because of his educational and class background, as well as his hue. Garvey's experiences in Jamaica, Central America, South America, and England led him to advocate the need to rally the black race diasporically. With that understanding Garvey left for the United Sates and arrived in Harlem on March 23, 1916. The U.N.I.A. became incorporated in the United States on July 2, 1918. The association's paper, *Negro World*, first appeared in 1918, a few months after the U.N.I.A. was legally established under New York laws. During the Garvey era, *Negro World* was *the* prominent organ of mass propaganda for blacks around the world. Throughout the 1920s and 1930s Garvey organized the International Convention of the Negro Peoples of the World in New York, and later, in Jamaica. He also built black businesses and nurtured the artistic and intellectual developments of blacks for the collective progress of the race. The International Conventions attracted black delegates from the Diaspora and adopted the Declaration of Rights of the Negro Peoples of the World as the doctrine of the race.[37] In 1923 Garvey was arrested and incarcerated under allegations of mail fraud, and in 1927 he was deported to Jamaica. In 1929 he organized the Peoples' Political Party (PPP). While in Jamaica Garvey published the *Blackman* paper, and later in 1933, he published the *Black Man* magazine. In 1935 he moved to England and continued to monitor the P.P.P. and the U.N.I.A. Garvey died in London, in June 1940. His major text, *Philosophy and Opinions of Marcus Garvey*, was published posthumously by his wife Amy Jacques-Garvey in 1968.

Zora Neale Hurston (1901–1960)

Zora Neale Hurston celebrated January 7, 1901, as her birth date and acknowledged Eatonville (Florida) as her birthplace. There is, however, an ambiguity surrounding the date of Hurston's birth, for researchers have reported that Hurston was born in 1891 and her birthplace is listed as Alabama.[38] According to the 1900 census, Hurston was born in Notasulga, Alabama, where two generations—or more—of the Hurston family lived. Hurston was the fifth child and the second daughter in her nuclear family. The family moved from Notasulga, Alabama, to Eatonville, Florida, sometime between 1893 and 1895, while Zora was still very young. Nonetheless, even though Zora might have been born in Notasulga, Eatonville was her hometown, from a very early age. Five of her siblings were also born in Notasulga: Hezekiah Robert, John Cornelius, Richard William, Sarah Emmeline, and Clifford Joel.[39]

Hurston's mother, Lucy Potts Hurston, was a schoolteacher. Lucy was an important source of ideological inspiration for the young Zora; she taught her daughter to "jump for the sun" and to aim beyond her horizon.[40] After the death of her mother in 1904, and her father's second marriage, the thirteen-year-old Zora was left alone to survive—practically an orphan.[41] The years following her mother's death, Hurston wandered in space and spirit. In *Dust Tracks* she explains that the moment her mother breathed her last breath, she "began [her] wanderings. Not so much in geography, but in time. Then not so much in time as in spirit."[42] Hurston lived with relatives and worked as a maid to support herself. Later, she enrolled in night school at Morgan College in Baltimore, and in 1918 she became a student at Howard University in Washington, D.C., where she attended classes part-time, most of the time. While attending Howard, she worked different jobs for financial subsistence. She worked as a waitress at the Cosmos Club and a manicurist in George Robinson's barbershop on G Street.[43] At Howard, Hurston specialized in literature. She became a member of the *Stylus*, Howard's literary club, which was sponsored by Alain Locke and Montgomery Gregory. In the *Stylus'* second magazine issue, Hurston published "John Redding" (a short story) and "O Night" (a poem).[44] Later she published two poems entitled "Passion" and "Journey's End" in the Universal Negro Improvement Association's *Negro World*. During the 1920s, Hurston published numerous short stories and poems.

In 1925 Hurston enrolled at Barnard College in New York where she undertook studies in anthropology. During the second half of the 1920s she became increasingly interested in fiction than poetry, and by the 1930s she began to focus her attention on history and world politics. She published *Mules and Men*—a collection of African-American folktales—in 1935; *Their Eyes Were Watching God*—a novel which depicts the struggles and empowerment of the protagonist, Janie Crawford—appeared in 1937. *Tell My Horse*—a volume based on cultural investigations in Haiti and Jamaica—appeared in 1938, and in 1939 she published an allegorical novel of American slavery entitled *Moses, Man of the Mountain*. In addition to her major works, during the 1930s Hurston continued to publish articles and short stories. In 1942 Hurston published her autobiography, *Dust Tracks on a Road*.

Hurston was a productive writer; regrettably, her roughly three-decade long literary career ended by the mid-1940s. During the remaining years, she worked as a newspaper reporter, a librarian, and a substitute teacher. After a stroke in 1959 Hurston was admitted to a welfare home in Florida where she died on January 28, 1960.

Amy Jacques-Garvey (1895–1973)

Amy Jacques-Garvey was born in Kingston, Jamaica, on December 31, 1895, in a middle-upper-class family. Amy Jacques' genealogy is rooted in an upper-class English lineage. Amy's mother, Charlotte Henrietta, was the offspring of a black woman and an English farmer.[45] Amy's paternal great-great-grandfather, John Jacques, was the first mayor of Kingston. Because of his well-to-do family background Amy's father, George Samuel Jacques, received a formal education and occupied a managerial position at the La Paloma Cigar Factory in Kingston.

In her autobiography, Amy Jacques-Garvey stated that her father was the biggest influence in her life. As a young child her father would often give her random translation and writing exercises to increase her knowledge and develop her analytical skills. Jacques-Garvey recollected that on Sundays after dinner "[her father] would collect foreign newspapers, and [she] had to get a dictionary, and read the editorials and news items."[46] The education Amy received at home from her father was complementary to her formal education. She started school at St. Patrick and continued her primary schooling at one of the twelve Deaconess Home Schools for boys and girls, which was known for preparing Jamaican women to be parochial workers, nurses, and teachers.[47] The Deaconess Home Schools were Anglican schools run by English nuns who framed the curriculum according to the Cambridge Local Examinations. The courses offered included religion, English language and literature, arithmetic and mathematics, history, geography, music, and drill.[48] After her years at Deaconess Home School, Amy attended Wolmers Girls' School to begin her secondary studies. In *Veiled Garvey*, Taylor underlines that the students at Wolmers Girls' School, which represented the "essence of elite secondary school," were required to take classes in Latin, English language and literature, modern languages, bookkeeping, and shorthand.[49] Taylor further explains that, in addition to academic skills, "Wolmers acculturated its students to adopt the essentialized values and lifestyle of the British. . . . In many ways, Wolmers provided a training ground not only for occupations but also for the social roles individuals were expected to play as adults."[50] Amy Jacques attended Wolmers from 1911 to 1913.

After the death of her father in 1913, Amy accepted an employment offer as a clerk in the MacMillian office and took over as head of the family. Because of multiple ailments: malaria, eye strain, arthritis, rheumatism, and excessive weight loss, Amy suffered chronic health problems. After her doctor's recommendation of a colder climate to cure her malaria, in 1917 Amy decided to move to New York; she could not go to England because of the First World War in Europe.[51] In 1919 Amy Jacques initiated her affiliation with the U.N.I.A. in Harlem, working as a private secretary to Marcus Garvey. As Garvey's secretary and, later, as his wife and partner, Amy Jacques-Garvey began her journey as an organization activist and leader. Her activist career spanned a little over fifty years. During that time she worked internationally with numerous black leaders throughout the Diaspora, among whom were W. E. B. Du Bois, Kwame Nkrumah, Nnamdi Azikiwe, and George Padmore.[52] Jacques-Garvey focused her writings on sociopolitical essays and manifestoes. She died on July 25, 1973, after long decades of unfailing dedication to Garveyist and Pan-Africanist thoughts and actions.

Aimé Césaire (1913–2008)

Aimé Césaire was born on June 26, 1913, in Basse-Pointe, Martinique. His mother worked as a seamstress and his father as an inspector for tax agencies. Aimé Césaire's father, Fernand, is described as an intellectual, who after hours of work would read French classics to his children.[53] Similar to his son, Césaire's paternal grandmother was also an intellectual influence on her grandchildren. Although she was not very educated, she taught her grandchildren to read, and taught the history of blacks in Martinique. Owing to the tutoring of his father and grandmother, Césaire was reading with ease by the age of four.

In 1924 Césaire received a scholarship to the high school of Fort-de-France, Lycée Schoelcher, where he met Léon-Gontran Damas. In 1931 he received a scholarship to study in France. He arrived in Paris in September of that year and enrolled at Hypokhâgne, Louis-le-Grand. The first African Césaire met in Paris was a Senegalese student named Ousmane Socé, whom he met three or four days after his arrival from Martinique.[54] A few days following his encounter with Socé, Césaire met Léopold Sédar Senghor on his way to lycée Louis-le-Grand. Their friendship would later prove to mutually stimulate and influence each other's philosophies and creative thoughts. By 1935 Césaire was among the black students living in France who contributed to the evolution of the journal *l'Etudiant martiniquais* to the renowned *l'Etudiant noir*. In 1939 he published his major literary work, *Cahier d'un retour au pays natal,* whose final version was published in 1956. After the 1939 publication of the *Cahier,* Césaire returned to Martinique. He started to teach in October 1940, at the lycée Schoelcher. Among his students were Frantz Fanon and Edouard Glissant, whom we know today as remarkable theoreticians on the issues of race, nationality, class, and gender.[55]

Césaire later stopped his academic career to engage in Martinique's politics. In November 1945 he was elected deputy of the National Assembly, and in May of the same year he became the mayor of Fort-de-France. In 1946 he published *les Armes miraculeuses*, a collection of poems which included the famous dramatic poem *Et les chiens se taisaient*. In 1948 and 1950 he published two consecutive collections, *Soleil cou coupé* and *Corps perdu*. Later, in 1960, he published *Ferrements*, and in 1961, *Cadastre*. He published his latest poetry collection in 1982, entitled *Noria et Moi, laminaires*. In 1950 he published his manifesto *Discours sur le colonialisme*. During the 1950s Césaire began to increasingly affirm his activist position. In 1956 Césaire resigned from the French Communist Party (Parti Communiste Français)—of which he had been an official member since the second half of the 1940s—after he observed that the party was not operating in the best interest of blacks in the Metropolis and the Caribbean. In 1960 he published his major historical text, *Toussaint-Louverture: la Révolution Française et le Problème Colonial*, which outlines the development of the French Revolution in relation to the Haitian Revolution. Throughout the 1960s he published three plays which reflect the tragedy of black leaders within the colonial and neo-colonial contexts, and the notion of autonomy for black folk: *La Tragédie du Roi Christophe* (1963), *Une Saison au Congo* (1966), and *Une Tempête* (1969).

In the midst of his political career, Césaire was elected president of the Parti Progressiste Martiniquais (P.P.M.) in 1983; he was reelected to the same office in 1986, but resigned in 1988. Césaire's resignation, nevertheless, did not curtail his involvement in the Martinican community. At an advanced age, Césaire continued to be a source of information for inhabitants of Martinique as well as for foreigners, during the 1990s and 2000s. He continued to volunteer his time to the queries of locals and visitors. Césaire died in Martinique on April 17, 2008, at the age of 94.

Nicolás Guillén (1902–1989)

Nicolás Guillén was born in Camagüey on July 10, 1902. His mother, Argelia Batista Y Arrieta, became a single mother after the assassination of her husband in 1917. Guillén's father, Nicolás Guillén Y Urra was a senator and a journalist who was assassinated during a political scuffle. After graduating from high school, Guillén started to publish his poems in the journal *Camagüey Gráfico*. In 1922 he published *Cerebro y corazón*. During the same year he commenced studies in law at the Universidad de La Habana. He withdrew soon after to focus on poetry and journalism. Upon his return to Camagüey Guillén founded the journal *Lys*; later he became the editor of *Camagüeyano*.

In 1930 Guillén published his first major work, *Motivos de son*. His father had introduced him to Afro-Cuban music at an early age; later, the verses of

Motivos the son expressed the rhythm of the music to which his father exposed him. In *Man-Making Words* Roberto Márquez explains the merit of Guillén's seminal work within the context of Hispanic America. *Motivos de son* "gave a new, less picturesque texture, an element of more penetrating realism and increased social density, to the Afro-Hispanic poetry movement of that time and previewed the seminal, constitutive importance of that indigenous popular form."[56] In 1931, Guillén published *Sóngoro Cosongo; poemas mulatos*. In 1934 he published *West Indies, Ltd.*, with a Pan-Caribbean scope. Through the 1930s Guillén insistently wrote about sociopolitical injustices in Cuba, the Caribbean, and the world. In 1937 he travelled to Mexico and Spain, respectively, to participate in 1) the congress, *Liga de Escritores y Artistas Revolucionarios de México* (Leagues of Revolutionary Mexican Writers and Artists), 2) *II Congreso Internacional de Escritores para la Defensa de la Cultura* (Second International Congress of Writers for the Defense of Culture). After experiencing the civil war in Spain, Guillén joined the Communist Party, of which he stayed a member until his death.

Just as Guillén's writing encompassed Afro-Cuba, Cuba, the Caribbean, North and South America, and Europe, he travelled extensively making alliances with various writers and activists. Guillén died on July 17, 1989, leaving behind a large and diverse body of work.

Kwame Nkrumah (1909–1972)

Kwame Nkrumah's birth date is recorded as September 21, 1909, although there is a discrepancy on whether he was born on September 18 or 21. Nkrumah was born in the village of Nkroful in Nzima, of a mother whom he describes in his autobiography as "a most worthy and vigilant protector . . . there was something about her presence, her quiet, decisive movements, that placed her above most people and gave her a natural leadership."[57] He describes his father as "a man of strong character, extremely kind and very proud of his children." Nkrumah underwent primary education under the influence of a German Roman Catholic priest named George Fischer. After eight years at the elementary school, Nkrumah became a pupil-teacher for one year at Half Assini.

In 1927 he moved from Half Assini to Accra, in order to train as a teacher at the Government Training College at Achimota. He graduated in 1930 and left Achimota to begin a position as a primary school teacher at the Roman Catholic Junior School at Elmina. A year later he was promoted to head teacher at the Roman Catholic Junior School at Axim, and two years later he taught at a Roman Catholic Seminary at Amissano. In 1935 Nkrumah traveled to England with the plan to attend Lincoln University in the United States. He arrived in the United States in October 1935 and attended Lincoln University, from where he graduated in 1939 with a Bachelor of Arts in economics and sociology.

Later, he simultaneously enrolled at Lincoln Theological Seminary and the University of Pennsylvania. While studying theology at Lincoln Seminary, Nkrumah spent much of his unoccupied time preaching at Negro churches. In his autobiography, Nkrumah recollects that "Almost every Sunday [he] was booked to preach at some church or other and [he] really enjoyed doing it."[58] In 1942 he graduated from Lincoln Theological Seminary with a Bachelor in Theology as well as a Master of Science in education. In 1943 he obtained a Master of Arts in philosophy, from the University of Pennsylvania. While at the University of Pennsylvania he helped to set up an African Studies Section. It was at the University of Pennsylvania that he began to organize the African Students' Association of America and Canada, whose official newspaper became known as the *African Interpreter*.[59] At the association's first conference he was elected president, a position he held until he left for England in 1945. During those years, Nkrumah also worked as a full instructor in philosophy, first year Greek, and first year Negro history.

Nkrumah spent ten years in the United States and moved to England in 1945, where he met George Padmore. In London, he joined the West African Students' Union, and later became the vice-president of the organization. In 1946 Nkrumah first published *The New African*, which became—for a short period, before its collapse due to lack of funds—the voice of the West African National Secretariat in London.[60] While *The New African* became the voice of the West African National Secretariat in London, *Pan Africa*, which was founded by Makonnen and Kenyatta, became the organ of the Pan African Federation, propagating the idea of African cooperation and unity in Africa and abroad.[61] The African Students' Association of America and Canada was able to use *The New African* to call the first West African Conference in London. The first West African Conference was significant in that it assembled Anglophone and Francophone Africans to hold a dialogue on Africa's needs. Nkrumah recalls that he went to Paris to meet "the African members of the French National Assembly—Sourous Apithy, Leopold Senghor, Lamine Gueye, Houphouet-Boigny, and others. [They] had long discussions and planned, among other things, a movement for the Union of West African Socialist Republics."[62] As a result of their meetings in Paris, Sourous Apithy and Léopold Senghor went to London to represent the Francophone West Africans at the West African Conference.

After a journey of activism in England, Nkrumah returned to the Gold Coast in 1947, and in 1956, with the help of Padmore and other constituents, he led the Gold Coast to independence. Nkrumah's various writings on Pan-Africanism and African Unity include *Ghana: The Autobiography of Kwame Nkrumah* (1957), *I speak of Freedom* (1961), *Africa Must Unite* (1963), *Consciencism* (1964), and *Dark Days in Ghana,* (1968). Nkrumah died in 1972.

Malcolm X (1925–1965)

Malcolm X was born Malcolm Little on May 19, 1925, in Omaha Nebraska. His mother, Louise Little, was from the Caribbean island of Grenada; his father, an African American, was a militant Baptist minister who supported and adhered to the views of Marcus Garvey. Malcolm's mother was the progeny of a rape act. In his autobiography, Malcolm explains that she "looked like a white woman. Her father was white. She had straight black hair, and her accent did not sound like a Negro's. Of this white father of hers, I know nothing except her shame about it. . . . But still later, I learned to hate every drop of that white rapist's blood in me."[63] The sentiment Malcolm expressed against his white "grandfather," from the very beginning of his autobiography, emphasizes his contempt for physical and psychological abuse, particularly against the black woman. On the other hand, Malcolm describes his father, Reverend Earl Little as a

> Baptist minister and a dedicated organizer for Marcus Aurelius Garvey's U.N.I.A With the help of such disciples as my father, Garvey, from his headquarters in New York City's Harlem, was raising the banner of black-race purity and exhorting the Negro masses to return to their ancestral African homeland—a cause which had made Garvey the most controversial black man on earth.[64]

Earl Little moved his family from Omaha to the outskirts of East Lansing in 1929, after two white men had set his house on fire. Later, the Little family moved from the outskirts of East Lansing into the country, to escape the constant harassment of whites. According to Malcolm, in 1931, Earl Little was assassinated by a group of whites, most likely by members of the Black Legion—whose members wore black robes contrary to the white robes of the members of the Ku Klux Klan—who had been threatening the family. By 1934 extreme poverty and desperation began to take a toll on the family and Louise Little began to psychologically deteriorate. Finally, in 1937 Louise was admitted to a mental institution, where she died in the 1960s.[65] As a result of this horrific outcome, Malcolm and his siblings were separated and were sent from foster homes to foster homes.

In 1937 Malcolm was sent to a detention home in Mason, Michigan, and later he entered seventh grade at Mason Junior High School. In 1940 he moved to Boston to live with his half sister, Ella. From Boston he migrated to Harlem, where he soon became involved in a life of crime and drugs. In 1946 he was arrested for robbery and was sentenced to ten years in prison. While incarcerated, he began to educate himself on the teachings of Elijah Muhammad, through daily correspondence. Malcolm was discharged from prison in 1952. Upon his release he visited the Detroit Temple Number One where he received the Muslims' "X." "The receipt of my 'X' meant that forever after in the nation of Islam, I would be known as Malcolm X. Mr. Muhammad taught that we would keep this 'X' until God Himself returned and gave us a Holy Name from his own mouth."[66]

In 1954 Malcolm was appointed minister of the Harlem Mosque Number Seven. From that moment he continued to rise to national and, later, to international prominence. Malcolm became the voice of many blacks, irrespective of religion. At the height of Malcolm's career, by the early 1960s, the chasm between Malcolm and Elijah Muhammad began. In 1963 Malcolm made a pilgrimage to Mecca. In *The Messenger* Karl Evanzz points out that by the end of 1964 the

> Messenger [Muhammad] was impressed too—and envious. On a second trip to Africa, which began in late August and lasted until November, Malcolm had effectively replaced Muhammad as America's prominent Muslim power broker. He had become acquainted with nearly every prominent African and Arab leader and had not come home empty-handed.[67]

After his pilgrimage to Mecca, Malcolm severed his relations with Elijah and the Nation of Islam. Instead, he became engaged in the teachings of orthodox Islamic principles, as he continued his teachings of black liberation and advancement, through the organization he founded and headed in 1964, namely the Muslim Mosque, Inc. Malcolm X was assassinated in Harlem on February 21, 1965. His writings and speeches, *The Autobiography of Malcolm X* (1965) and *Malcolm X Speaks* (1965) were published after his death.

Notes

1. Blyden, *Selected Letters*, 4.
2. Blyden, *Selected Letters*, 4.
3. Ibid., 7.
4. Ibid., 7.
5. Ibid., 8.
6. Ibid., 8.
7. Delany, *Blake*, vx.

8. Ibid., xvi.

9. Martin R. Delany, *Martin Delany: A Documentary Reader*, ed. Robert S. Levine (Chapel Hill: The University of North Carolina Press, 2003) 14.

10. Delany, *The Condition*, preface.

11. Delany, *Blake*, xiv.

12. Ibid., xiv.

13. William Nesbit and Samuel Williams, *Two Black Views of Liberia: Four Months in Liberia, Four Years in Liberia* (New York: Arno Press, 1975) introduction.

14. Ibid., xix.

15. David Levering Lewis, *W. E. B. Du Bois—Biography*, 13, 20–21.

16. Ibid., 22.

17. Ibid., 155.

18. *W. E. B. Du Bois: A Biography in Four Voices*, producer/director Louis Massiah (San Francisco: California Newsreel, 1995).

19. W. E. B. Du Bois, *The Souls of Black Folk*. 1903. (New York: Fawcett Publications, Inc., 1961) ix.

20. Rudwick, "W.E.B. Du Bois: Protagonist of the Afro-American Protest," 76.

21. The Niagara Movement was mainly composed of northern college-educated professional men. Members of the movement met yearly on the Canadian side of the Niagara Falls to discuss issues of injustice and disfranchisement against African Americans (68–69).

22. Rudwick, "W.E.B. Du Bois: Protagonist of the Afro-American Protest," 82.

23. Shannon, *Jean Price-Mars: The Haitian Elite and the American Occupation*, 15. (Jean Price-Mars, "Les Origines et le destin du nom Jean-Baptiste Belley Mars, l'ancêtre," *Revue de la Société d'Histoire et de Géographie d'Haïti*, 12, No. 36 (1940) 1–24).

24. Ibid., 15. Jean Price-Mars' "Pan," *La Relève*, III, No. 7 (1942) 2.

25. Ibid., 16.

26. Ibid., 16.

27. Berrou, Pompilus, *Histoire de la Littérature Haïtienne*, 716.

28. Ibid., 718.

29. Ibid., 760.

30. Ibid., 719.

31. Garvey, *Philosophy*, 124.

32. Ibid., 124.

33. Ibid., 124.

34. Ibid., 124.

35. Levine, "Marcus Garvey and the Politics of Revitalization," 107.

36. Martin, *Race First*, 4–5.

37. Garvey, *Philosophy*, 93.

38. See Robert Hemenway's introduction to *Dust Tracks* (1984); Cheryl Wall, *Women of the Harlem Renaissance* (1995); Roger M. Valade III., *The Essential Black Literature Guide* (1996).

39. Wall, *Women of the Harlem Renaissance*, 143.

40. Ibid., 145.

41. Valade III., *The Essential Black Literature Guide*, 124–25.

42. Zora Neale Hurston, *Dust Tracks on a Road* (Urbana: University of Illinois Press, 1984) 65.

43. Wall, *Women of the Harlem Renaissance*, 145.

44. Ibid., 146.

45. Taylor, *The Veiled Garvey*, 7–8.

46. Ibid., 11.

47. Taylor, *The Veiled Garvey*, 11.

48. Ibid., 10–11.

49. Ibid., 12.

50. Ibid., 12.

51. Ibid., 3, 7.

52. Ibid., 5.

53. Ngal, *Aimé Césaire: Un Homme à la Recherche d'une Patrie*, 29.

54. Ibid., 46.

55. Ibid., 112.

56. Guillén, *Man-Making Words*, x.

57. Nkrumah, *Ghana*, 5.

58. Ibid., 41.

59. Ibid., 43.

60. Ibid., 57.

61. Ibid., 57.

62. Ibid., 57.

63. Malcolm X, *The Autobiography of Malcolm X*. 1964. (New York: Ballantine Books, 1999) 2–3.

64. Ibid., 1.

65. Ibid., 21–22.

66. Ibid., 203.

67. Karl Evanzz, *The Messenger: The Rise and Fall of Elijah Muhammad*. 1999. (New York: Vintage Books, 2001), 307.

Bibliography

Asante, S. K. B. *The Political Economy of Regionalism in Africa: A Decade of the Economic Community of West African States.* New York: Praeger, 1986.

Banks, William M. *Black Intellectuals.* New York: W.W. Norton & Company, Inc., 1996.

Balandier, Georges. "Messianism and Nationalism." *Perspectives on the African Past.* Ed. Martin A. Klein and G. Wesley Johnson. Boston, Little, Brown [1972], 465–482.

Beard, John R. *The Life of Toussaint L'Ouverture: The Negro Patriot of Hayti.* London: Ingram, Cooke, and Co., 1853.

Benjamin, Robert C. O. *The Life of Toussaint L'Ouverture, Warrior and Statesman, with an Historical Survey of the Island of San Domingo from the Discovery of the Island by Christopher Columbus, in 1492, to the Death of Toussaint, in 1803.* Los Angeles: Evening Express Print Co., 1888.

Berrou, Raphaël, and Pradel Pompilus. *Histoire de la Littérature Haïtienne*, Tome I-II. Port-au-Prince: Editions Caraïbes, 1975.

Blyden, Edward W. *Christianity, Islam, and the Negro Race.* Edinburgh: University Press, 1967.

———. *Selected Letters of Edward Wilmot Blyden.* Ed. Hollis R. Lynch. New York: KTO Press, 1978.

———. *African Life and Customs.* London: African Publication Society, 1969.

Carmichael, Stokely, and Charles V. Hamilton. *Black Power: The Politics of Liberation in America.* New York: Random House, 1967.

Césaire, Aimé. *Cahier d'un Retour au Pays Natal.* Paris: Présence Africaine Editions, 1971.

———. *Notebook of a Return to the Native Land.* Trans. Clayton Eshleman and Annette Smith. Connecticut: Wesleyan University Press, 2001.

———. *Toussaint Louverture: La Révolution Française et le Problème Colonial.* Paris: Présence Africaine, 1961.

———. *Discours sur le Colonialisme.* Paris: Présence Africaine, 1953.

———. *Une Tempête.* Paris: Editions du Seuil, 1969.

———. *La Tragédie du Roi Christophe.* Paris/Dakar: Présence Africaine, 1963.

———. *The Tragedy of King Christophe.* Trans. Ralph Manheim. New York: Grove Press, Inc., 1970.

———. *Une Saison au Congo.* Paris: Editions du Seuil, 1973.

———. *A Season in Congo.* Trans. Ralph Manheim. *Theater and Politics: An International Anthology.* Washington, D.C.: Ubu Repertory Theater Publications, 1990.

———. *Aimé Césaire: A Voice for History.* San Francisco: California Newsreel, 1994.

———. *Et les Chiens se Taisaient.* Paris: Présence Africaine, 1956.

Chrisman, Robert, ed. "Langston Hughes: Six Letters to Nicolás Guillén." Trans. Carmen Alegría. *The Black Scholar* 16.4 (1985): 54–60.

Cleaver, Kathleen, and George Katsiaficas. *Liberation, Imagination, and the Black Panther Party: A New Look at the Panthers and Their Legacy.* New York: Routledge, 2001.

Clifford, James. *Routes: Travel and Translation in the Late Twentieth Century.* Cambridge: Harvard University Press, 1997.

Cobb, Martha. *Harlem, Haiti and Havana: A Comparative Critical Study of Langston Hughes, Jacques Roumain, Nicolás Guillén.* Washington, D.C.: Three Continents Press, Inc., 1979.

Cole, Hubert. *Christophe King of Haiti.* New York: The Viking Press, 1967.

Cone, James H. *A Black Theology of Liberation.* Maryknoll, New York: Orbis Books, 1990.

Cooper, Anna Julia. *Slavery and the French Revolutionists, 1788–1805.* Trans. Frances Richardson Keller. New York: The Edwin Mellen Press, 1988.

———. *The Voice of Anna Julia Cooper: Including a Voice from the South, and Other Important Essays, Papers, and Letters.* Ed. Charles Lemert and Esme Bhan. New York: Rowman & Littlefield Publishers, 1988.

Crummell, Alexander. *Africa and America, Addresses and Discourses.* 1891. Miami: Mnemosyne Publishing, Inc., 1969.

Curtin, Philip D. *Cross-Cultural Trade in World History.* Cambridge: Cambridge University Press, 1984.

Davies, Carole Boyce. *Black Women, Writing, and Identity: Migrations of the Subject.* New York: Routledge, 1994.

Delany, Martin R. *The Condition, Elevation, Emigration, and Destiny of the Colored People of the United States.* 1852. Baltimore: Black Classic Press, 1993.

———. *Blake; or, The Huts of America.* 1861. Boston: Beacon Press, 1970.

———. *Martin R. Delany, A Documentary Reader.* Ed. Robert S. Levine. Chapel Hill: The University Press of North Carolina Press, 2003.

De Saint-Méry, Moreau. *Description de la partie française de Saint-Domingue.* Philadelphia, 1797.

Diop, Cheikh Anta. *The African Origin of Civilization.* Trans. Mercer Cook. Chicago: Lawrence Hill & Co., 1974.

Dodson, Howard, et al. *Jubilee: The Emergence of African-American Culture.* Washington, D.C.: National Geographic Society, 2002.

Dorsainvil, Justin Chrysostome. *Psychologie Haïtienne: Vodou et Magie.* Port-au-Prince: N. Telhomme, 1937.

Douglass, Frederick, *Narrative of the Life of Frederick Douglass, an American Slave. Written by Himself.* 1845. New York: The Library of America, 1994.

Du Bois, W. E. B. *The Souls of Black Folk.* New York: Fawcett Publications, Inc., 1961.

———. *Crisis.* New York: Crisis Pub. Co., 1910–1934.

———. *Black Reconstruction in America.* New York: Maxwell Macmillan International, 1992.

———. *Du Bois on Religion.* Ed. Phil Zuckerman. New York: Altamira Press, 2000.

———. *Dusk of Dawn.* 1940. New York: Kraus-Thomson Organization Limited, 1975.

———. *Selected Poems.* Accra: Ghana University Press, 1964.

———. *The World of Africa.* New York: The Viking Press, 1947.

———. *The Correspondence of W.E.B. Du Bois: Volume I Selections, 1877–1934.* Ed. Herbert Aptheker. Amherst: University of Massachusetts Press, 1973.

———. *The Correspondence of W.E.B. Du Bois: Volume II Selections, 1934–1944.* Ed. Herbert Aptheker. Amherst: University of Massachusetts Press, 1976.

———. *The Correspondence of W.E.B. Du Bois: Volume III Selections, 1944–1963.* Ed. Herbert Aptheker. Amherst: University of Massachusetts Press, 1978.

———. *Against Racism: Unpublished Essays, Papers, Addresses, 1887–1961.* Ed. Herbert Aptheker. Amherst: University of Massachusetts Press, 1985.

Echenberg, Myron J. *Colonial Conscripts: The Tirailleurs Sénégalais in French West Africa, 1857–1960.* Portsmouth: Heinemann, 1991.

Edwards, Brent Hayes. *The Practice of Diaspora.* Cambridge: Harvard University Press, 2003.

Esedebe, Olisanwuche P. *Pan-Africanism: The Idea and Movement, 1776–1963.* Washington, D.C.: Howard University Press, 1982.

Evanzz, Karl. *The Messenger: The Rise and Fall of Elijah Muhammad.* New York: Random House, Inc., 2001.

Fabre, Michel. *From Harlem to Paris: Black American Writers in France, 1840–1980.* Chicago: University of Illinois Press, 1991.

Fanon, Frantz. *Black Skin, White Masks.* Trans. Charles Lam Markmann. New York: Grove Press, 1967.

———. *The Wretched of the Earth.* Trans. Constance Farrington. New York: Grove Press, 1963.

———. *Toward the African Revolution.* Trans. Haakon Chevalier. New York: Grove Press, 1967.

Fick, Carolyn E. *The Making of Haiti: The Saint Domingue Revolution from Below.* Knoxville: University of Tennessee Press, 1990.

Firmin, Joseph-Anténor. *De l'Egalité des Races Humaines.* New York: Garland Publication, 2000.

Garvey, Marcus. *Philosophy and Opinions of Marcus Garvey*. New York: Arno Press, 1968.

———. *Negro World*. New York: African Communities League, 1918–1934.

———. *The Poetical Works of Marcus Garvey*. Ed. Tony Martin. Dover: The Majority Press, 1983.

———. *Marcus Garvey: Toward Black Nationhood*. Princeton: Films for the Humanities, 1983.

Geggus, David Patrick. *Slavery, War, and Revolution: The British Occupation of Saint Domingue, 1793–1798*. New York: Clarendon Press, 1982.

———. *Slave Resistance Studies and the Saint Domingue Slave Revolt: Some Preliminary Considerations*. Miami: Florida International University, 1983.

———. *Haitian Revolutionary Studies*. Bloomington: Indiana University Press, 2002.

Geiss, Imanuel. *The Pan-African Movement: A History of Pan-Africanism in America, Europe, and Africa*. Trans, by Ann Keep. New York: African Publishing, 1974.

Gomez, Michael A. *Exchanging Our Country Marks*. Chapel Hill: The University of North Carolina Press, 1998.

González, José Luis, and Mónica Mansour. *Poesía Negra de America*. México: Ediciones Era, S.A., 1976.

Gregory, James M. *Frederick Douglass: The Orator*. New York: Thomas Y. Crowell Company, 1971.

Guillén, Nicolás. *Sóngoro Cosongo: Motivos de Son, West Indies Ltd. Espa a*. Buenos Aires: Editorial Losada, S.A., 1952.

———. *El Son Entero: Cantos para Soldados y Sones para Turistas*. Editorial Losada, S.A.: Buenos Aires, 1952.

———. *Elégies et Chansons Cubaines*. Trans. Claude Couffon. Paris: Editions Pierre Seghers, 1959.

———. *Le Grand Zoo*. Trans. René Depestre. Paris: Editions Pierre Seghers, 1967.

———. *Man-Making Words*. Trans. Roberto Márquez and David Arthur McMurray. Amherst: University of Massachusetts Press, 1972.

———. *Nueva Antología Mayor*. La Habana: Editorial Letras Cubanas, 1979.

Harlan, Louis R. "Booker T. Washington and the Politics of Accommodation," *Black Leaders of the Twentieth Century*. Ed. John Hope Franklin and August Meier. Urbana: University of Illinois Press, 1982. 1–18.

Hinks, Peter. *To Awaken My Afflicted Brethen: David Walker and the Problem of Antebellum Slave Resistance*. University Park: Pennsylvania State University Press, 1997.

Hobsbawm, E. J. *Nations and Nationalism since 1780*. Cambridge: Cambridge University Press, 1990.

Holloway, Karla F. C. *The Character of the Word: The Texts of Zora Neale Hurston*. Westport: Greenwood Press, 1987.

Hooker, James R. *Black Revolutionary: George Padmore's Path from Communism to Pan-Africanism*. London, New York: Praeger Inc., 1967.

Hughes, Langston. *The Negro Mother and Other Dramatic Recitations by Langston Hughes*. 1931. Salem: Ayer Company, Publishers, Inc., 1984.

———. *Big Sea*. 1940. New York: Thunder's Mouth Press, 1986.

———. *The Collected Poems of Langston Hughes.* Ed. Arnold Rampersad. New York: Alfred A. Knopf, 2002.

Hurston, Zora Neale. *Mules and Men.* 1935. Bloomington: Indiana University Press, 1978.

———. *Their Eyes Were Watching God.* 1937. New York: HarperCollins Publishers, 2000.

———. *Tell My Horse.* New York: J. B. Lippincott, 1938.

Hymans, Jacques Louis. *Léopold Sédar Senghor: An Intellectual Biography by Jacques Louis Hymans.* Edinburgh: Edinburgh University Press, 1971.

Kellas, James G. *The Politics of Nationalism and Ethnicity.* New York: St. Martin's Press, 1991.

Kohn, Hans. *The Idea of Nationalism.* New York: The Macmillan Company, 1944.

Jackson, Richard L. *Black Writers in Latin America.* Albuquerque: University of New Mexico Press, 1979.

———. *Black Literature and Humanism in Latin America.* Athens: University of Georgia Press, 1988.

———. *Black Writers and Latin America: Cross-Cultural Affinities.* Washington, D.C.: Howard University Press, 2001.

Jacques-Garvey, Amy. *Garvey and Garveyism.* Kingston: Amy Jacques Garvey, 1963.

———. *Black Power in America: Marcus Garvey's Impact on Jamaica and Africa.* Kingston: United Printers Ltd., 1968.

James, C. L. R. *The Black Jacobins.* New York: Random House, Inc., 1963.

Jerome, Yves J. *Toussaint L'Ouverture.* New York: Vantage Press, 1978.

July, Robert W. "Nineteenth-Century Negritude: Edward W. Blyden." *Journal of African History* V.1 (1964): 73–86.

Langley, J. Ayodele. *Pan-Africanism and Nationalism in West Africa, 1900–1945.* Oxford: Clarendon Press, 1973.

Lawler, Nancy E. *Soldiers of Misfortune: Ivorien Tirailleurs of World War Two.* Athens: Ohio University Press, 1992.

Legum, Colin. *Congo Disaster.* Baltimore: Penguin Books, 1961.

———. *Pan-Africanism: A Short Political Guide.* London: Frederick and A. Praeger, Inc., 1965.

Levine, Lawrence W. "Marcus Garvey and the Politics of Revitalization," *Black Leaders of the Twentieth Century.* Ed. John Hope Franklin and August Meier. Urbana: University of Illinois Press, 1982. 105–138.

Lewis, David L. *W. E. B. Du Bois—Biography of a Race, 1869–1919.* New York: H. Holt, 1993.

Lewis, Rupert, and Patrick Bryan, eds. *Garvey: His Work and Impact.* Trenton: Africa World Press Inc., 1991.

Lumumba, Patrice. *Congo My Country.* Trans. Graham Heath. New York: Frederick A. Praeger, 1969.

———. *Lumumba Speaks: The Speeches and Writings of Patrice Lumumba, 1958–1961.* Boston: Little, Brown and Company, Inc., 1972.

Lynch, Hollis R. "Edward W. Blyden: Pioneer West African Nationalist." *Journal of African History* VI.3 (1965): 373–388.

Madiou, Thomas. *Histoire D'Haïti*, Tome I-VIII. Port-au-Prince: Editions Henri Deschamps, 1989.

Malcolm X. *The Autobiography of Malcolm X*. New York: Ballantine Books, 1999.

———. *Malcolm X Speaks: Selected Speeches and Statements*. New York: Pathfinder, 1989.

———. *The Black Book: The True Political Philosophy of Malcolm X (El Hajj Malik El Shabazz)*. Atlanta: Clarity Press, 1986.

Martin, Tony. *Literary Garveyism: Garvey, Black Arts and the Harlem Renaissance*. Dover: The Majority Press, 1983.

———. *Race First: The Ideological and Organizational Struggles of Marcus Garvey and the Universal Negro Improvement Association*. Westport, Connecticut: Greenwood Press, 1976.

McCartney, John T. *Black Power Ideologies*. Philadelphia: Temple University Press, 1992.

McDonald, Gordon, Donald W. Bernier, et al. *Area HandBook for People's Republic of the Congo (Congo Brazzaville)*. Washington, D.C.: U.S. Government Printing Office, 1971.

Mintz, Sidney Wilfred. *An Anthropological Approach to the Afro-American Past: A Caribbean Perspective*. Philadelphia: Institute for the Study of Human Issues, 1976.

Mossell, Charles C. *Toussaint L'Ouverture: The Hero of Saint Domingo, Soldier, Statesman, Martyr; or Hayti's Struggle: Triumph, Independence, and Achievements*. New York: Ward & Cobb, 1896.

Mullen, Edward J. *Langston Hughes in the Hispanic World and Haiti*. New York: Archon Book, 1977.

———. *Critical Essays on Langston Hughes*. Boston: G. K. Hall & Co., 1986.

———. *Afro-Cuban Literature: Critical Junctures*. Westport: Greenwood Press, 1998.

Nardal, Jane. "L'Internationalisme Noir." *La Dépêche africaine*. Paris, 1928.

Nardal, Paulette. "L'Eveil de la Conscience de Race." Trans. Jacques Louis Hymans. *Léopold Sédar Senghor: An Intellectual Biography by Jacques Louis Hymans*. Edinburgh: Edinburgh University Press, 1971.

Nesbit, William, and Samuel Williams. *Two Black Views of Liberia: Four Months in Liberia, Four Years in Liberia*. New York: Arno Press, 1969.

Ngal, Georges. *Aimé Césaire: Un Homme à la Recherche d'une Patrie*. 1975. Paris/Dakar: Présence Africaine Editions, 1994.

Nichols, David. *From Dessalines to Duvalier: Race, Colour and National Independence in Haiti*. Cambridge: Cambridge University Press, 1979.

Nkrumah, Kwame. *Africa Must Unite*. New York: F. A. Praeger, 1963.

———. *Consciencism: Philosophy and Ideology for Decolonization and Development with Particular Reference to the African Revolution*. New York: Monthly Review Press, 1964.

———. *Ghana: The Autobiography of Kwame Nkrumah*. New York: International Publishers, 1957.

———. *Kwame Nkrumah and the West Indies*. San Juan, Trinidad: Print by Vedic Enterprises for C. L. R. James, 1962.

Ott, Thomas O. *The Haitian Revolution, 1789–1804.* Tennessee: University of Tennessee Press, 1973.

Owusu-Sarpong, Albert. *Le Temps Historique dans L'Œuvre Théâtrale d'Aimé Césaire.* Paris: Editions L'Harmattan, 2002.

Padmore, George. *Pan-Africanism or Communism? The Coming Struggle for Africa.* New York: Roy Publishers, 1956.

———. *Africa: Britain's Third Empire.* London: D. Dobson 1949.

Parkinson, Wenda. *"This Gilded African" Toussaint L'Ouverture.* New York: Quartet Books, 1980.

Pérez-Stable, Marifeli. *The Cuban Revolution: Origins, Course, and Legacy.* Oxford: Oxford University Press, 1999.

Pillsburg, W. B. *The Psychology of Nationality and Internationalism.* New York: Appleton, 1919.

Plant, Deborah G. *Zora Neale Hurston: A Biography of the Spirit.* Westport: Praeger Publishers, 2007.

Price-Mars, Jean. *La Vocation de l'Elite.* 1919. Port-au-Prince: Editions de Presses Nationales d'Haïti, 2001.

———. *Ainsi Parla l'Oncle.* Port-au-Prince: Imprimerie de Compiègne, 1928.

———. *Silhouettes de Nègres et de Négrophiles.* Paris: Présence Africaine, 1960.

Raboteau, Albert. *Slave Religion: The "Invisible Institution" in the Antebellum South.* New York: Oxford University Press, 1978.

Rampersad, Arnold, and David Roessel. *The Collected Poems of Langston Hughes.* New York: Alfred A. Knopf, 2002.

Rauschenbusch, Walter. *Christianity and the Social Crisis.* New York: Harper & Row, 1964.

Rodney, Walter. *Comment l'Europe Sous-Développa l'Afrique.* Trans. Catherine Belvaude and Sàmba Mbuup. Paris: Editions Caribéennes, 1986.

Roumain, Jacques. *Masters of the Dew.* 1944. Trans. Langston Hughes and Mercer Cook. Portsmouth: Heinemann Educational Publishers, 1978.

———. *When the Tom-Tom Beats.* Trans. Joanne Fungaroli and Ronald Sauer. Washington, D.C.: Azul Editions, 1995.

———. *Analyse Schématique.* Port-au-Prince: Editions Idées Nouvelle, Idées Prolétariennes, 1999.

Rudwick, Elliot. "W. E. B. Du Bois: Protagonist of the Afro-American Protest," *Black Leaders of the Twentieth Century.* Ed. John Hope Franklin and August Meier. Urbana: University of Illinois Press, 1982. 63–83.

Schmidt, Hans. *The United States Occupation of Haiti, 1915–1934.* New Brunswick: Rutgers University Press, 1971.

Senghor, Léopold Sédar. *On African Socialism.* Trans. Mercer Cook. New York: Praeger, 1964.

———. *Anthologie de la Nouvelle Poésie Nègre et Malgache.* Paris: Presses Universitaires de France, 1948.

———. *Prose and Poetry.* Trans. John Reed and Clive Wake. London: Heinemann Educational, 1976.

Shannon, Magdaline W. *Jean Price-Mars: The Haitian Elite and the American Occupation, 1915–1935.* New York: St. Martin's Press, 1996.

Sharpley-Whiting, T. Denean. *Negritude Women.* Minneapolis: University of Minnesota Press, 2002.

Shepperson, George. "Notes on Negro American Influences on the Emergence of African Nationalism." *Journal of African History* I.2 (1960): 299–312.

Slade, Ruth. *The Belgian Congo.* London: Oxford University Press, 1960.

Stewart, Maria W. "Religion and the Pure Principles of Morality, The Sure Fondation on Which We Must Build," *Classic African American Women's Narratives.* Ed. William L. Andrews. Oxford: Oxford University Press, 2003.

Suárez, Dominga González. "Análisis de las causas de la immigración en Cuba (1902–1932)." *Revista de la Universidad de Oriente.* Publicación trimestral. 55 (1984): 159–71.

Sundquist, Eric J., ed. *Frederick Douglass: New Literary and Historical Essays.* New York: Press Syndicate of the University of Cambridge, 1990.

Taylor, Ula Yvette. *The Veiled Garvey: The Life and Times of Amy Jacques Garvey.* Chapel Hill: The University of North Carolina Press, 2002.

Têtêvi Godwin, Tété-Adjalogo. *Marcus Garvey: Père de l'Unité Africaine des Races, Garveyisme et Panafricanisme* (Tome I, II). Paris: Editions L'Harmattan, 1995.

Thiong'o, NũgĩWa. *Decolonising the Mind: The Politics of Language in African Literature.* Portsmouth: Washington, D.C., 1986.

Trouillot, Hénock. *Les Origines Sociales de la Littérature Haïtienne.* Port-au-Prince: Editions Fardin, 1986.

Trouillot, Michel-Rolph. *Haiti: State Against Nation.* New York: Monthly Review Press, 1990.

———. *Silencing the Past: Power and Production of History.* Boston: Beacon Press, 1995.

Vandercook, John Womack. *Black Majesty.* New York: The Literary Guild of America, 1928.

Vaucaire, Michel. *Toussaint Louverture.* Paris: Firmin-Didot et Cie, 1930.

Walker, David. *David Walker's Appeal to the Coloured Citizens of the World.* University Park: Pennsylvania State University Press, 2000.

Wall, Cheryl A. *Women of the Harlem Renaissance.* Bloomington: Indiana University Press, 1995.

Wells-Barnett, Ida B. *The Autobiography of Ida B. Wells.* Chicago: The University of Chicago Press, 1970.

Wells-Barnett, Ida B., and Jane Adams. *Lynching and Rape: An Exchange of Views.* New York: American Institute for Marxist Studies, 1977.

Weisbord, Robert G. *Ebony Kinship: Africa, Africans, and the Afro-American.* Westport: Greenwood Press, 1973.

Williams, Michael W. "Nkrumahism as an Ideological Embodiment of Leftist Thought Within the African World," *Journal of Black Studies* 15.1 (1984): 117–34.

Woodson, Carter Godwin. *The Mis-Education of the Negro.* 1933. Washington, D.C.: The ASALH Press, 2005.

Index

Abako, 151

Abbeokuta, 65

abolitionism, 14

Accra Evening News (newspaper), 183, 184

Achille, Louis T., 85

Africa: independence movements in, 25, 149, 186–89; languages in, 182; postcolonial period in, 93, 139, 149–58, 185–87; powerlessness of, 187; religion in, 127–28; repatriation to, 12–14, 65, 107–9, 189, 201–2, 204–5; self-determination/governance in, 93, 100–108; unity in, 53, 149, 157, 183, 185–89

African-American literature: depiction of blacks in, 111; stages of, 89

African Americans, and World's Columbian Exposition, 47n28. *See also* blacks

African Association, 117n3

African Church, 57

African descendants: self-determination/governance of, 100–108; and tree metaphor, 45; unity of, 44, 102, 109–10, 149, 186 (*see also* Pan-Africanism)

African Diaspora. *See* black Diaspora

African Institution, 13–14, 29n14

African Interpreter (newspaper), 216

African Lodge, 13

African National Congress (South Africa), 20

African Nationalism, 185, 188

African Personality, 49, 186

African religion, 59, 127–28

African Repository (journal), 203

African Students' Association of America and Canada, 216

African Times and Orient Review (journal), 17

Afrocriollo movement, 2, 7, 165–77, 198

Afro-Cuban culture, 164–77

Afro-diasporic studies, 2–4

agriculturism, 15–16, 51, 73, 141

Alexander High School, Liberia, 202

Alexis, Nord, 126

All-African People's Conference, 93, 149, 160n45, 185

Allen, Richard, 13, 14

About the Author

Kersuze Simeon-Jones, PhD, completed her Bachelor and Master degrees in French and Francophone Studies at Rutgers University. She holds an interdisciplinary doctoral degree in the History and Literature of the Black Diaspora from the University of Miami, Florida. Dr. Simeon-Jones currently serves in a joint position in the Department of World Languages and the Department of Africana Studies at the University of South Florida.